Philanthropy in Practice

Philanthropic foundations are experiencing a crisis of professional identity. They attract considerable hopes due to an unusually high degree of independence and freedom of manoeuvre, which theoretically places them in a privileged position to find novel solutions to societies' most severe and intractable problems. However, the field suffers from a pervasive lack of orientation as to how these aspirations can be realised. Compared to other professions, it can be said that there exists neither reliable knowledge nor established practices which might guide the strategy development and the daily practice of foundations. This void is frequently filled by changing fads which present easy-to-grasp recipes and often make bold promises of how foundations can change the world.

Yet, none of them has ever met these expectations. *Philanthropy in Practice* shows how philanthropic organisations can effectively address this predicament. Drawing on the public philosophy of Pragmatism, it argues that, to be effective, they need to go for the solution of social problems of middle range.

The book puts at centre stage the crucial role of niches in terms of bounded, protected and stable social spaces which are rich in resources. They render possible the experiments required to develop effective interventions and facilitate the retention of novel solutions to social problems. The model builds upon and is illustrated by four in-depth case studies from the UK, Germany and Switzerland.

With its sharp analytical eye and substantial evidence, *Philanthropy in Practice* will reshape the way we think about the questions of what impact philanthropy can reasonably hope to achieve, and by which means.

Ekkehard Thümler is Director of the Department "Personal Development" at the Joachim Herz Foundation in Hamburg, Germany.

Routledge Studies in the Management of Voluntary and Non-Profit Organizations

Series Editor: Stephen P. Osborne (University of Edinburgh, UK)

This series presents innovative work grounded in new realities, addressing issues crucial to an understanding of the contemporary world. This is the world of organised societies, where boundaries between formal and informal, public and private, local and global organizations have been displaced or have vanished, along with other nineteenth-century dichotomies and oppositions. Management, apart from becoming a specialized profession for a growing number of people, is an everyday activity for most members of modern societies.

Similarly, at the level of enquiry, culture and technology, and literature and economics, can no longer be conceived as isolated intellectual fields; conventional canons and established mainstreams are contested. Management, Organization and Society addresses these contemporary dynamics of transformation in a manner that transcends disciplinary boundaries, with books that will appeal to researchers, students and practitioners alike.

Also available from Routledge

The Management of Non-Governmental Development Organizations
An Introduction
David Lewis

Financial Management in the Voluntary Sector
New Challenges
Paul Palmer and Adrian Randall

Strategic Management for Nonprofit Organizations
Roger Courtney

Regulating Charities
The Inside Story
Edited by Myles McGregor-Lowndes and Bob Wyatt

Philanthropy in Practice
Pragmatism and the Impact of Philanthropic Action
Ekkehard Thümler

Philanthropy in Practice

Pragmatism and the Impact of
Philanthropic Action

Ekkehard Thümler

LONDON AND NEW YORK

First published 2017 by Routledge

2 Park Square, Milton Park, Abingdon, Oxfordshire OX14 4RN

52 Vanderbilt Avenue, New York, NY 10017

Routledge is an imprint of the Taylor & Francis Group, an informa business

First issued in paperback 2019

Copyright © 2017 Taylor & Francis

The right of Ekkehard Thümler to be identified as author of this work has been asserted by him in accordance with sections 77 and 78 of the Copyright, Designs and Patents Act 1988.

All rights reserved. No part of this book may be reprinted or reproduced or utilised in any form or by any electronic, mechanical, or other means, now known or hereafter invented, including photocopying and recording, or in any information storage or retrieval system, without permission in writing from the publishers.

Notice:
Product or corporate names may be trademarks or registered trademarks, and are used only for identification and explanation without intent to infringe.

Library of Congress Cataloging-in-Publication Data
Names: Thèumler, Ekkehard, author.
Title: Philanthropy in practice : pragmatism and the impact of philanthropic action / by Ekkehard Thèumler.
Description: New York : Routledge, 2017. | Includes bibliographical references.
Identifiers: LCCN 2017009621 | ISBN 9781138210684 (hardback) | ISBN 9781315454733 (ebook)
Subjects: LCSH: Charities—Management. | Nonprofit organizations—Management.
Classification: LCC HV41 .T558 2017 | DDC 361.7—dc23
LC record available at https://lccn.loc.gov/2017009621

ISBN: 978-1-138-21068-4 (hbk)
ISBN: 978-0-367-88414-7 (pbk)

Typeset in Sabon
by Apex CoVantage, LLC

PhD Thesis, Heidelberg University 2016

To my parents

Contents

Analysis   135

10 From Exploration to Exploitation: The Pragmatic
    Model of Action in Philanthropic Practice   137

11 Explanations for Social Impact: The Door-Opener Mechanism   151

12 Towards a Model of Philanthropic Niches and Intelligent
    Niching   166

13 Conclusion and Outlook   183

    Appendix A: List of Cases   191
    Appendix B: Interview Schedule   193
    References   197
    Index   217

Figures

Acknowledgements

The pragmatist account of intelligent social action requires that the process of problem solving be conducted in distributed and interactive ways, based on a community of dedicated inquirers. This is a nice description of how this book came about and I am indebted to many colleagues, contributors and supporters.

First, I am grateful to Volker Then, who initiated the "Strategies for Impact in Philanthropy" project and who offered me the opportunity to join the project team at the Centre for Social Investment of Heidelberg University as a successor to Fatiah Bürkner. Thank you, Volker for being such a loyal, unwavering and reliable supporter of the project through all its highs and lows.

As members of the project team, Nicole Bögelein and Annelie Beller played critical roles and they were my closest companions during a long stretch of the research journey. Thanks to you both for getting the work going and for being my sparring partners in innumerous attempts to make sense of the puzzling corpus of raw data. Many thanks also to Helmut K. Anheier, who served as the project's principal investigator and who was a constant source of ideas on questions of method and theory.

I owe a further intellectual debt to Steffen Sigmund, who was a very constructive adviser to my dissertation. His response to my study, along with Michael Hoelscher's feedback, helped greatly in improving the manuscript.

The discussions with Christopher K. Ansell in Heidelberg and Berkeley, as well as his seminal book on pragmatist democracy, were a major and constant source of inspiration. Along with Tobias Jung and Regina List, he participated in a highly consequential workshop on an early version of the outcomes of the "Strategies for Impact in Philanthropy" project.

Thanks also to Kellie Liket, Georg Mildenberger and Kathia Serrano-Velarde for many seminal discussions and for constant encouragement. Many thanks go to the group of researchers who helped the CSI team prepare the case studies. Among them are Wolfram Bergande, Steffen Bethmann, Deborah Bolognesi, Raquel Campos Franco, Christopher Gohl, Pernilla Hultén, Susanna Krüger, Diana Leat, Regina List, Robert Münscher and Paolo Palenzona. Special thanks to Keith Povey Editorial Services for proofreading and editorial assistance.

The project "Strategies for Impact in Philanthropy" was made possible by a grant awarded by the Calouste Gulbenkian Foundation, King Baudouin Foundation and Stiftelsen Riksbankens Jubileumsfond, provided through the Network of European Foundations, as well as the Compagnia di San Paolo. Their support is gratefully acknowledged

I am also obliged to my editor David Varley and Megan Smith for editorial assistance. I very much appreciate having the opportunity to publish at Routledge. I further sincerely thank three anonymous reviewers for Routledge. They provided prudent and constructive analyses of the draft manuscript which helped me to improve the final version greatly.

I would also like to thank the many foundation and non-profit representatives and stakeholders who participated in the expert interviews. It was their kind willingness to offer their time, share information—sometimes confidential in nature, and to expose their work to public discussion that made our research possible in the first place.

Finally, I owe my greatest debt to Eva Blome, "without whom not".

1 Introduction

Contemporary Philanthropy and Its Problems

There is a straightforward and widespread narrative according to which organised philanthropy is particularly well suited to help solve complex social problems of contemporary societies. It proceeds from the premise that the prosocial motivation[1] of making a beneficial difference to individuals and society is an important aspect of the institution of modern philanthropy.[2] It is further assumed that philanthropic organisations[3] may operate in more systematic, sustainable and knowledgeable ways than individuals and on a much broader scale and scope. Philanthropic foundations attract particular hopes due to an unusually high degree of independence, flexibility and freedom of manoeuvre, all of which supposedly puts them in a privileged position to find novel solutions to societies' most severe and intractable problems. These assumptions are mirrored both in foundations' self-perceptions and aspirations as well as the hopeful expectations they mobilise among their observers (Nielsen 1972; Adloff 2004, 2010; Anheier 2005; Anheier and Leat 2006; Frumkin 2006; Gerber 2006; Fleishman 2007; Hammack and Anheier 2010; Zunz 2012).

However, philanthropic actors who seek to contribute to the solution of complex social problems are frequently confronted with a quite puzzling situation. When it comes to questions such as how migrants can best be integrated in society, how public schools can be improved or poverty alleviated, they have to deal with contentious ends and means and a lack of effective instruments. Furthermore, some philanthropists seek to further the public good in rather abstract ways as they tackle problems which reside on a "systemic level" and remain unrelated to individual welfare. Others address socially distant target groups whose needs may not be obvious to societal elites. Hence, philanthropic assumptions of what serves individuals and society may represent merely idiosyncratic preferences of detached donors or managers rather than responding to actual societal problems. In sum, it is often difficult to judge how desirable states of affairs would look like, why they should count as beneficial, how they can be brought about and how the size of the challenge can be met.

The above observations point at the fact that, in a historical perspective, foundations were not created with the intention to serve as tools for the effective solution of social problems. Being ambiguous organisations with roots in the gift economy (Adloff and Sigmund 2005; Adloff 2010), based on multiple rationales (Sigmund 2000) and often shaped as tools for expressive rather than instrumental ways of giving (Frumkin 2006), they frequently lack the organisational prerequisites to meet these complex demands (e.g., Nielsen 1972; Bacchetti and Ehrlich 2007; Adloff 2010). Furthermore, there is no such thing as a profession of philanthropy. There exists neither a reliable technique nor an established body of knowledge which might guide the practice of philanthropic organisations. As a result, the organisational field of philanthropy can be regarded as semi-professional at best. The situation is further aggravated by the fact that foundations as non-membership organisations lack important sources of democratic legitimacy which may render their interventions problematic from a political point of view.

Finally, while the assets of many foundations look impressive at first glance, they actually remain marginal in relation to the needs they address. Largely regardless of the country or field in which they operate, be it education, science, health, the arts or social services, their share is usually no more than around 1 per cent of total expenditures and often much less (Hammack and Anheier 2010; Thümler et al. 2014a).[4] Foundations are certainly neither willing nor able to substitute for a welfare state in retreat (Anheier and Daly 2007a: 30–31). Under these conditions, they may find it difficult if not impossible to contribute to the solution of social problems in responsive, effective and comprehensive ways.

1.1 Philanthropy's Role in Society and the Rationalisation of Charity

Due to material as well as ideological changes in Western societies, the question of whether, why and to what degree foundations succeed or fail in realising their (more or less) prosocial agendas is no longer a concern of individual philanthropists or philanthropic organisations only: the results of philanthropic action are relevant from a societal point of view, as well.

Recent decades have seen a rapid growth in the financial assets of philanthropic foundations in Europe (European Foundation Centre 2008) and the USA (Foundation Center 2012). New philanthropic actors like Bill Gates and his "giving pledge", an attempt to commit the wealthiest families and individuals in the USA and worldwide to give the majority of their fortunes to philanthropic causes, stir the imagination, and the criticism, of public observers. These developments are partially due to a growth of wealth in modern societies that is distributed highly unequally, giving rise to large fortunes in the hand of a few "high-net-worth" individuals (Adloff 2010: 145–150). In times of austerity, the role of the public welfare state is decreasing in many countries, and demands for a stronger engagement of private actors—foundations among them—to fill the emerging gaps, complement public systems under strain, provide funding for public services and solve social problems with their very own assets, methods and competencies are heard more often (Anheier and Toepler 1999: 255; Anheier and Freise 2004; Harrow 2010: 121). It is in this context that many observers (and foundations themselves) regard philanthropy as a particularly important institution of society.

Yet, this new attention does not come without strings attached. Scholars diagnose a utilitarian turn in societal attitudes towards philanthropy that renders more traditional gift-oriented practices problematic. Increasingly, the mere unconditional handing out of grants is regarded as inadequate, even illegitimate, behaviour. In particular, it is criticised for being irresponsive vis-à-vis complex social problems and, hence, an ineffective waste of tax-free resources (Porter and Kramer 1999).[5]

What is more, critical voices point out that inadequate philanthropic action may actually harm individuals or collectives if social problems are tackled in irresponsible or dilettantish ways. Historically, this has resulted in the loss of human life and the destabilisation of communities (Damon 2006: 4–7). A more recent and less dramatic example for this diagnosis is the Gates Foundation's small schools programme. This aimed at breaking down large urban school systems into smaller independent units based on the erroneous belief that this would regularly result in higher levels of student performance. An approach that was praised for its potential to leverage[6] private assets by means of the redirection of an "ocean of public dollars" (Greene 2005: 72) turns out to have resulted in the waste of *public* resources (Shear et al. 2008).

Foundations thus face a serious dilemma. They are confronted with external demands and their own ambitions to help solve major social problems, and they thrive due to the hopes they mobilise in this regard. At the same time, they lack the necessary intellectual, financial and organisational resources to cope with these new expectations. As a way out of this dilemma, foundations frequently choose the option of "functional dilettantism" (Seibel 1994), addressing social problems by utterly inadequate means and in merely symbolic ways which results in "successful failure" (Seibel 1996; Thümler 2011). In these cases, foundations strive more for the public credits they earn for announcing bold initiatives, while at the same time shying away from the risks inherent in tackling complex and controversial issues long term and in adequate ways. Thus, they consolidate the status quo rather than fostering social change (Nielsen 1972; Adloff 2004; Fioramonti and Thümler 2011; Thümler 2011), which has led to the portrait of foundations as maximisers of legitimacy rather than societal welfare (Hall 1992: 226).

Research further suggests that, under conditions of ambiguous or contentious goals and high uncertainty regarding the appropriate means for tackling particular problems, actors may take refuge in the alleged certainty of ideology (Schön 1971), thus replacing experimentation and processes of self-critical learning with a firm belief in prevailing rational myths. In this context, scholars have pointed at the role of foundations as drivers of the marketisation (Nickel and Eikenberry 2009; Edwards 2010) and financialization (Thümler 2016) of society and even of the very process of rationalisation of which they are objects themselves (Hwang and Powell 2009).

In both scenarios, society might ultimately be worse off and the institution of philanthropy itself might experience a loss of trust and legitimacy if it cannot come up to the expectations of its audiences, nurtured by its own ambitious aims and promises.

1.2   From Strategic Philanthropy to Emergent Strategy and Beyond

The current discourse on strategic philanthropy can be regarded as a response to these concerns. It is based on the Weberian ideal of rational bureaucracy and aspires to maximise value for money by deliberative and instrumental means and by imposing a high degree of control over processes and ends. It further implies the political project of establishing this framework as the *standard* approach to philanthropy. While not based on a unified and coherent doctrine, its proponents typically subscribe to the following set of beliefs.

First, the production of a particular type of outcome—*social impact*—is conceived as the very rationale of philanthropic action and the major criterion of success. Social impact in terms of the demonstrable, measurable and attributable effect of a philanthropic cause is regarded as the only legitimate aim and desirable "social return" of philanthropic action. Just as the performance of a business or a financial investment is judged by a look at the bottom line, the success of philanthropy is supposed to be determined by reference to the degree of impact it brings about (Porter and Kramer 1999; Prewitt 2006; Brest and Harvey 2008; Ebrahim and Rangan 2010; Liket 2014; Harrow and Jung 2015).

Second, the attempts to model impact as the allegedly straightforward new "currency" of philanthropy go along with an increase in attempts at *standardising* and *measuring* the effects of philanthropic action, because otherwise performance cannot be assessed and compared reliably. Scholars and practitioners try to capture impact in quantifiable and even monetary dimensions (Emerson et al. 1999; Rauscher et al. 2012; Kroeger and Weber 2014; Liket 2014) which are strongly influenced by the logics, methods and concepts of business (Ebrahim and Rangan 2010: 8) and, increasingly, the financial industry (Salamon 2014; Thümler 2016).

Third, effective performance is regarded as being dependent on the existence of a *strategy* in terms of an encompassing and coherent approach to problem solving which combines high precision in terms of goals, a detailed knowledge of the problem situation and alternative options for action, sophisticated plans which specify how to reach the goals and a close alignment between organisational resources, means and objectives

(Porter 1996; Porter and Kramer 1999; Frumkin 2006; Brest and Harvey 2008).

The underlying logic has been formulated most clearly by Brest and Harvey (2008: 7). They stipulate:

> accomplishing philanthropic goals requires having great clarity about what those goals are and specifying indicators of success before beginning a philanthropic project. It requires designing and then implementing a plan commensurate with the resources committed to it. This, in turn, requires an empirical, evidence-based understanding of the external world in which the plan will operate. And it requires attending carefully to milestones to determine whether you are on the path to success.

Rational philanthropic behaviour under conditions of resource scarcity is further framed as a kind of *social investment* (Frumkin 2003; Knott and McCarthy 2007; Thümler and Bögelein 2012; Zunz 2012). According to this line of thinking, foundations are supposed to achieve *maximal* social return on investment with the overly limited resources at hand by way of "leveraging" their contributions, thus generating impacts significantly beyond their financial inputs (Frumkin 2000; Hess 2005a; Katz 2005; Bishop and Green 2008; Adloff 2010; Hammack and Anheier 2010).[7]

As a response to the overwhelming dimensions of many social problems, this approach is frequently combined with demands to trigger processes of growth. Acknowledgement of unsatisfied demands comes first, followed by a close study of the nature of the problem. As a next step, philanthropists are supposed to develop a prototype and test and refine it in practice. In the case of success, it is turned into a standardised product ready to be distributed to end users by different means of societal diffusion or organisational scaling up. The more users adopt the innovative product, the higher the social impact will be (Dees et al. 2004; Gerber 2006: 342; Fleishman 2007: 59; Weber et al. 2013).

In what follows, this conception of philanthropic action will be labelled the "bureaucratic model". Far from being a theoretical ideal only, this approach flourishes in practice as well as in practitioner's discourse. It is actively promoted by an emerging industry of consulting firms and nonprofit rating agencies such as the German Phineo, the UK-based New Philanthropy Capital or Charity Navigator in the USA (Gordon et al. 2009; Kail and Lumley 2012; Phineo 2012; Kurz and Kubek 2013). This is further reflected in the reliance on *projects* as highly controlled, but temporarily limited organisational forms (Institute for Philanthropy 2009).

1.2.1 The Bureaucratic Project and its Challenges

A wide body of scholarship sheds doubts on the claims that organisational behaviour based on the bureaucratic model represents the state of the art of organisational effectiveness, that it adequately describes what effective problem solvers *do* and that it represents the ideal of what organisations in pursuit of effectiveness are *supposed* to do. These assumptions have repeatedly and convincingly been refuted by research on a broad range of issues such as the effectiveness and evaluation of non-profit organisations (DiMaggio 2001; Ebrahim and Rangan 2010), organisational decision making (Cohen et al. 1972; Brunsson 2006), industrial and corporate innovation (Nelson and Winter 1977; Van de Ven et al. 2008), corporate strategy development (Mintzberg 1979a; Hayes 1985; Grant 2003; Wiltbank et al. 2006), managerial problem solving (Wagner 1991), urban planning (Blanco 1994), entrepreneurship (Sarasvathy 2001), the psychology of complex problem solving (henceforth CPS) (Funke 2003), management under conditions of complexity (Levinthal and Warglien 1999; Snowden and Boone 2007) and public school reform (Cohen et al. 2014).

In particular, critics point at the weakness of the bureaucratic ideal when it comes to action under conditions of unclear problem situations, contentious and ambiguous goals, environmental complexity and dynamic change as well as a lack of reliable problem-solving technology, which are regarded as being characteristic of and increasing in contemporary societies (e.g., Rittel and Webber 1973; Crozier 1982; Chisholm 1995; Kettl 2009). Under these initial conditions, actors can neither formulate clear preferences, *predict* outcomes with a sufficient degree of precision nor exert *control* over the process of problem solving. Instead, an adequate definition of problems, the formulation of prudent ends and the generation of new or better causal knowledge are the *result* rather than the point of departure of the process of problem solving. In other words, the bureaucratic model provides no answer to the question of how to cope with profound uncertainty and how to generate novelty. This is the proper domain of (social) innovation rather than strategic planning (Moore and Westley 2011).

Second, the preference for processes of growth to match the size of social problems is problematic for a number of different reasons. For instance, successful problem solving in the field of school improvement in general is often highly idiosyncratic to the local problem situation (Tyre and von Hippel 1997). In these cases, problem solvers generate "sticky" knowledge that cannot easily be transferred to other sites (von Hippel 1994). What is more, there is a manifest trade-off between effectiveness on the one hand and growth on the other. Rather than multiplying the impacts by multiplying solutions, effectiveness decreases as solutions are more widely distributed. This phenomenon has been explained by the variation inherent in local situations and the necessary degree of required adaptation to local needs, which results in a loss of effectiveness of interventions (Slavin, personal communication). Research on the diffusion and institutionalisation of civil service reforms has shown that the adoption of new practices is driven by considerations of superior performance only in the early stages of the process. The pace accelerates as the sources of adoption change from an emphasis on performance to a focus on legitimacy (Tolbert and Zucker 1983). Finally, the very concept of growth may frequently be inadequate to the requirements of civil society actors. For instance, scholars of innovation at the grassroots level have observed that the sustainability of local projects can be undermined by support that is targeted at growth and diffusion. Even if support is granted with the best of intentions, it may overwhelm the capacity of these actors and contradict their values (Seyfang and Smith 2007).

The concept of leverage hasn't been addressed convincingly, either. While frequently used in practice, it didn't receive much systematic scholarly attention and no coherent definition has been put forward so far. The discussion does not go far beyond the provision of long lists of leveraging "tactics" (e.g., Frumkin 2000; Frumkin 2006: 190–203) which do not provide answers to the pervasive problems inherent in this concept. What can it possibly mean to generate outcomes which are significantly larger than inputs, given that the two dimensions are usually different in kind? Hence, use of the concept often boils down to the questionable assumption that the mobilisation of more and additional inputs would result in an enhanced level of impact.

Finally, strategic philanthropy rests on a voluntaristic conception of social value, regarding as beneficial whatever philanthropic actors intend to bring about (Frumkin 2006; Hammack and Anheier 2010: 6; Liket 2014: 53). However, examples such as the somewhat absurd case of a Swiss foundation aiming at "providing the nuns and the priest of the local Cistercian Monastery at Easter with one Schoggi-Chocolate Easter Egg filled with 300g of candies each" (Alberg-Seberich and Meibom 2009: 41) demonstrates that philanthropic intentions can be utterly meaningless in societal terms. A related and more profound line of criticism is put forward by the advocates of "effective altruism". Sparked by the considerations of moral philosopher Peter Singer on the ethical implications of severe global poverty (Singer 1972), they urge the development of a more rational approach towards decisions on the aims and purposes of philanthropic giving. For instance, Pogge argues that, in ethical terms, "we should, for the most part, direct our grossly insufficient contributions for maximum effect: toward the most cost-effective harm protection projects" (Pogge 2011: 65). This points at the tension that arises as scholars of philanthropy focus exclusively on the *means* of effective philanthropic action, including an advanced debate on increasingly sophisticated techniques of project planning, monitoring and evaluation, while at the same time regarding ends as given, left at the discretion of the funder or executives (Schambra 2014). Moreover, strategic philanthropy underestimates the value-laden and contentious nature inherent in attempts at fostering the public good by means of solving complex social problems (e.g., Lindblom 1959; DiMaggio 2001: 269; Cho 2006). This point is vividly illustrated by the fact that critical observers of philanthropy have frequently blamed foundations for pursuing illegitimate neo-liberal agendas (Roelofs 2003; Schöller 2006) and pointed at severe unintended consequences of philanthropic action (Nickel and Eikenberry 2009; Edwards 2010; Thümler 2016).[8]

Summing up the discussion, there are good arguments and strong empirical evidence that the strategic project, at least if regarded as a universal panacea to the philanthropic predicament, may often make things *worse,* rather than leading to new levels of rationality and efficacy in tackling complex social problems. Research suggests that the application of bureaucratic practices to "situations to which they are profoundly ill suited" (DiMaggio 2001: 250) may result in a *loss* of organisational effectiveness, caused by an increase in organisational complexity, permanent attempts at reform and a diversion of resources from core activities to the implementation and operation of control systems which remain ultimately dysfunctional (Bromley and Powell 2012). Scholars further suggest that exclusive reliance on the model of rational bureaucracy may result in a depoliticised philanthropy, causing it to turn away from contentious issues, themes which reside on a more discursive level or which require the change of complex social systems (DiMaggio 2001: 269) because of a bias "in favour of work that can readily be measured, such as delivery of services in education or healthcare, at the expense of work where the outcomes are harder to measure, such as in policy advocacy, democratization, or civil rights" (Ebrahim and Rangan 2010: 9).

Hence, the proposition that the bureaucratic model should be adopted as the *standard* procedure of philanthropy, regardless of the concrete problem situation, is untenable. This is not to say that this approach does not work at all. But it means that it works under specific circumstances only, and fails in others. Funke and Frensch (2007: 38) assert that:

> it is true that a lot of problem solving and thinking can be reconstructed as a series of rules which are followed by the problem solver. In certain environments, the use of plans will be helpful and lead to the goal. But there are other situations in which the control of action is more triggered by the events and the environment than by following a fixed plan.

The task is, then, to determine more precisely which types of situations require alternative responses and how these need to be designed. Furthermore, the discussion shows that the mere intention to do good is of little value when it comes to the question of what constitutes a beneficial difference to individuals or society. The value of the results of philanthropic action can only be determined in the framework of a suitable normative theory such as pragmatism or the capability approach which needs to provide a tenable explanation of which results of philanthropic initiatives can be regarded as morally good and societally desirable, and why.

1.2.2 *From Strategic to Emergent Philanthropy*

In recent years, some of the most important proponents of strategic philanthropy have conceded that this approach might be inadequate when it comes to tackling complex social problems (Heifetz et al. 2004; Kania and

Kramer 2011; Hanleybrown et al. 2012; Kania and Kramer 2013, Kania et al. 2014). They have made amendments to the bureaucratic framework to enhance flexibility and responsiveness (Brest et al. 2015).[9]

For instance, drawing on Mintzberg et al. (1998) and the insights of complexity theory, Kania et al. (2014) maintain that the scope of application of bureaucratic models is restrained to the solution of simple problems under stable environmental conditions. They suggest adopting the approach of "emergent strategy" as the method of choice in the face of problem complexity (2014: 29). This approach is supposed to retain the virtues, yet remedy the shortcomings, of overly rigid conceptions of strategic philanthropy. It emphasises the importance of clear objectives, yet opens up latitude for a much higher degree of flexibility and adaptability when it comes to finding the path towards goals. In other words, instead of a detailed strategy in terms of a fixed plan or roadmap that predetermines a linear succession from problem situation towards goal situation, they favour a combination of clear goals with an organic approach which is triggered by environmental responses to organisational activities as well as serendipitous events.

What is more, the subjects of remedial action are now conceived as alliances of collaborators rather than single organisations. Problem solving is no longer regarded as isolated and effects are no more directly attributable. Rather, strategies are co-produced, implementation is collective and the emphasis on control and planning shifts to an emphasis on learning (Heifetz et al. 2004; Kania et al. 2014).

However, as progress is made in the discussion on adequate philanthropic strategies, a number of shortcomings of the new approach come into view as well. To begin with, more open and experimental approaches are in danger of losing the distinctive advantages of strategic philanthropy such as the orientation that comes along with the focus on outcomes and clear goals as well as the discipline characteristic of planned strategies, as they replace the language of logical models with entirely vague concepts such as "working the attractors" (Kania et al. 2014: 30–31).

Furthermore, conceptions of emergent strategy are subject to some of the same objections which apply to strategic philanthropy. In particular, the discussion largely brackets normative questions and tends to take the moral relevance of successful attempts at problem solving as given. It thus underestimates the prevalence of unclear goals in processes of social problem solving and provides no answer to the case of contentious or meaningless ends of philanthropic action either.

Moreover, a number of crucial aspects of philanthropic action are not covered by this discussion at all. In particular, the almost exclusive focus on *strategy* results in the neglect of important other variables of problem-solving action. For instance, research on corporate strategy points at the dependence of strategy on adequate *structures* (Chandler 1962; Mintzberg 1979b; Miller 1988). Considerations such as these are almost entirely absent in current research on philanthropy.

Finally, the current scholarship circles around the determinants of effective action in terms of an increasingly broad set of variables which are supposed to be relevant for problem solving. However, the identification and addition of success factors is unable to provide *explanations* for the phenomenon under investigation, just as managerial strategies for the development of an effective pharmaceutical drug fall short of providing the mechanism by which it works. The discussion on the role of social mechanisms in Chapter 11 is an attempt to show how these limitations can be overcome in a systematic way.

1.3 Research Questions, Objectives and Design

In sum, while it seems straightforward to demand that philanthropic organisations should make a beneficial contribution to society, this ambition can neither easily be realised in practice, nor captured in conceptual and theoretical terms. Yet, under conditions of a profound lack of orientation, misguided philanthropic efforts may be in vain or even outright harmful. Given the apparent weaknesses of the bureaucratic project which flourishes in the current practice of philanthropy, there is an urgent need for a more advanced approach to philanthropic problem solving. Furthermore, as long as the knowledge on the actual and potential effects of foundations on society is limited, it is almost impossible to determine more precisely what to hope, or fear, from them. A better understanding of what this type of organisation actually contributes to the public good would be desirable from a practical and societal as well as a more political point of view.

This is where my study comes in. It puts centre stage philanthropic organisations which tackle complex social problems and investigates how they manage to generate social impact by means of addressing these problems in new and effective ways. The research was guided by the following questions: What does it mean to say that philanthropic action is beneficial in the first place? That is, what kind of difference constitutes an advantage, for whom and why? If advantageous states of affairs come about, how can these results be explained and how can they be causally related to philanthropic action? This is the perspective of social impact.

How can such a difference be made if philanthropic actors are confronted with complex social problems which elude readily available solutions? How can they develop, implement and sustain novel solutions to these problems? This is the perspective of social innovation.

How can philanthropic organisations match the size of social problems under conditions of scarce resources and how can they make the best possible use of the available assets? Is it possible to "leverage" them in such a way as to make an impact which is disproportionally larger than the resources invested and what could that possibly mean, given that inputs and outcomes are usually incommensurable? This is the perspective of social investment.

Finally, how can the answers to these questions be related systematically to the particular strengths and weaknesses, competencies and resources, of organised philanthropy?

1.3.1 The Research Project "Strategies for Impact in Philanthropy"

These questions guided the research project "Strategies for Impact in Philanthropy" (SIP), coordinated by the Centre for Social Investment at the University of Heidelberg, Germany, from January 2007 to December 2009.[10] The initial research situation was rudimentary and fragmented, characterised by weak empirical data, limited availability of research (often semiscientific in nature) and lack of a coherent theory, including convincing hypotheses.

In cases such as these, an explorative procedure is recommended (Friedrichs 1983: 156). SIP thus adopted an inductive research design. The project sought to identify, portray and analyse examples of European philanthropy with high social impact. Accordingly, it was not supposed to identify statistically measurable correlations, but rather to reconstruct complex mechanisms or patterns of social interaction (Mayntz 1983) and to build theory based on these results.

The investigation was confronted with a particular methodological difficulty, namely the question of how to establish reliable instances of social impact under conditions of conceptual, causal and normative uncertainty. There is no doubt that this problem is not endemic to the field of philanthropy. Just as in research on public policy reforms or the effects of social movements:

> all propositions involving effectiveness as a dependent variable face the problem that this variable is notoriously difficult to operationalise. . . . Methodologically more difficult is the fact that effectiveness is the result not of a single factor, and not even of an additive combination of factors, but of a specific interactive relationship between sets of factors.
>
> (Mayntz 1997: 147)

The project thus proceeded on the "shaky ground" (Giugni 1999: xxiv) of what might be considered as a scholarly "swamp" (for the imagery see Schön 1987: 3). To balance these problems, it aimed at carving out a viable and stable core based on the description, analysis and explanation of comparatively uncontroversial instances of philanthropic impact. It was assumed that, once scholars were equipped with this theoretical grid, it would be easier to explore further more unstable regions of the swamp, including the more messy and ambiguous phenomena of widespread, disruptive or systemic social change.

For the project, a mixed methods approach was chosen, based on case study analysis (Yin 2003) to gain sufficiently differentiated insights into the most relevant aspects of philanthropic programmes. To improve the chance of determining a causal link between activities and societal effects by means of a comparison of different interventions and their outcomes, the project was set up as a collective case study, addressing the issue under investigation by means of "multiple case studies to illustrate the issue" (Creswell 2007: 74).

The project investigated cases from Belgium, Germany, Italy, the Netherlands, Portugal, Sweden and the UK. The countries were selected on the basis of a balanced proportion of different welfare states and non-profit regimes. In addition, access to data played an important role. SIP took into account different kinds of interventions targeted at the issues of "equal participation and integration in society". The aim was to identify an issue wide enough to find a sufficient number of interesting activities across Europe and at the same time be specific enough to allow for meaningful comparison. Hence, the final sample included programmes working on issues as diverse as the integration of migrants into the labour market, the establishment of intercultural gardens and advocacy for freedom of information legislation.

The cases were selected by means of a multi-step procedure (the "funnel" approach). First, about 130 instances of allegedly successful[11] interventions were collected. To this purpose, experts in the field, including civil society researchers, foundation staff members and members of philanthropic associations, were asked for recommendations, and the project team conducted own research, as well. Out of this first collection, 45 cases were chosen to be portrayed in "vignettes", that is, short descriptions of actors and activity including the precise approach and presumed impact. On the basis of the vignettes, a smaller number of 20 cases were selected to be examined by means of in-depth research case studies,[12] which were investigated and prepared by the project team, other CSI staff and external investigators. In each of these cases, semi-structured interviews with five to ten participants in different roles (directors of foundations; project directors, project staff, grantees and partners outside the foundation; members of the target group; and external observers and critics, if available) were conducted, based on standardised templates.[13] All the interviews were recorded as audio files and transcribed professionally. Additional to this, use was made of other types of documents, such as reports by professional associations, research by other scholars of philanthropy as well as documents provided by the foundations or their partner organisations, including project reports, publications and evaluations. Comprehensive case study reports which summarised the major findings of the single cases were prepared by the case authors, again, along a standardised structure based on the interview template.

A critical review of these 20 cases showed that most of them could not be regarded as promising candidates for social impact in the demanding sense introduced above. Some remained overly vague and did not allow a comprehensive understanding of the initiative. Others did not present the data necessary to make a robust assessment of results. Some of the initiatives were not regarded as convincing by the foundations themselves and were cancelled after some time. However, we identified a group of seven cases which were characterised by the following properties:

1   There were visible results in terms of evident and sustainable change in the foundation's environment. For instance, the UK-based Nuffield Foundation succeeded in the establishment of the Nuffield Council on Bioethics, which organises the production and distribution of non-partisan scientific reports on problems of bioethics.

2   These changes were not limited to mere outputs (such as the number of trainings realised). Rather, there occurred developments on the level of the target group which were described as positive and largely un-controversial. This is evident in the case of The Chance Foundation for Vocational Training in Eastern Switzerland, which helps disadvan-taged youth to complete vocational training and to find permanent jobs.

3   It seemed plausible to assume a causal relation between foundation activities and beneficial results. Even if the comprehensive freedom of information legislation in the UK was enacted by Parliament and not an NGO, observers agreed that the result was due to the sustained en-gagement of the Campaign for the Freedom of Information. For a long period of time, this organisation had been the only relevant actor in the UK to engage in systematic lobbying for such a law. Its work would not have been possible without long-term support provided by the Joseph Rowntree Charitable Trust.

4   Finally, the selected cases seemed to generate "high" impact. Take the case of the Foundation Interkultur, an advocacy organisation which contributed to the strong growth of the number of intercultural gardens in Germany. They were initiated and run by a large number of vol-unteers, requiring only a very moderate amount of philanthropic seed funding.

According to the standard approach to the analysis of qualitative data, characteristic issues of each of these seven cases were identified, followed by an analysis across all cases looking for common themes (Yin 2003). In this phase, we found that all our cases shared a number of common properties.

First, the approaches foundations chose and the ambitions they displayed seemed to be rather *pragmatic* in character. They all addressed and solved social problems which could neither be characterised as the most complex "super wicked" (Levin et al. 2012) challenges of modern societies, nor as merely marginal disturbances. They could better be described as *problems of moderate complexity* which were addressed in *adequate* ways. In other words, actors neither aspired to save the world nor to provide mere impulses. Instead, they sought to find serious and sustainable solutions for problems of limited scale and scope. In this context, we introduced the concept of "niching", which was supposed to capture attempts at coherently tackling problems of medium complexity and relevance. Yet, we were unable to determine the meaning of these fundamental concepts and ideas with sufficient precision. Moreover, we observed that the solution of problems always relied on the experimental development of novel arrangements instead of the use or diffusion of standard instruments. Thus, a close connection between social impact and social innovation became visible at an early stage of analysis.

In the following phases, we aimed at the development of a new conception of philanthropic action which was supposed adequately to describe, explain and classify *this particular group of cases*. It needs to be emphasised that the aim of this study is limited to this very ambition. It does not seek to discard the bureaucratic model in favour of an ideal of pragmatic philanthropy as the new paradigm of effective philanthropic action, for bureaucracy has its merits. Neither does it claim that philanthropic organisations should not attempt to contribute to the solution of the large, systemic challenges of modern societies (for they should).

In this book, the emerging "pragmatic" model of philanthropic action is based on the discussion of only four out of the seven impactful cases due to limitations of space and the need to reduce complexity. These are the Foundation anstiftung and Foundation Interkultur (Germany), the Joseph Rowntree Charitable Trust and the Campaign for Freedom of Information (UK), the Nuffield Foundation and the Nuffield Council on Bioethics (UK) and The Chance Foundation for Vocational Training in Eastern Switzerland.

The cases were prepared based on the pool of data mentioned previously. They are supposed to illustrate major characteristics of the emerging model. The selection was guided by the intention to present a broad and diverse spectrum of organisations, approaches and outcomes. They feature grant-making, operating and hybrid types of foundations. These actors operate in different societal environments and exhibit and reflect the different logics and traditions of these fields. Accordingly, and most importantly, the cases exhibit four different types of social impact. Foundation Interkultur triggered a grassroots movement for intercultural gardens, which enhances the quality of life of gardeners and fosters encounters among different social groups. The Nuffield Council provided expertise to scientists and policymakers, helping them to make better informed decisions in a very sensible domain of action. The Joseph Rowntree Charitable Trust supported a political campaign which resulted in a piece of comprehensive Freedom of Information legislation, granting citizens access to previously confidential governmental files. The Chance developed social services which help disadvantaged youth to complete vocational training and find permanent jobs. While it would have been an option to include additional cases from other countries to show how philanthropy works in different societal environments, this would have been redundant in terms of the impact created.

1.3.2 Theoretical Background and Contributions

The case analysis suffered from the lack of a relevant and comprehensive theory. Moreover, the central concepts were unclear. For instance, there exists no study which elucidates the causal and normative components and implications of the concept of social impact. Hence, as the next step of analysis, a suitable theoretical repertoire had to be developed, along with an adequate vocabulary for the description and analysis of the phenomena under investigation. The pragmatic model originates as a crossover between different disciplines, in particular pragmatist philosophy and research on technology transitions. Both theories share a concern for the question of how a deviation from routinised action and dominant structures is possible; how variation in terms of creative, innovative action comes about and how it unfolds; and how new practices are retained in such a way as to bring about ultimate change and enhancement of the initial situation. However, neither pragmatism nor transition research can simply be turned into the necessary framework for the analysis of philanthropic action. Each has its own strengths and weaknesses; the challenge is to combine strengths, remedy shortcomings and, where necessary, complement both with additional research on problem solving and innovation strategies from different social sciences.

To begin with, the public philosophy of pragmatism proved to be particularly well suited to serve the purposes of this investigation. It systematically addresses the question of how intelligent social action looks in those puzzling problem situations which are characterised by high degrees of causal and normative uncertainty in which the bureaucratic model fails. The pragmatist theory of action focuses on the circulation between stable habitual action and creative phases of problem solving in processes of evolutionary learning and highlights the importance of the generation of novel solutions which emerge from and shape this circle (e.g., Joas 1992). It thus provides basic assumptions and the conceptual framework which are needed to organise research on the impact and effectiveness of philanthropic action in new and more coherent ways. Pragmatism further makes some—if quite tentative—suggestions regarding the structural conditions of social problem solving and provides a normative framework that explains which kind of social action counts in moral terms, and why. Finally, it suggests a number of more far-ranging societal consequences which may help to challenge overly limited and merely instrumental perspectives on philanthropic action (West 1989; Campbell 1992; Talisse and Aikin 2008; Ansell 2011).

However, while the practical relevance of pragmatism has frequently been posited, it has never been tested empirically in the context of non-profit action and it must be demonstrated how the pragmatist theory of action can be applied to empirical instances of philanthropic interventions. Furthermore, pragmatism as a public philosophy proved to be too abstract to inform the research project in sufficiently specific ways. When it comes to questions of the nature of social problems and their properties, available strategies of action as well as the structures underpinning these strategies, additional scholarly sources needed to be tapped.

The sociology of social problems provides important background knowledge both on empirical instances and sources of such problems as well as the complex ways in which they are discursively construed, negotiated and adopted or rejected as valid or invalid claims (e.g., Blumer 1971; Kitsuse and Spector 1973; Merton 1976). In particular, it emphasises the structural causes and the longevity of the most severe social problems, which are

> so entrenched in societal arrangements and so much an intrinsic part of societal pursuits that the most any intervention methods at the operative level can achieve is to control the extent or the intensity of the problem.
>
> (Jamrozik and Nocella 1998: 60)

However, the sociological literature on social problems tends to bracket the question of *solutions*. Moreover, whenever the issue of problem solving *has* been addressed, *public* actors such as the social professions and law enforcement agencies have been the focus of attention (cf. Jamrozik and Nocella 1998; Kaufmann 1999). In contrast, the roles of civil society actors in general and philanthropic organisations in particular constitute a blind spot in the research.[14]

Other disciplines provide a much more comprehensive repertoire of relevant knowledge on adequate problem solving *strategies*. For instance, there is a substantive literature on public problem solving (e.g., Mayntz 1983; Chisholm 1995; Ansell 2011), (urban) planning (e.g., Cartwright 1973; Blanco 1994) as well as corporate strategy (e.g., Miller 1988) and industrial innovation (e.g., Nelson and Winter 1977; Levinthal 1998) which circles around the reconstruction and analysis of effective strategies for action in situations of high complexity and low certainty. The discussion on complex problem solving in psychology (e.g., Frensch and Funke 1995; Funke 2003) proved to be particularly relevant as it helps to determine the fundamental concepts of (complex) problems and problem-solving behaviour with more precision.

Although not all the results of these diverse strands of research can be transferred to the field of philanthropy, they still broaden the discussion considerably, help avoid the overly optimistic exuberance that characterises much of the discussion on philanthropy and vicinal fields such as social entrepreneurship or social innovation, and provide a number of important and fundamental, if somewhat fragmented, conceptual and theoretical tools which serve as important building blocks of the framework which is under construction here.

The discussion on the *structures* of problem solving relies on research on radical technological change and the approach of strategic niche management (SNM). They both were motivated by the attempt to explain and shape processes of socio-technological innovation to further transitions towards a more sustainable economy (Kemp et al. 1998; Geels 2002). The major insight of this strand of research can be put as follows. Comprehensive, maximally complex and contentious processes of transformation of dominant socio-technological systems cannot be planned in advance and steered top-down. They rather depend on the existence of innovative niches in terms of supportive ecosystems which protect and foster the emergence, co-evolution and sustainability of a multitude of independent local niche experiments which may ultimately result in the development of complex new alternatives to incumbent technological systems (Verheul and Vergragt 1995; Kemp et al. 1998; Geels 2002; Schot and Geels 2007). In this study, it will be shown how the approach of SNM can be extended beyond the domain of technology and issues of large-scale systemic change to be made fruitful for the analysis of much more moderate processes of social problem solving. Moreover, the above-mentioned discussions of problem-solving strategies help to zoom in on questions of agency, thus complementing the focus on grand structures and long-term trajectories of change which are characteristic for transition studies.

Given the lack of coherent theory, the required analytical framework could not simply be derived from the available literature. Rather, the analysis proceeded in multiple recurrent phases that involved moving between the data, emerging categories, concepts and relationships, as well as a growing body of relevant research. This multi-step approach resulted in the pragmatic framework of philanthropy that is the essential outcome and the major contribution of this book. As its development was based on and shaped by the discussion of the data, it is tailor-made to guide their analysis.

1.4 Structure of the Study

Part I sets the theoretical stage for the remainder of the study. It aims to develop a provisional theoretical and conceptual framework, which, though still somewhat fragmentary, might guide both the presentation and the analysis of the case studies. Chapter 2 introduces the public philosophy of pragmatism, with a particular focus on the work of John Dewey. The pragmatist perspective grounds the development of the major themes of my work, namely, a remedial theory of action with an evolutionary perspective on societal learning and development. The concepts of social problems and problem solving, habits/routines and change of routines, as well as situated experimental action and evolutionary learning lie at the basis of pragmatist thought and are of crucial importance for the development of a coherent theory of philanthropic problem solving.

Chapter 3 unpacks the concept of complex social problems. I begin by developing a basic and generic model of problems and proceed by determining sources of complexity which are characteristic of social problems.

Drawing on the key notions of uncertainty and resistance as well as a lack of resources and control, I develop a more fine-grained account of social problems and thus lay the foundation for a tailor-made discussion of problem-solving strategies. They are addressed in Chapter 4, where I begin by formulating a number of well-established heuristics relevant to problem solving, such as the reduction of complexity and the notion of fit. I then go on to present and discuss the characteristics and the range of application of different types of strategies which include, but are not limited to, bureaucratic and experimental approaches.

Chapter 5 explores the structural foundations of problem solving, with a particular focus on the concept of niches in terms of bounded, protected and stable spaces as the locus of innovation and the production of value. This is based on the approach of strategic niche management and explores its potential relevance for philanthropic action.

Part II contains the descriptive part of the study. The empirical case studies are presented in detail in order to make visible a broad range of problem-solving behaviour and impact phenomena, which are sometimes straightforward and clear, sometimes more subtle. Chapter 6 discusses the case of The Chance Foundation for Vocational Practice in Eastern Switzerland. The organisation was set up to fight youth unemployment by means of an evidence-based, intense and long-term mentoring programme which targets adolescents in six Swiss cantons. Chapter 7 introduces the case of the Foundation anstiftung and Foundation Interkultur. Based on the values and logics of civil society and an orientation towards action at the grassroots, these organisations fostered the emergence and growth of the intercultural garden movement in Germany. Chapter 8 portrays the UK-based Nuffield Foundation and its offspring, the Nuffield Council on Bioethics. The Council was founded to explore ethical dilemmas in the domain of the biosciences and to prepare recommendations which address a wide audience of policymakers, researchers and the broader public. The Joseph Rowntree Charitable Trust and the Campaign for Freedom of Information are presented in Chapter 9. The Campaign successfully lobbied for the enactment of Freedom of Information legislation in the UK and keeps working to safeguard and improve the newly established system. These activities and achievements have been made possible by the long-term support of the Joseph Rowntree Charitable Trust which has lasted for over 25 years.

The analysis of the case studies follows in Part III. Equipped with the theoretical and conceptual repertoire which was developed in Part I on the one hand, and the empirical case studies of Part II, on the other, it aims to develop a coherent model of pragmatic philanthropic action. In Chapter 10, the pragmatist theory of action is applied to the case studies. The data analysis suggests that the model is valid, if with some modifications. It reconfirms the relevance of the pragmatist concern with the change of habits through phases of experimental learning which are triggered by problems of action. In all my cases, early episodes of exploration and experimentation are followed by a stage of exploitation during which actors make continuous and sustained use of new knowledge and practices of problem solving in order to "produce" or facilitate the production of solutions on a permanent basis. It is in this latter phase that social impact comes about, but the organisational capability to do so depends on a prior period of successful social innovation.

In Chapter 11, I suggest a generic explanation for the observed effects of philanthropic action. I show that all the interventions under investigation address a lack of access to valued resources on behalf of the target groups of philanthropic organisations. Their beneficial effects are a result of the "door-opener" mechanism. This term designates the mobilisation of these resources by means of opening up access to members of the target group. It explains why the addressees of philanthropic interventions change their behaviour in predictable and stable ways, and why this matters in normative terms. In Chapter 12, I show how the notion of innovative "niches" as developed in the context of research on socio-technological transformation can be adapted to the purposes of the study of philanthropy. I arrive at the concept of "philanthropic niches" as spaces in which novel solutions to social problems are developed and sustained. I go on to discuss varieties of niching behaviour in terms of different types of action which are directed at establishing, sustaining and facilitating philanthropic niches. The chapter closes with a discussion of the practical and organisational relevance and implications of niching.

Concluding in Chapter 13, I sum up the major results of my study. Based on my findings, I put forward a tentative suggestion of how the role of philanthropic foundations might be framed in a macro-perspective. Taking up the notion of intelligent niche management and building on theories of institutional and regime change, an alternative role for philanthropy is suggested that emphasises the societal relevance of successful, yet bounded, instances of social problem solving for processes of evolutionary change. Finally, I offer some open questions and directions for future research which come into view as a consequence of the above discussion.

Notes

1 Prosocial behaviour is defined as the willingness to benefit others voluntarily, if not necessarily at great personal costs or without any personal gains (Bierhoff 2002, 2010).
2 Prosocial motives are regarded as a major cause of charitable giving and philanthropic action (Timmer 2005; Bekkers and Wiepking 2011). Of course, philanthropy cannot be reduced to prosocial intentions alone. Philanthropic action may frequently be dominated by the desire to gain in reputation, demarcate social status, simply do justice to social conventions or produce the "warm glow" (Andreoni 1990) of personal satisfaction and righteousness (Sigmund 2000, 2004; Adloff 2010: 414; Bekkers and Wiepking 2011). However, research refutes the assumption that all prima facie instances of prosocial behaviour turn out to be veiled egoism at closer inspection. Rather it suggests that the prosocial

motivation to make a positive difference in the world and to help alleviate the fates of others is a fundamental trait of human nature (Piliavin and Charng 1990; Monroe 1994; Bierhoff 2002; Tomasello 2009). Hence, I contend that self-portrayals, public perceptions and existing instances of prosocial philanthropy should be taken seriously. The meaning of philanthropic action cannot be captured adequately if attempts "to make the world a better place" are dismissed as mere window-dressing. Even if not *all* philanthropic action can be characterised in this way, a portrait of philanthropy that entirely disregards this aspect would be incomplete in important respects.

3 In a broad sense, the modern understanding of the term "philanthropy" denotes the use of private goods for individual or public benefit (Sulek 2010: 204). In a more restrictive sense it refers to the institution of endowed philanthropic foundations only (Anheier 2005: 301). This study investigates the behaviour of philanthropic *organisations,* with a particular focus on philanthropic *foundations.*

4 In the USA, this unfavourable ratio has significantly *decreased* in recent decades (Hammack and Anheier 2010: 8).

5 Foundations have thus become objects of the "rationalisation of charity", that is, a development towards the professionalisation of non-profit organisations. The new paradigm is based on the ideal of rational bureaucracies, including professional managerial logics and techniques. It demands, among other things, strategic plans to structure future activities as well as a systematic orientation towards, and assessment of, organisational effectiveness (Hwang and Powell 2009). These pressures are not confined to philanthropy in particular or the broader organisational field of non-profit and development aid organisations in general (Ebrahim and Rangan 2010). Similar discussions play prominent roles in the discourse on the effectiveness of public bureaucracies, innovation policy and public planning. Better management, a closer focus on measurable results and a general orientation towards business logics are seen as the rational method of choice in these fields as well, although outcomes and effectiveness are similarly difficult to determine (Blanco 1994; Ansell 2011; Nill and Kemp 2009). These developments can be explained as expressions of a more general societal trend towards heightened expectations of due performance along with increasing attempts at controlling conformity to these standards that has come to be known under the label of the "audit society" (Power 1999).

6 In this case, the concept of leverage refers to the redirection of the flow of public resources into more effective areas of application. It is assumed that limited philanthropic inputs can thus "have a massively outsized impact—like a small rudder steering a big ship" (Hess 2005b: 297).

7 Porter and Kramer (1999: 122–123) even maintain that endowed foundations have the moral *obligation* to increase their social impact. They base their argument on the observation that these organisations, working with the revenues of tax-exempt assets, operate with a high share of public money foregone and a low payout rate compared to other non-profit organisations.

8 Strategic approaches are further plagued by a certain fetishism of measurement regardless of persistent problems to determine and attribute effects reliably. Against the background of research on the unintended consequences of social action (Merton 1936; Fine 2006), fundamental problems with the determination of means-ends relations in the context of organisational action in general (Bromley and Powell 2012) and the non-profit sector in particular (DiMaggio 2001), a lack of control over the outcomes of organisational action (Ebrahim and Rangan 2010), the non-linear character of processes of innovation which evades attempts at maximising results (Nelson and Winter 1977; Schot 1998; Van de Ven et al. 2008) as well as the collective nature of outcomes (Kania and

Kramer 2011), these attempts at determining, weighing and attributing impact tend to appear simplistic and reductionist.

9 There is yet another line of thinking which advocates "entrepreneurial" behaviour as an alternative or amendment to the rational bureaucracy (e.g., Hess 2005a), thus drawing on yet another societal myth. However, while the literature makes bold promises regarding the ability of social entrepreneurs to generate systemic or disruptive change (Alvord et al. 2004; Light 2006; Martin and Osberg 2007; Dorado and Ventresca 2012), the empirical basis for these claims is weak and there is little consensus as to how entrepreneurs manage to achieve these effects. Remarkably, the few attempts at providing explanations for entrepreneurial creation of value draw on arguments which are very similar to the discussion on adequate strategies.

10 To catch up with recent developments, additional interviews were conducted and documents were collected and analysed in 2015.

11 While the project explicitly sought to identify instances of successful philanthropy, a number of cases turned out to be failures at closer inspection, which allowed to study instances of both.

12 See Appendix A for a complete list of cases.

13 See Appendix B.

14 I further tie my research in with a long and ongoing discussion in sociology that asks for shapes and consequences of and alternatives to the project of the rationalisation of society (e.g., Rowan 2002; Boli 2005; Hwang and Powell 2009; Bromley and Powell 2012).

Part I

Theory

2 Pragmatism and the Evolution of Intelligent Social Action

In the introduction I outlined the tenets of strategic philanthropy, varieties of which dominate the current discourse on effective philanthropic action. At its core lies a model of philanthropic behaviour which is based on the ideal of rational bureaucracy. I have argued that this approach is both impoverished and misleading and I have pointed to the need to formulate the outlines of a viable alternative which must be informed by a comprehensive theory of social action. This needs to provide an account of individual and collective behaviour that is both scientifically tenable and morally relevant and that helps to formulate new and better answers to my questions. It must be applicable to philanthropic organisations and the situations they typically confront, namely action under considerable resource constraints and both causal and normative uncertainty. Finally, it should help to integrate the rather limited question concerning the beneficial societal contributions of organised philanthropy into a broader societal (macro-) perspective. In what follows I will introduce the pragmatist theory of social action as a promising candidate that satisfies these multiple demands.

2.1 Which Pragmatism, and Why?

The philosophy of pragmatism emerged in the USA in the late 1800s during a period of particularly intense and rapid social change (Feffer 1993; Anderson 2014). It is neither a coherent philosophical theory based on a set of widely shared propositions nor a school organised around a central doctrine or method of how to approach philanthropic problems. Rather, it must be regarded as a more or less loosely coupled collection of similar themes and arguments which have been formulated and elaborated in distinct ways in the canonical writings of its central figures, namely Charles Sanders Peirce, William James, John Dewey and George Herbert Mead (Talisse and Aikin 2008, 2011; but see Pape 2000). Among these, Dewey is the most relevant source for the purposes of my study, though I will occasionally also draw on the writings of Peirce and Mead whenever this is appropriate for the argument.

There are at least three good reasons for basing my inquiry on the philosophy of pragmatism. To begin with, pragmatism provides a *sui generis* theory of action that has frequently been regarded as a viable alternative to rational choice theory. It focuses on the question of how to cope intelligently with the uncertainty and contention inherent in and characteristic of the processes of social problem solving, in which initial conditions, means and ends are contested and unclear (Joas 1992; Whitford 2002; Beckert 2009). Pragmatists model adequate problem-solving behaviour along the paradigm of the natural sciences and emphasise the ability of rational actors to improve both empirical and moral knowledge and problem-solving capacity through continuous and collective processes of open inquiry, reflection, deliberation and experimentation (Scheffler 1974; Nagl 1998; Kitcher 2005; Talisse and Aikin 2008; Ansell 2011). Hence, pragmatism promises an opportunity to investigate the questions I raise in novel and original ways.

Second, pragmatists emphasise the necessity for a conception of meaningful action which aims at the integration of both instrumental and normative aspects. Historically, pragmatism has often been mistaken as the philosophical equivalent of a pragmatic attitude in a colloquial or even cynical sense of the term: as action that focuses on 'what works' regardless of ethical or political considerations. In fact, however, the very opposite is true: pragmatism represents a major attempt to reconcile these two strands (Campbell 1992; Joas 1992; Nagl 1998; Talisse and Aikin 2008; Dewey 2011 [1917]; Anderson 2014). Dewey, in particular, was concerned with the project to "address the difficulties involved in giving an account of value—moral, aesthetic, epistemic, political—that is consistent with experimental natural science" (Talisse and Aikin 2011: 2). On the other hand, I maintain that the theory of pragmatism offers an answer to the problem of action under resource constraints if it is conceived as pragmatic in the best literal sense of the term: not because it suggests doing what is feasible just because it is feasible, but rather because of its emphasis on the patient and piecemeal development of prudent remedies for complex concrete problems which are rooted in practical experience, and its rejection of excessive claims for shortcuts to wholesale societal and systemic transformation which are so eagerly traded in the marketplaces of philanthropic fashions.

Third, pragmatism fits well the particular properties and demands of actors in civil society. Philanthropic organisations in general and foundations in particular are neither suitable vehicles for the routine provision of basic social services such as public bureaucracies nor instruments for social struggles such as movements or political parties. They lack the size and the motivation to be the former and the constituency and legitimacy to be the latter. But due to a comparatively high degree of both political and financial independence, they are well positioned to enact the collaborative and consensus-oriented type of inquiry pragmatists favour as an intelligent response to social problems (Anheier 2005; Anheier and Leat 2006: 910; Anheier and Daly 2007a). Accordingly, both Dewey and Mead emphasise the relevance of problem-solving processes that operate "in and through voluntary associations" (LW 3: 144) and emphasise "the power of voluntary action based upon public collective intelligence" (LW 11: 299).

In the following I do not attempt to provide an encompassing account of pragmatist thought but rather highlight those aspects which are of central importance to this study. In particular, I will focus on Dewey's quasi-evolutionary perspective on intelligent social action. While it is certainly not sufficiently concrete to generate testable hypotheses, it still has to offer a highly original and very coherent outlook on social problems and problem-solving action that differs from conventional wisdom in a number of fundamental respects.

2.2 Core Themes of Pragmatism

Pragmatism is characterised by a shared commitment to naturalism and humanism: it is "a philosophy that fully respects the modern scientific worldview without thereby losing contact with the world of human practice" (Talisse and Aikin 2011: 4). The naturalist point of view, put very roughly, implies a dual commitment. On the one hand it maintains that natural things are the only real things. There are no metaphysical entities such as the articles of religion which exist independently of empirical cognition. On the other hand naturalism posits that all real things should be studied in accordance with the most advanced scientific methods and theories available (Talisse and Aikin 2008: 85–86). This position implies a rejection of all claims to a priori truths, be they of religious or philosophical origin, acknowledging that all our beliefs and theories are in principle fallible as they may be falsified by new evidence. Consequently, pragmatists maintain that human knowledge is essentially uncertain and provisional and potentially the object of revision (2008: 85; Ansell 2011: 12).

In the case of Dewey, who was profoundly influenced by Darwinist thought, the commitment to naturalism takes a distinctive evolutionary shape. Dewey argued that, in the light of Darwin's insights, the traditional problems of philosophy appear meaningless. They should be abandoned in favour of an entirely new set of questions (Dewey 2011 [1910]). This evolutionary conception of pragmatism is captured in the proposition that "the fundamental philosophical datum is activity of living creatures interacting with various factors and materials within their environments" (Talisse and Aikin 2011: 2). Dewey conceived human beings as the inhabitants of a natural and social environment which is subject to permanent processes of change and thus requires the continuous capability for successful adaptation (MW 6: 364–365).

However, unlike animals, the relationship of humans to their environment is not simply a matter of reaction and reflex. Since human beings are endowed with intelligence, their behaviour need neither be blind and random, nor based on dogma and tradition. Pragmatists thus put in focus the human ability to cope actively and creatively with the demands of the situations they face (Joas 1992). Dewey conceives the relationship between man and the environment as an active interplay. Humans do not simply adapt to their environment, but purposefully shape it (MW 6: 393–395). Hence, "adaptation . . . is as much adaptation *of* the environment to our own activities as our activities *to* the environment" (Thayer, 1981: 177, italics in the original) and the permanent reconstruction of the natural and social world is a characteristic property of human action (MW 6: 393–395).

Dewey's pragmatism thus combines evolutionary and instrumental perspectives as two basic "motors" of change (Van de Ven et al. 1995) in what can be conceived as a quasi-evolutionary conception of human agency. It is evolutionary because it portrays human action as a continuous process of variation, selection and retention that is aimed at successful adaptation to a changing environment. But Darwin holds that variation is essentially blind, and selection and retention of new variations are determined by the traits of the environment (Sydow 2013). Opposed to this, Dewey emphasises the importance of intelligent variation and purposeful selection, thus subscribing to a quasi-evolutionary model of evolution according to which "actors anticipate on selection and work towards linkages between variations and selections. Variation comes subsequently pre-packaged in the right direction" (Schot and Geels 2007: 614–615).

Finally, pragmatism is characterised by its *humanist* orientation. Dewey maintained "that action and opportunity justify themselves only to the degree in which they render life more reasonable and increase its value" (LW 2: 19). Given that human action in pursuit of life and well-being is supposed to constitute the major and fundamental theme philosophy has to deal with, and given the premise that the old metaphysical sources of knowledge are discredited, the question arises as to how successful orientation in and adaptation to changing environments can be achieved in ways which are adequate and reliable in cognitive, instrumental and normative terms. In the context of pragmatism, the methods of the natural sciences play a central role in answering this question.

2.3 The Pragmatist Theory of Action and the Scientific Method

The pragmatist theory of action emerged in the context of evolutionary epistemology as developed by Charles Sanders Peirce. Peirce argued that the project of epistemology should neither consist in the search for the sources of epistemic certainty nor in attempts at the justification of our present body of empirical knowledge (Kitcher 2005: 72). Rather, he proposed that we should:

> treat our current corpus of belief as a starting point from which we can hope to improve. Epistemology . . . must begin with what has been

passed on to us, and it must devise tools for inquiry, so that we can bequeath to our successors something better than what we inherited.

(Kitcher 2005: 72)

His own attempt to meet this challenge led to the development of the outlines of a pragmatist theory of action in his (2011 [1877]) article "The Fixation of Belief" which develops the doubt-belief model of inquiry. Inquiry is the process by which humans try to escape a puzzling and uneasy state of doubt in order to achieve a desirable state of belief. Peirce criticises inadequate methods of inquiry such as: "tenacity" (2011 [1877]: 43), that is the inclination to ignore doubt; "authority" (2011 [1877]: 44) as the fixation of belief based on doctrine; or metaphysical "a priori" arguments (2011 [1877]: 46)—and he argues for the merits of the scientific method as the most reliable method of inquiry available.

This model was later adopted by Dewey to serve a different purpose. In Dewey's hands, Peirce's tools for the rational generation of warranted claims for knowledge in the context of an evolutionary process of epistemic improvement were transformed with the intention of addressing practical problems in intelligent ways. His argument is motivated by considerations which are actually quite similar to Peirce's. The project is concerned with the analysis and reconstruction of appropriate methods to settle practical problems in such a way as to generate a conception of intelligent inquiry which might become the basis of a collective process of intelligent societal reconstruction and the object of continuous further scrutiny and refinement (Joas 1992: 299). This transfer was motivated by the observation that the state of empirical knowledge had massively improved since around the sixteenth century due to the introduction of experimental methods for the purposes of investigating natural phenomena (Kitcher 2005: 72–73). Dewey maintained that, by contrast:

> our moral, social, and political practices are still constrained by a legacy of dogmatism and over reliance on the powers of reason; [hence] the most important project of philosophy is to undertake the same kind of transformation in the human sphere, introducing the experimental method, both by describing how it would work and actually applying it.
>
> (Kitcher 2005: 73)

To overcome this predicament and to meet the challenge, he urged the sciences to explore systematically the ways in which collective problems can be solved effectively and responsibly. Just like Peirce, Dewey regarded the orientation towards the empirical sciences both as an antidote to the inclination to settle problems and conflicts too early, too easily and based on the wrong reasons and as a paradigm for the development of a more adequate and more effective method of collective action.

This does not imply the claim that the scientific method is to be conceived as a panacea for all problems. Just as science will not yield uncontroversial answers to *all* its questions, there is no guarantee that the experimental method of social inquiry will reliably result in the reconciliation of opposing points of view or that it will produce the causal knowledge necessary to solve social problems in each and every case. Rather, so the argument goes, intelligent and reflective methods of problem solving are the best and most promising instruments we have to date (Campbell 1992: 106–109). Hence, "change for the better is in no way guaranteed, but it certainly is not impossible" (Campbell 1992: 102).

Pragmatists further argue that, in Western societies which are deeply impregnated by the values and methods of science and technology, the treatment of practical problems needs to come up to the level of sophistication that governs these other societal sectors—not by subjecting all practical questions to a rational-scientific treatment, but by orienting the solution of practical problems to the high standards which have been reached elsewhere (Joas 1992: 304).

Both in "Human Nature and Conduct" (MW 14) and in "Logic: The Theory of Inquiry" (LW 12), Dewey analysed inquiry (that is, problem-solving action) as a complex process departing from habits which constitute the basis of most human behaviour. According to Dewey, the process of intelligent action unfolds as follows.[1] It begins with the recognition of an empirical situation *as being* problematic. In this early stage, the precise properties and features of the situation are still unclear and perceived as a state of disturbance and unease (LW 12: 109–110). Actors may simply leave it at that. But if they decide that the problematic situation needs to be resolved, they begin the process of inquiry (LW 12: 111). As the situation may still be completely opaque in this phase, the problem must be defined; that is, the situation must be "converted into a problem having definite constituents" (LW 12: 112). This transformation requires empirical observation of the relevant facts and considerable attempts to understand causal connections between them. It also includes the search for better interpretations of the situation, including provisional formulations of adequate ends. The phase of problem definition is particularly important because it essentially determines the further course and fate of inquiry: "a problem well put is half-solved", whereas "to mistake the problem involved is to cause subsequent inquiry to be irrelevant or to go astray" (LW 12: 112). The definition of the problem leads to the subsequent search for possible solutions. It begins with the occurrence of ideas which are at first vague. They guide further observation and reasoning and become more specific in the subsequent course of inquiry:

> Ideas are anticipated consequences (forecasts) of what will happen when certain operations are executed under and with respect to observed conditions. . . . The more the facts of the case come to light in consequence of being subjected to observation, the clearer and more pertinent

become the conceptions of the way the problem constituted by these facts is to be dealt with.

(LW 12: 113)

These early ideas are not simply enacted. Instead, problem solvers theoretically probe different possible options for action in thought experiments (Kitcher 2005: 76) and develop more elaborate yet tentative hypotheses. Hypotheses express informed opinions as to which intervention most likely leads to desired ends and thus involve causal as well as normative judgements: "they say that if something were done, then certain consequences would follow, which would be liked or valued" (Anderson 2014: para. 12).

Dewey emphasises that problems cannot be resolved theoretically but only by means of practical action. Hence, hypotheses need to be tested empirically: actors design a plan of action and implement solutions tentatively and incrementally to modify the problem situation. This process of variation takes place as long as action fails to deliver the predicted results. If a new course of action proves to be successful, it is selected by the problem solver(s) due to its perceived effectiveness and retained in the individual or collective repertoire of action as a new and refined habit. As such, it may again become an object of doubt in the future, for the process of problem solving never comes to a final end and solutions never reach bedrock. At best, it leads to "warranted assertibility" which may be revised in the light of new situations and experiences (LW 12: 15–17).

Importantly, this model of inquiry is not to be perceived as a linear process. In complex problem situations, observation, practical reasoning and action unfold in multiple parallel and recursive loops. They are guided by the original problem definition but they also may modify it. New observations influence the way actors think about a problem. Reasoning about the nature of the problem guides observations, too. Action is needed to test hypotheses, and the results of these tests feed back into problem definition, reasoning and observations (LW 12: 117). Hence, inquiry is the more intelligent:

> the more articulate the definition of one's problem in light of more observant uptake of its relevant features, the more imaginative one is in coming up with feasible solutions, the more comprehensive and accurate one's view of the consequences of implementing them, and the more responsive is one's decision to its anticipated consequences, relative to the consequences of alternatives.
>
> (Anderson 2014: para. 11)

At first glance, Dewey's model of intelligent inquiry and the bureaucratic model of strategic philanthropy have important similarities. Both emphasise the relevance of a precise problem definition, require a thorough investigation of the facts, and are based on the exploration of alternative ways of action and a weighing of possible consequences. However, there are also a number of fundamental differences. To clarify them further, I will discuss the central tenets and concepts of the pragmatist model of intelligent action in more detail.

2.3.1 Habitual Action and Problems of Action

The pragmatist theory of action maintains that most action is *habitual*. Habits are developed and employed by individuals as well as collectives. The term generally refers to a *disposition* to respond to a particular situation in an adequate way, based on acquired skills (Camic 1986: 1044; Cohen 2007: 779). This definition might suggest a likely misunderstanding, for in colloquial language, habits are closely related to routines. This latter concept has recently become an important topic in organisational studies and scholars tend to equate routine with rigid, mundane and mindless types of action (Cohen 2007: 774–775). However, the pragmatist notion of habit ranges far beyond routine in this limited sense, leaving room for much more demanding kinds of action. Otherwise, the concept could hardly serve as the central building block for a humanist philosophy of action. Dewey himself stipulates that "repetition is in no sense the essence of habit. Tendency to repeat acts is an incident of many habits but not of all. . . . The essence of habit is an acquired predisposition to *ways* or modes of behaving" (MW 14: 32).

Similar to routines, habits serve as repositories of the lessons of prior experiences and thus play an important role when it comes to economising the energy of human organisms (Ansell 2011: 25). Hence, they make the conduct of actors "fluid, and enable them to reliably produce certain results" (Anderson 2014: para. 8). But habits in the demanding sense of the term are much more complex entities, including cognitive, emotional and even aesthetic components. They are associated with skill, competency, capacity and character (MW 14: 29–30, 50–52) and thus become sources of satisfaction and meaning. Dewey illustrates this demanding conception with the following example:

> How delicate, prompt, sure and varied are the movements of a violin player or an engraver! How unerringly they phrase every shade of emotion and every turn of idea! Mechanism is indispensable. If each act has to be consciously searched for at the moment and intentionally performed, execution is painful and the product is clumsy and halting. Nevertheless the difference between the artist and the mere technician is unmistakable. The artist is a masterful technician. The technique or mechanism is fused with thought and feeling. The "mechanical" performer permits the mechanism to dictate the performance. . . . We are confronted with two kinds of habit, intelligent and routine.
>
> (MW 14: 51)[2]

Under conditions of environmental change or internal conflicts, habits may become problematic and even obsolete. In these cases, crises of action arise out of the confrontation with a concrete and thus unique empirical situation (LW 12: 74, 109). The course of mundane habitual action is interrupted, becomes impossible, or is conceived as inadequate to present circumstances. Pragmatism emphasises the profoundness of the puzzle and its embeddedness in particular problem situations: if inquiry is to be intelligent, it neither begins with mere inspiration nor with doubts for doubts' sake regardless of concrete practical demands. Rather, inquiry in the proper sense of the term begins with "real and living" doubt (Peirce 2011 [1877]), triggered by a real situation. This scenario is, again, an implication of the evolutionary conception of human agency: "what stimulates inquiry is . . . an instance of breakdown or disturbance in organism-environment transactions" (Burke et al. 2002: xv).

Serious doubt occurs if remedies in terms of causal knowledge or effective instruments are unavailable, if normative conflicts occur, or both. In problematic situations there is no blueprint which might guide the search for a solution and uncertainty is pervasive as the nature of the problem state, the effective remedies (the means) and the precise properties of the desirable goal state (the end) may all be unclear and/or contentious (LW 12: 110). However, as has been shown in the discussion on the process of inquiry, it is by no means *all* pervasive. One cannot doubt everything at once:

> for if we did we should have no tools to work with. But we can question different habits as different problems arise, always however against the background of received habits which in that situation are taken for granted. Inquiry must therefore be piecemeal to be effective.
>
> (Murphey 1983: xiv)

This conception of habits and practices has important consequences for the study of the processes of social problem solving. It favours a cautious, incremental approach and suggests the adoption of new practices if and only if they prove to be of a higher problem-solving value than existing arrangements (Oelkers 2008). This position has been labelled "progressive conservatism" (Ansell 2011: 13). The term captures the fact that pragmatism values both habits as preserved experience *and* the readiness and capability to revise them if necessary, since "lessons, skills, and values learned . . . are cumulative, but they are also constantly tested" (Ansell 2011: 14). It also expresses the insight that, if no one can reasonably claim to know the one best way ahead, it is most prudent to proceed incrementally, considering a wide range of perspectives and counter-arguments (Talisse and Aikin 2011: 8). For these reasons, pragmatists share a preference for *meliorism,* which is the seeking of better, but not necessarily perfect, solutions to complex social problems (Campbell 1992: 102).

2.3.2 Experimentalism as a Generic Method of Inquiry

Dewey vehemently advocated for the adoption of experimental methods for the purposes of social problem solving. He regarded them as the human equivalent of the search processes of living organisms which try to adapt to the changing demands of their natural environments.

Dewey argued that the overwhelming success of the natural sciences demonstrated the superiority of experimental methods in situations of high uncertainty which are characteristic of social problems. Hence, he suggested that these should be adopted as the paradigmatic method of social problem solving (Kitcher 2005: 72, 75; Talisse and Aikin 2008: 121).

This raises the question of what, precisely, the concept refers to. Experimentalism in a pragmatist sense is definitely not equivalent to the colloquial understanding of experimenting as trying out new things creatively. Neither is it confined to the adoption of rigid scientific methods as a means to settle social problems (Weber 2011; Ansell and Bartenberger 2015).[3]

Dewey conceived of experiments as the method by which scientific hypotheses are tested "by bringing about their antecedents and seeing if the results are as they predicted" (Anderson 2014: para. 24). The experimental modification of a situation based on empirically and theoretically grounded hypotheses "supplies the data for confirming or disconfirming them" (Anderson 2014: para. 24). Importantly, experimental behaviour is not simply "random trial-and-error", but it relies on a "skilled projection of prior . . . regularities to analogous novel situations" (Anderson 2014: para. 24).

However, experimentalism requires much more than conducting experiments. To work properly in the context of collective problems of action, experiments need to be embedded in comprehensive and highly demanding social practices. Dewey argued that, similar to the process of the scientific production of knowledge, social problem solving should be shaped as a collective and distributed process driven by the voluntary collaboration of different actors with diverse sets of knowledge in communities of inquiry under conditions of face-to-face interaction. He further emphasised the importance of the *public* basis of inquiry, that is, the requirement to include citizens (particularly those who are affected by remedial action) in the definition of problems and attempts at collaborative problem solving (Ansell 2011: 12).

Now the claim that the collective quest for answers to practical problems should be oriented towards the methods of the natural sciences seems not to be excessive (given that experimentalism is not confined to social experiments in the narrow sense of the term) as long as the solution of problems requires the generation of causal knowledge. However, social problems are obviously not simply a matter of a lack of knowledge but also arise in cases of contention. Dewey himself acknowledged that "there are situations . . . which feature *disordered* values and are therefore *morally problematic*" (LW 13: 221, italics in the original).

Remarkably, Dewey maintained that experimental inquiry is not limited to the generation of causal knowledge but a generic property of *all* intelligent remedial action, conceived as "the use of reflective intelligence to revise one's judgements in light of the consequences of acting on them" (Anderson 2014: para. 2). In other words, there is *only one generic* standard of good inquiry, regardless of the field to which it is applied (Talisse and Aikin 2008: 120), be it mundane instrumental problem solving, normative conflicts in the realms of politics and ethics or sophisticated research in scientific laboratories. Just like empirical inquiry always involves normative elements, inquiry in contentious situations includes investigations into both the empirical and causal components of the problem in question. Conflicts may arise due to ignorance in terms of wrong causal beliefs. If these are addressed systematically, participants may give up their erroneous positions. Similar considerations apply in cases of conceptual or normative error, the close scrutiny of which may sometimes dissolve the conflict (Kitcher 2005: 78). For instance, a scientific attitude would require participants to "explore whether or not some of them are affected by some form of apparent bias, overrating what is due to some people or overemphasizing certain qualities" (Kitcher 2005: 78).

What is more, the very experimentalist framework which makes intelligent inquiry possible in the first place is required for moral deliberation as well: it must be conducted collectively and in public and be based on the commitment of all participants to subject their beliefs and norms to serious scrutiny—empirical as well as moral. They need to avoid ideological bias in favour of an open process of deliberation. Finally, they need to subscribe to impartiality, recognising the legitimacy of the convictions and needs of others, be they members of the same community or not (Kitcher 2005: 77).

2.4 The Ends and Value(s) of Action

The discussion up to this point leaves open the question of the *ends* of action. Where do ends come from and what role do they play in the context of action? In particular, my discussion has bracketed the *normative* dimensions of this model: which ends *ought* to be pursued?

However, Dewey is notorious for his abstinence when it comes to specifying the normative implications of his framework of action. Scholars have frequently been puzzled by the fact that, while his philosophy places remedial action and social reform centre stage, there is no account of what, precisely, this entails in normative regards and no answer to the question of which values should be pursued in practice.[4] For these reasons, Dewey was criticised for being a moral formalist:

> Not to choose concrete sides and face the moral and power implication of such choice makes more central, and more abstract, the

universal-problem-solver. It makes "method" itself the seat of value. It makes "intelligence" *the* good.

(Mills 1966: 395)

This claim is certainly unwarranted and there are a number of good reasons for Dewey's emphasis on method. They become clear if his conception of ends and values is examined in more detail.

2.4.1 Means, Ends and Novelty

In the context of the bureaucratic model of action, ends are regarded as unproblematic, stable and given. Rational actors are motivated by preferences which are formulated independently of the situation in which action takes place and of the means available. They calculate the advantages and disadvantages of the available courses of action and decide in favour of the option that maximises value (Elster 1989; Whitford 2002; Beckert 2009).

In Dewey's view, this conception is empirically and normatively untenable. He argued that there are no intrinsically valuable ends understood as imaginary states of affairs which exist prior to and independently of situations of action and provide guidance to actors. To begin with, actors in problematic situations typically lack detailed conceptions of appropriate ends. Rather, action is guided by provisional *ends-in-view*: ideas of the state of affairs to be attained which are not identical with the *actual* outcomes of action (Scheffler 1974: 229–230). In the beginning of the process of inquiry, ends-in-view are quite vague and emergent and only become concretised in the course of action and with regard to the available means and expected consequences (Joas 1992: 227; Whitford 2002: 339–340; Beckert 2009: 9). To specify ends, this "complete package" (Anderson 2014: para. 30) is required since:

> a judgment of the value of ends apart from the means needed to get there . . . cannot provide the basis for rational action. . . . Our judgments of the worth of an end are inextricably tied up with our judgments of the costs of achieving it, both in terms of the means needed to get there and the unintended consequences of getting there.
>
> (Anderson 2014: para. 30

Second, Dewey posits that the seemingly clear distinction between means and ends is untenable, as well. On the one hand, ends-in-view guide action and thus also function as means. For instance, a plan of a house provides a model of how the edifice is supposed to look in the future. At the same time it directs the activities of the construction workers and thus serves as a means to erect it (MW 14: 184). On the other hand, Dewey maintains that means need to be infused with value if they are to fulfil their role properly: the quality of the future results depends on the degree of the commitment and individual involvement which is invested today. Accordingly, the architect of the house to be built may be compared to a:

> skilled artisan who enjoys his work [and who] is aware that what he is making is made for future use. Externally his action is one technically labeled "production". It seems to illustrate the subjection of present activity to remote ends. But actually, . . . the sense of the utility of the article produced is a factor in the present significance of action due to the present utilization of abilities, giving play to taste and skill, accomplishing something now. The moment production is severed from immediate satisfaction, it becomes "labor", drudgery, a task reluctantly performed.
>
> (MW 14: 186)

Finally, and most importantly, Dewey emphasises that the process of intelligent inquiry is not to be equated with a somewhat more liberal view of how actors reach their aims. Opposed to bureaucratic models which measure the success of action against the attainment of pre-existing ends, the most important achievements of problem-solving processes are to be regarded in terms of the creation of *novelty*. The human capacity for creativity must not be misunderstood as a context-free generation of new ideas. Rather, it is mobilised relative to and dependent on the problem situations in which actors operate (Joas 1992: 190, 196). All situations contain a potentially indefinite number of elements and, hence, a broad range of possible options for modification. These options are mobilised by means of abduction, that is, inference to the best explanation. The concept was developed by Peirce as a third logical type beyond the classical modes of induction and deduction (Joas 1992: 197–198). Abductive reasoning proceeds from the observation of a set of facts $(F_1 \ldots F_n)$ to a hypothesis which seeks to provide a coherent explanation of the facts. Medical diagnoses and the development of scientific theories are pertinent examples of abduction (Sebeok and Umiker-Sebeok 1979; Bartelborth 1996).

By means of this type of inference, problem solvers develop ideas though "educated guesses" (Ansell 2011: 25). These are assumptions as to how action may build "new bridges" between the actual and the desired state of affairs (Joas 1992: 196). They guide the gathering of new data and may thus grasp new aspects of reality (Joas 1992: 190) which feed back into problem definition and the further elaboration of the hypothesis. These multiple perspectives are present in Dewey's characterization of experimental behaviour in terms of a "dramatic rehearsal" (MW 5: 292–293), that is, the probative yet patterned arrangement and rearrangement of different elements of the problem situation in search of coherent results. Once more, the case of science serves as a helpful paradigm. It shows that the process from the development of a promising initial idea to an elaborate hypothesis can be a complex, long and demanding endeavour which requires "affectionate care"

(Joas 1992: 199, my translation) before a sufficiently elaborate hypothesis can be put forward which may or may not be verified by empirical testing.

If successful, the creative exploration and development of hypotheses may result in an enhanced repertoire of action due to a better grasp of the problem or the availability of new means. In Dewey's view:

> the function of mind is to project new and more complex ends—to free experience from routine and from caprice. Not the use of thought to accomplish purposes already given. . . , but the use of intelligence to liberate and liberalize action, is the pragmatic lesson.
>
> (Dewey 2011 [1917]: 137)

This creative potential plays a particularly important role in situations of conflicting values since, in these cases, the very ends of action are contested (LW 7: 185). Under these conditions, intelligent processes of deliberation may lead to the identification of new common ground and, hence, the formulation of a viable compromise for all participants (see for example Ansell 2011: 166–167).

2.4.2 Ends and Well-being

Yet, while there may be good reasons for a contextual and creative conception of ends, there remains a difficulty. Philanthropic organisations do not solve their own problems but seek to enhance other people's welfare. Hence, for purposes of orientation it would be helpful to know more about the states of affairs which are supposed to be attained as a result of successful philanthropic action as well as the appropriate means to bring them about. A rudimentary conception of what it means to further human well-being can be derived from the discussion on the merits of habitual action. Recall that intelligent action results in new and refined habits in terms of action that integrates cognitive, emotional and aesthetic components and thus becomes a source of satisfaction and meaning. Against this background, Dewey argued that human welfare cannot be achieved by means of a direct transfer of resources but rather by the creation of conditions that individuals can use. Accordingly, he holds that:

> a person's happiness depends upon the degree to which his activity has meaning. And this, in turn, is a matter of the effectiveness of his choice or agency, his ability to meet the urgent difficulties of the present through actions that reconstruct the conditions of his future. Action is thus effective only if it is not isolated—only as it branches out in causal, emotional, and conceptual connections to other elements of life. . . . To foster conditions that widen the horizon of others and give them command of their own powers, so that they can find their own happiness in their own fashion, is the way of "social" action.
>
> (Scheffler 1974: 234–235)[5]

This complex conception of happiness also works the other way around as it determines what happiness is *not*. In what can be regarded as a critical commentary to contemporary philanthropic practices, Dewey maintains:

> that it cannot be *given* to others; welfare cannot "consist in a soup-kitchen happiness". . . . To "make others happy" except through liberating their powers and engaging them in activities that enlarge the meaning of life is to harm them.
>
> (Scheffler 1974: 235)

However, even thus specified, the model might still seem to be unconvincing in normative terms. A conception of moral good that is assigned to individual action aiming at individual satisfaction in the context of concrete situations of action seems to be spinning in the void. Actors obviously have all sorts of motivations, preferences and conceptions of the good, and many of them are distorted by prejudice, selfishness or factual error. How, then, can successful problem solving in terms of a reconstruction of habits serve as a measure of morally valuable action?

Dewey argued against this assumption that there is no instance outside human practices to which one might take refuge in order to construe a more robust foundation of moral knowledge. All the moral convictions and intuitions we have rely on the inherited "moral material" (Kitcher 2005: 73) that is already there, including all distortions and errors. This is why we should focus on improving our moral practices instead of construing a truly unbiased instance of correction. When it comes to collective action, this process requires, above all, the identification of an appropriate means of inquiry. If moral deliberation is to be intelligent, it needs to meet the familiar standards of inquiry. It must be organised in collective and public ways and aim at correcting factual errors, at submitting all normative commitments to serious inquiry and at taking seriously the needs of other humans (Kitcher 2005: 75–77). Individual action is subject to similar methodological considerations:

> the moral life, then, is not a life in which certain kinds of psychological states, such as pleasure, are frequently realized; rather, the moral life is the life of cultivating by means of practice the skills involved in moral inquiry. Hence Dewey identified the "only moral end" as *growth*.
>
> (Talisse and Aikin 2008: 122, italics in the original)

2.5 Implications of Dewey's Theory of Action

The pragmatist conception of social action is particularly demanding as it presupposes habits of deliberation and inquiry which cannot simply be assumed as being given. On the contrary, pragmatists believe that human nature does not necessitate the altruistic and rational behaviour that lies at the core of intelligent problem-solving processes. For instance, Mead wrote that the "primal stuff of which we are made up is not under our direct control" (Mead 1929: 396). And Dewey maintained that man "is naturally or primarily an irrational creature" (MW 13: 247), thus "impulse and habit, not thought, are the primary determinants of conduct" (MW 14: 153). Hence, they both saw the need to "shape and channel individual conduct" (Campbell 1992: 100) in adequate ways. Dewey argued that "native human nature supplies the raw materials, but custom furnishes the machinery and the designs" (MW 14: 78) and inferred that it is "through the reconstruction of the customs and institutions that many hold to be human nature that selfishness can be addressed" (Campbell 1992: 101).

This is consistent with Peirce's original argument that humans do not abandon habits easily. They have a strong inclination to perpetuate familiar ways of behaviour and "experience disruptions of their habits with alarm, displeasure, offense, even outrage" (Anderson 2014: para. 10). If problems occur, they often try to quiet doubts or take refuge in merely symbolic problem solving (Campbell 1992: 29). This tendency is reflected in the strength of ideology and dogma both of which "represent current customs as right and inviolable. These facts pose obstacles to deliberate social change" (Anderson 2014: para. 10).

Hence, the above considerations have implications which reach far beyond the theory of inquiry. They point at the major importance of the question of how to generate the societal conditions necessary for the realisation of intelligent social action. West thus maintained that Dewey's "conception of social experimentation. . . 'goes all the way down'; that is, it embraces the idea of fundamental economic, political, cultural, and individual transformation in light of . . . ideas of accountable power, small-scale associations, and individual liberties" (West 1989: 218).

At the core of Dewey's social philosophy lies the following idea. A future society supposed to be able to solve its own problems intelligently and competently in the ways outlined above relies on adequate institutions which enable and foster both the possibility and the ability of ordinary citizens to contribute to this process (Campbell 1992: 104). Importantly, the relation between individual action and social structures is not regarded as a one-way street but as being mutually dependent: structures shape individual preferences and enhance individual capacities and thus open up room for individual growth, which, in turn, is supposed to foster collective values and to contribute to societal evolution (LW 7: 350).

Three societal institutions are of particular importance as they are regarded as conditions of the very possibility of widespread intelligent inquiry: a demanding version of democracy as a "way of life" (Dewey 2011 [1939]), education as the means to educate competent and compassionate problem solvers and an active civil society (Campbell 1992; Kitcher 2009).

Democracy is assigned a privileged position by virtue of its participatory and self-correcting nature. Ideally, it offers all citizens the opportunity to make their concerns heard, contribute to the public and collective formulation of social problems, and, even more importantly, to participate in attempts at solving them (Dewey 2011 [1939]). A democratic society, thus understood, resists inclinations for allegedly effective top-down diagnoses and solutions and embraces the participatory and incremental method of collective inquiry:

> if we are to have any hope of success as a society, we must develop democratic community. We need to abandon our attempts to short-circuit its slow and complex process of development through the quick fixes of technological breakthroughs or expert management, which lead only to new dependencies and new problems.
>
> (Campbell 1992: 104)

To work well, democracy further requires involved citizens in vital communities who are able and willing to contribute actively to common affairs (Campbell 1992: 104). Dewey regards collective attempts at self-administration and problem solving through civic associations as the primary unit and the ideal form of societal coordination. Civil society, thus conceived, functions as a bulwark against tendencies for a bureaucratization, professionalisation and corporatization of society and needs to be defended against these forces (Adloff 2005: 48). If civil society is to flourish, a number of demanding prerequisites need to be in place: "Social integration, a fair distribution of resources and the feeling of being able to make a valuable contribution to the commonwealth are the social preconditions for deepening political participation" (Adloff 2005, my translation).

Finally, both the conception of democracy as a way of life and a strong civil society rely on citizens who are committed to furthering the common good, who are willing to participate in discussions of matters of public concern and who are competent contributors to processes of collective inquiry. Both institutions require that children and youth be educated in such a way as to abandon reliance on dogmatism and to develop the habits and virtues required for intelligent and impartial collaborative inquiry which have been described above (Kitcher 2005: 77). Hence, the ultimate aim of the system of education is to build "a wise citizenry that is both self-critical and concerned with social issues" (Campbell 1992: 104).

2.6 Conclusion

The following elements of the pragmatist position are of particular importance, as they will shape the further course of this study. The first is a quasi-evolutionary framework of action which conceives of human behaviour as a response to problems in terms of highly contingent and ambiguous, yet urgent situational demands. This reaction can be shaped and unfolds in more or less adequate ways. It both adapts to and impacts its natural and social environment. The second is a model of action which alternates between complex habits as the carriers of value and the meaningful building blocks of most human behaviour, and experimental search for novel solutions triggered by problems of action. If conducted in intelligent ways and if successful, this search process results in new and improved habits and, thus, contributes to a process of growth of individuals and collectives. The third is the recognition that experimental strategies are necessarily distributed and long term, presupposing the existence of interactive and interdependent, committed and competent, communities of inquiry as problem-solving agents. Importantly, the different themes can be kept separate for analytical purposes only. To match the complexity of the issue of social problems, they need to be bound together in a holistic perspective because each single component is a necessary but not sufficient building block of an intelligent problem-solving endeavour.

However, as a philosophical theory formulated almost a century ago, the pragmatist perspective resides on an overly generic level. Pragmatism alone is not specific enough to inform a more thorough scientific analysis of philanthropic action and to provide guidance to practitioners of philanthropy. Hence, in what follows, the pragmatist framework needs to be specified and expanded. As a first step, I will explore the central concept of complex social problems so as to specify the target of all subsequent considerations.

Notes

1 The model is not intended to describe what problem solvers actually and necessarily *do*. Dewey rather seeks to further our understanding of how intelligent action should be shaped if it is to be effective and responsible. Neither does he claim that the model is the last word on the issue. The idea was rather to trigger a much broader scientific process of inquiry into the methods and means of intelligent responses to practical problems, hoping that his own framework might increasingly be refined in the future (Kitcher 2005: 75–76).

2 According to Dewey, the distinction between dead routines and vital habits has important political dimensions as well since modern societies in an increasingly globalised world rely on an unjust division of labour: standardised, mechanical work processes in the agricultural, industrial and service sectors are assigned to a servant class, the labour of which is reduced "to a tedious, mindless, meaningless mechanical exercise" (Anderson 2014: para. 58). The products of this labour are reaped by a leisure class in European, North American and emerging economies. Dewey concludes that "the challenge of the modern day is to consider how work, and human activity generally, can be reformed so that it has aesthetic value and is thus no longer valued merely instrumentally" (Anderson 2014).

3 This approach was proposed by Donald Campbell in his seminal article on reforms as experiments (1969). It regained prominence in recent discussions in the context of development economics (e.g., Banerjee and Duflo 2011).

4 Yet, in his practical work, Dewey, like Mead, actively engaged in the very fields of action one would expect progressivists to address, such as education reform, the

provision of better housing, penal reform, women's rights and reforming urban health services (Levine 1995: 260).

5 This conception of successful social action is hardly consistent with accounts that seek to determine the results of problem-solving action by means of generic quantitative measures (Kroeger and Weber 2014). Yet, while it might seem to be too diffuse to guide action, I will argue in Chapter 11 that it is actually highly compatible with theories such as the capability approach, which can be operationalised very well.

3 Mapping the Space of Social Problems

Pragmatism directs attention to the relevance of problems as a point of departure for meaningful social action and highlights the importance of attempts to tackle and solve them in intelligent ways. This focus on problem solving is a common theme in the literature on the effectiveness of philanthropic organisations, as well (Anheier and Leat 2006; Brest and Harvey 2008; Cutler 2009; Ebrahim and Rangan 2010, 2014; Kania et al. 2014; Liket 2014; Brest et al. 2015).

Yet, problems are such familiar phenomena that scholars often deal with them too briefly, noticing only that the pivotal insight of modern philanthropy is the addressing of the "underlying causes" of problems rather than the symptoms (e.g., Anheier and Leat 2006: 20). Against this I maintain that a close analysis of those dimensions that render problems problematic in the first place must precede and inform any substantial discussion on problem solving, as it uncovers the full extent of the challenge. In particular, the basic phenomena of complexity and the barriers they present to problem solvers remain underexposed in the discussion. Hence, as the first step, I will clarify the concept of (social) problems. I will then unpack the sources and dimensions of complexity inherent in social problems and show how they may operate in concert. For these purposes I will draw on a wide range of literature from different disciplines such as the sociology of social problems, the psychology of complex problem solving, political science, urban planning as well as research on philanthropy and (social) innovation.

In doing so I aim at the development of a conceptual apparatus that is sufficiently nuanced to match the complexity of social problems and to demonstrate the challenges inherent in problem-solving action, yet concise enough to guide both scientific analysis and practice. As clarity of the basic terms is an important building block for the development of a coherent framework of problem-solving action, I will begin the discussion with some fundamental conceptual distinctions.

3.1 What's the Problem With Problems?

There are a number of characteristic properties a situation must exhibit for it to be considered a problem. To begin with, problems do not exist independently of human cognition and valuation. There needs to be at least one actor who "produces" the problem by perceiving a particular state of affairs as being unsatisfactory according to certain values or standards (e.g., knowledge, justice or effectiveness) (Frensch and Funke 1995: 18; Funke 2003: 20). Similar to the definition of the situation that plays a major role in almost all sociological theories of action (Esser 1996), actors thus determine the essential characteristics of the problem situation (Jonassen 2000: 65). In other words, problems are not entirely natural or objective states of affairs or events, but are *created* out of empirical and normative raw material, as it were.

Three further components need to be distinguished: the actual problem state, the hypothetical goal state and the wider environment.[1] Obviously, problems do not exist in a void but they occur in concrete situations in time and space that constitute the specific properties of *this* problem and, accordingly, determine important conditions of problem solving (Frensch and Funke 1995: 18). The problem state is the empirical immediate realm of action that can (at least potentially) directly be influenced by problem-solving actors (see Parsons 1968: 43–44 on the basic properties of action). This is contrasted by the actor(s) with a different, supposedly more favourable, goal state (Funke 2003: 14–15). The goal state may be a mere idea or a real state of affairs which exists elsewhere. Initially, the knowledge and understanding of these two is often vague, erroneous and subject to revision and a sufficiently detailed conception emerges only in the course of the process of problem solving. The societal environment constitutes the wider context of social problems, including hypothetical or actual solutions and the discourses pertaining to them, other stakeholders who may react in unpredictable ways and thus change the terms of engagement (Kaufmann 1999: 923), cultural conditions like norms and institutions (i.e., patterns of thought and action that are taken for granted by stakeholders) (Parsons 1968: 44–46) and opportunity structures that constrain or expand the range of possible activities (Kern 2008: 153). Usually, the conditions of the wider problem situation can hardly be influenced. At the same time, they essentially determine and restrain the available scope of action.

A problem occurs if and because the undesirable current state of affairs cannot easily be transformed into the goal state, since there is a "barrier" (Frensch and Funke 1995: 18) between them. If action which transfers the problem state into the goal state is entirely unproblematic, then it is called "routine" rather than "problem solving". On the other hand, a remedy needs to be possible at least in principle: states of affairs that are entirely resistant to change are seen as "God's will" or fate, rather than problems (Jamrozik and Nocella 1998: 21).

Discussion further highlights the relevance of the resources that problem solvers command. For instance, inexperienced novices may be at a loss in a situation that is perfectly transparent to experts (Dörner 2007: 61–62), and what constitutes a problem for one actor may be a matter of routine for another. Generally speaking, resources can be conceived as any symbolic or material good, event or action over which actors have control and which is regarded as beneficial to individuals or collectives (Coleman 1990; Small 2006). In the literature, a very wide range of assets has been identified, such as economic (wealth), social (reputation, networks, power, access to target groups or organisations, legitimacy) or cultural (knowledge, information, skills) capital (Bourdieu 1982). Personal (staff), organisational, cognitive and emotional (motivation and commitment) capacities (Funke 2006: 442; Andersen 2008) and time (Mitroff et al. 1979) are important resources, as well. Shared expectations and supportive institutional and regulatory structures have also been regarded as important enabling resources (Farla et al. 2012). Precisely which resources are required depends on the characteristics of the problem situation. The combination of the different elements which are constitutive for problems is displayed in Figure 3.1.

This generic scheme can be applied to all kinds of problems, including those which are addressed by philanthropic actors, and the organisation of my case studies will be oriented according to this model. However, the problems tackled by philanthropy are obviously more demanding than for example simple problems of arithmetic. Rather, they belong to the family of *social* problems, which differ in important respects from other types of problems and require specific problem-solving strategies.

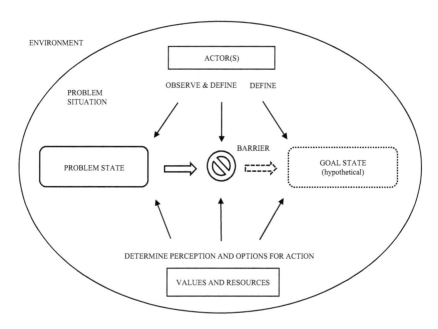

Figure 3.1 The Structure of Problems

3.2 Social Problems

There are all sorts of different problems, both large and small, in all fields of society, but not every problem is a social problem. Examples of social problems include crime in an urban district, unemployment or environmental pollution on a national level, as well as global climate change and terrorism. They are situated at different levels of society and vary in complexity, scale and scope.

The sociology of social problems has developed different definitions of the term "social problem", all of which are controversial (Merton 1976; Jamrozik and Nocella 1998; Peters 2002; Schetsche 2008). There is dissent regarding the very nature of problems which have been conceived as instances of individual pathology, social disorganisation or deviant behaviour (Jamrozik and Nocella 1998; Peters 2002). There has also been a lively debate on the ontological status of social problems, that is, the questions of whether some states of affairs can objectively count as problems, or whether they are entirely products of discourse (Blumer 1971; Kitsuse and Spector 1973).

In what follows, I define the term "social problem" as an actual social state of affairs that is collectively perceived by a community of observers as undesirable or threatening according to shared values or norms. Since a social problem is of social origin, it can also be remedied by society (Blumer 1971; Merton 1976: 40; Jamrozik and Nocella 1998: 1–2; Peters 2002: 40–45; Schetsche 2008: 42–45).

This definition resembles the generic model of problems presented above. Again, it is the *perception* of a social state of affairs as being a problem that makes it become a problem in the first place. However, there are also important additional requirements. To begin with, social problems are necessarily collective phenomena. Unlike other types of problems, for example earthquakes or sinking ships, social problems do not impose themselves on their observers *as* problems. Rather, they result from a sufficient level of agreement in a community of observers to regard the discrepancy between what is and what ought to be as being a problem (Merton 1976: 40).

In modern societies, there are countless perceived discrepancies, large and small. Yet, not every discrepancy counts as a problem but only those cases in which the gap is perceived as being "too large" (Merton 1976: 40). According to Merton, there are no fixed measures for this; it is, once more, a matter of definition and negotiation in any single case. Hence, the process of problem definition must be seen as an essentially constructive act that is guided by the shared values and norms as well as the interests and knowledge of the actors involved.

3.2.1 *Varieties of Social Problems and their Properties*

There are other distinguishing properties of social problems which are relevant for this study. In modern societies, problems increasingly tend to be *complex* (Rittel and Webber 1973; Crozier 1982; Chisholm 1995; Kettl 2009) and ill structured (Simon 1973), and the most severe problems are characterised as *wicked* rather than *simple* (Rittel and Webber 1973).

Accordingly, different types of problems can be identified which require different types of treatment.

In the case of simple problems, definitions and boundaries are clear, problem-solving technology and causal knowledge are readily available and there is a consensus of how to address them and of when a solution has been achieved (Rittel and Webber 1973; Simon 1973; Crozier 1982; Chisholm 1995; Kettl 2009). If, for instance, a city needs to accommodate a large number of newly arrived refugees, the challenge is mainly administrative in nature (assuming that there is no resistance to the process). It can be tackled by the problem-solving routines of local public administration. In the case of philanthropy, professional emergency relief or the treatment of curable diseases can sometimes be regarded as examples of largely administrative problems as they require the provision of standardised services to cater for basic and immediate needs.

Wicked problems such as global poverty, failing school systems or the instability of the financial industry are characterised by a number of properties that inhibit successful problem solving and even draw into question the very notions of solution and success. They are characterised by unclear problem states, contentious and ambiguous goals, environmental complexity and dynamic change as well as a lack of reliable problem-solving technology. Hence, wicked problems cannot be defined unambiguously, it is unclear when they have been solved and there is no consensus of what counts as a solution (Rittel and Webber 1973).

In between these two ends of the spectrum there are problems which exhibit an intermediate degree of complexity. They have also been labelled as "complicated" problems (Glouberman and Zimmerman 2002). The problems which are addressed in my sample cases fall into this latter category.

These three types of problems can be distinguished along the following four dimensions of the problem situation: complexity, intransparency, contention and non-linear change.

3.2.1.1 Complexity

According to Kohn (1976: 94) there is an inclination to consider only those problems as *social* problems that have a "seriously negative impact on the lives of sizeable segments of the population". Problems of this dimension are usually *complex* because they are composed of a large number of single elements which are highly interconnected but ill structured (Simon 1962; Chisholm 1995; Funke 2006: 440; Snowden and Boone 2007: 3). In other words, the complexity of a problem state depends on the number of relevant[2] variables and the density and intensity of connections between them (Dörner 2007: 59–60).

Consider as an example unjust school structures in Germany or the USA which lead to an "achievement gap", that is, systematic differences in student performance which are dependent on socio-economic background rather than cognitive abilities and social skills. These problems occur in thousands of schools[3] which are embedded in a highly complex and interdependent public (and increasingly public-private) governance system made up of a multitude of highly interconnected organisations and agencies which provide training, accreditation, budgeting, support and maintenance. What is more, the achievement gap is not the result of one single variable but the product of many different influences (for instance, the quality of instruction relies on the curriculum, the availability of staff, teacher training and technological equipment), some of which, such as poverty or racism, are beyond the reach of the educational system (Thümler et al. 2014a).

3.2.1.2 Intransparency

Complexity frequently entails intransparency. In such a "situation, the structure and status of the system are not entirely open and accessible" (Funke 2003: 134, my translation). In other words, information required to determine the precise and relevant properties of the problem state, as well as the variables relevant to achieve the goal state, are unavailable, unclear, incomplete or hard to attain (Funke 2006: 440; Dörner 2007: 63–64). There may be a number of different reasons for this. To begin with, complexity leads to an overwhelmingly large number of different options to describe the problem and to tackle it, particularly under conditions of dynamic change. Furthermore, relevant information may be unavailable simply because nobody knows it, or because powerful actors have an interest in withholding it (Schimank 2002: 90). For instance, when it comes to the regulation of the global financial system, the most relevant actors are often unknown to the public and act under conditions of very high confidentiality. Civil society organisations which are active in this field tend to focus attention on the World Bank or the International Monetary Fund as the most visible and prominent institutions. However, other actors such as the Bank for International Settlements are much more influential in this field, which is why activists tend to "bark at the wrong tree" (Scholte 2013; Scholte, personal communication).

3.2.1.3 Contention

While there are many examples of a broad consensus on desirable societal states of affairs and, accordingly, of problem states (for instance, in cases of youth delinquency or poverty), controversy arises in regard to many other situations. In fact, the common good is hard to determine and diverging notions of how it can be furthered are more the rule than the exception (Offe 2002). Different representations of the same reality may weigh and assess the same aspects in entirely different ways, to the effect that a "situation seen by one group as a problem may, therefore, constitute a solution in the eyes of another group" (Merton 1976: 40). At the extreme, one group's terrorist is the other group's freedom fighter.

Take the issue of migration. Many citizens are fundamentally opposed to migration, regarding it as a threat that needs to be minimised. For others, it is not a problem at all but a positive phenomenon that ought to be welcomed as an opportunity to develop a more diverse society. For migrants themselves it may simply be an inevitable necessity. In this situation, it may be very difficult to conduct a constructive dialogue on the question of how to integrate migrants for the best, and no solution in the proper sense of the word may be possible. Contention is, of course, of particular relevance if philanthropists act in opposition to incumbents of powerful positions who may render problem solving impossible.

3.2.1.4 Non-linear Change

Social problems may remain stable, but they need not. Some are moving targets, which change dynamically, independently of or parallel to the intervention, and in non-linear and unpredictable ways (Funke 2003: 131; 2006: 440; Snowden 2007). These processes may alter the character of the problem situation both for better and worse, with profound consequences for problem solvers. Take the case of emergency relief. Actors are often under pressure to act quickly, regardless of the availability of comprehensive information, as any delay may have severe consequences for the target group—particularly so in fragile contexts, in which relief agencies have to cope with a highly instable security situation. The terrorist attacks of 9/11 are a further, extreme example of a problem that is characterised by surprising and highly uncontrollable events that unfold quickly, following no predictable pattern (Snowden 2007; Kettl 2009).

3.2.2 Barriers to Problem Solving

The above-mentioned problem dimensions need not erect barriers to problem solving per se. There exist no wicked problems for a hypothetical omniscient and almighty higher being with complete knowledge of any problem situation and the consequences of action as well as the means to impose and implement solutions on whatever scale. For ordinary actors, the scale of a problem is a function of the above-mentioned dimensions and the resources they command. For instance, defects in highly complex technical systems may easily be repaired as long as operators have blueprints and instruction manuals. Conflicting opinions of stakeholders need not hinder problem solvers as long as opponents do not dare to resist the intervention. Dynamic change becomes more manageable the more an organisation is prepared to cope with it.

Hence, there is neither an absolute measure of problem complexity nor a clear boundary between simple, complex and wicked problems (Simon 1973). Depending on the properties of the concrete situation as well as the capacities of problem solvers, the latter are confronted with a multitude of more or less severe liabilities. I will constrain my analysis to those dimensions which play the most important role in the cases under investigation, namely uncertainty, resistance, lack of material resources and a lack of control.[4]

3.2.2.1 Uncertainty

Uncertainty is an essential property of problem solving as a kind of non-routine action (Funke 2003) and characteristic for innovation processes per se (Nelson and Winter 1977). The reasons for this are manifold. To begin with, the very nature of the problem may be contested and unclear. Once more, the global financial and economic crisis is a good example as only limited consensus of how to define the problem has emerged to date. While the crisis has largely been diagnosed in terms of a lack of accountability and regulation of financial markets (Fioramonti and Thümler 2013; for an example see Anheier 2012), other scholars have explained it as a result of the defeat of democratic states due to the sheer political power of the financial industry (Engelen et al. 2011; Streeck 2011). The different definitions entail fundamentally different and incompatible courses of action and there is no way to tell in advance which one is right. For instance, if the assumption is correct that the crisis has been caused by the hegemony of global finance, all containment strategies aiming at a better regulation are doomed to fail because the incumbents of financial power will ultimately outmanoeuvre public regulators (Fioramonti and Thümler 2013).

Second, uncertainty is frequently due to a lack of knowledge regarding means-ends relations. In these cases, there exists no established "technology" that reliably transforms the problem state into the goal state (Christensen 1985: 63 and *passim*). This is the case in the field of school improvement. While the problem may be clear and uncontentious, there are few proven remedies, not least due to the fact that a measurement of student achievement is difficult and expensive, which further contributes to the degree of uncertainty.

Third, uncertainty is caused by "informational and computational limits on rationality" (March 1978: 590). Even the most experienced and knowledgeable of experts may lack the capacities required to design an effective intervention based on all the information available, and to predict reliably a successful course of events. A multitude of non-linear interactions among different system components exceeds problem solvers' capacities to list all alternative options for action and to weigh their consequences. Dynamic change further inhibits reliable prognoses of future developments, particularly if change occurs very fast, very slow or over very long periods of time (Funke 2003: 132; Allen and Gunderson 2011).

Hence, both the lack of the necessary information as well as bounded rationality contribute to a fundamental inability of problem solvers to analyse complex problems exhaustively (Lindblom 1979). Under these conditions, they need to act based on an incomplete and blurred representation of the problem state (Funke 2003: 133).

3.2.2.2 Resistance

Discussions on philanthropic effectiveness tend to underestimate the controversial nature of social change and many scholars of problem complexity bracket the issue of contention (see, e.g., Hanleybrown et al. 2012; Kania and Kramer 2013; Kania et al. 2014). However, the ends of interventions are frequently disputed and attempts at realising them often meet vehement opposition (Christensen 1985).

For instance, research suggests that advocacy coalitions which try to outmanoeuvre their opponents are more likely to achieve the desired change in a shorter period of time compared to broader and more inclusive civic coalitions. However, this strategy may also trigger a higher level of resistance that tends to undermine the long-term sustainability of change (Ansell et al. 2009; Reckhow 2013). The fierce and widespread public critique of the German Bertelsmann Foundation (Schöller 2006; Wernicke and Bultman 2007) is an example of the fundamentally political character of interventions in society and the potential consequences that may arise if this fact is ignored.

Contention need not always be caused by disputes over values, though. It may also be due to psychological mechanisms by which stakeholders are inclined to perceive novelty itself in a critical way. Schumpeter observed that, in the case of innovation, "any deviating conduct by a member of a social group is condemned. . . . Even mere astonishment at the deviation, even merely noticing it, exercises a pressure on the individual" (Schumpeter 2012 [1934]: 86–87).

The larger and more profound the problem, the more it will be related to societal structures and schemes of distribution which favour some actors to the detriment of others. For instance, unequal achievement in schools is caused, in important regards, by the fact that so many students grow up in poverty (Portes 2005). Yet, interventions aimed at changing underlying structural conditions, namely unequal distributions of societal wealth, are likely to trigger the resistance of the incumbents of wealth and power (Jamrozik and Nocella 1998).

3.2.2.3 Lack of Material Resources

Problem solvers are further likely to suffer from a lack of material resources. This includes money and any other type of material asset which may be valuable for humans, be it water, food or shelter (Dörner 2007; Seelos and Mair 2014). In the context of this study, money is of particular relevance since the mere size of problems tends to make problem solving expensive. Consider again the problem of the achievement gap in the USA and Germany. Problem solvers are confronted with a large and complex school system that exhibits notoriously high degrees of inertia which makes change extraordinarily demanding and costly (Von Friedeburg 1992; Tyack and Cuban 1995). This situation is made worse by the fact that a wide range of relevant variables may play a role in processes of school improvement. For instance, while some emphasise the crucial role of the quality of instruction, others consider the quality of school management to be of major explanatory relevance (Hattie and Anderman 2013). In fact, however, only a combination of different means may bring about the necessary and sufficient conditions for substantial change. As a result, any reform requires the investment of considerable amounts of slack resources to explore different possible paths of action, only a few of which will be successful (Van de Ven et al. 2008).

3.2.2.4 Lack of Control

Social problem solvers do not operate in closed hierarchical organisations but under conditions of open social systems where they rely on the voluntary collaboration of autonomous stakeholders. Hence, they frequently suffer from a lack of control that inhibits the development and implementation of effective interventions (internal control) and causes unintended side-effects (external control). As the scholarly discussion has largely ignored this dimension, there is an urgent need to explore it in more depth (Ebrahim and Rangan 2010: 13).

Generally speaking, the term "control" refers to the ability of an organisation or its managers to determine intentionally the course of a process or the properties of a state of affairs in order to cause desired effects (Landau and Stout 1979: 149). This capacity is, among others, a function of actors' knowledge on means-ends relations, clarity of goals, predictability of environmental change, the ability to suppress interfering variables, repetitiveness of the problem-solving task as well as authority over other actors (Landau and Stout 1979; Hofstede 1981; Tsoukas 1994; Wiltbank et al. 2006; Seelos and Mair 2014). Control over the problem situation is of particular importance for processes of innovation as it is regarded as a necessary condition for the very possibility of learning and the attribution of effects (Weiss 2000; Van de Ven et al. 2008: 80).

Control problems are well known and pervasive in the field of educational reform. The implementation of programmes is often inhibited by the high autonomy of teachers, who are free to choose whether they carry them out faithfully, alter them or disregard them. This is a major impediment to processes of school improvement (Rowan and Miller 2007: 253). Control problems further arise if the properties of the problem situation change dynamically, as in the case of 9/11. Under these conditions it is impossible to know in advance if an intervention will cause the desired effects, or not. Or take the need to co-produce solutions, which is more the rule than the exception in processes of social innovation. A lack of authority-based control over the behaviour of the involved stakeholders may lead to coordination problems as the contributions and activities of different networked actors need to be aligned to serve a common goal (Chisholm 1992).

Unintended consequences, on the other hand, are due to a lack of *external* control over the societal effects of interventions. In the case of wicked problems it is impossible to test or evaluate all the effects of new solutions in a laboratory situation before implementing them in practice (Rittel and Webber 1973). Interventions may thus have unanticipated and unintended consequences as effects occur over long periods of time and ramify beyond the realm of the intervention (Merton 1936; Fine 2006). Hence, even those interventions which are based on the best of intentions may produce perverse outcomes:

> any solution, after being implemented, will generate waves of consequences over an extended—virtually an unbounded—period of time. Moreover, the next day's consequences of the solution may yield utterly undesirable repercussions which outweigh the intended advantage or the advantages accomplished hitherto. In such cases, one would have been better off if the plan had never been carried out.
> (Rittel and Webber 1973: 163)

For these reasons, responses to wicked problems have been characterised as "one-shot operations": if they fail to meet their targets at the first attempt, they may cause harm (Rittel and Webber 1973: 163). The Rockefeller Foundation's initiative to open up the third sector to investments from the global capital markets, which has been described as an instance of philanthropic best practice by Kania et al. (2014), is a good example of this: in the best case it may mobilise considerable additional resources for entrepreneurial solutions of social problems. In the worst case, it may contribute to a process of a financialization of the third sector which will be completely beyond the control of the actors who initiated the development in the first place (Thümler 2016).

At the same time it has to be kept in mind that unintended consequences may also be an important source of novelty. For instance, research on entrepreneurship has shown that, under conditions of uncertainty regarding means and ends, the ability to recognise and exploit unexpected opportunities is an important virtue (Sarasvathy 2001). The challenge for philanthropic problem solvers, then, is to manage unintended consequences in such a way as to minimise undesirable consequences and to harness those desirable discoveries and opportunities that non-linear developments may generate.

3.2.3 Types of Social Problems

I am now in a position to determine better the properties of different types of social problems. Wicked problems are maximally complex and non-transparent, the level of contention is high and the problem situation changes dynamically. Hence, problem solvers tend to suffer from uncertainty as well as a lack of material resources and control, and they are confronted with high degrees of resistance, all of which interact with and amplify each other. On the other side of the spectrum, there are rather "tame" or "simple" problems. They are clearly defined, problem-solving knowledge is available at least in principle, and they are uncontentious and situated in stable environments. In between the two there are moderate problems which neither fully exhibit nor lack all of these dimensions. Assuming that a single dimension is dominant while others are weak, four more problem types can be distinguished: innovation problems, characterised by a high level of uncertainty regarding means-ends relations; contentious problems, in which disagreement on ends, actors or means prevails; resource problems, the solution of which is expensive; and control problems, which inhibit the implementation of interventions due to a lack of authority over stakeholder behaviour or changes in the environment.

These results can best be illustrated by a widely quoted remark by Donald Schön who maintained that problem solvers face the following decision:

> In the varied topography of professional practice, there is a high, hard ground, overlooking a swamp. On the high ground, manageable problems lend themselves to solution through the application of research-based theory and technique. In the swampy lowland, messy, confusing problems defy technical solution. The irony of this situation is that the problems of the high ground tend to be relatively unimportant to individuals or society at large, however great their technical interest may be, while in the swamp lie the problems of greatest human concern. The practitioner must choose. Shall he remain on the high ground where he can solve relatively unimportant problems according to prevailing standards of rigor, or shall he descend to the swamp of important problems and nonrigorous inquiry?
>
> (Schön 1987: 3)

The discussion has shown that practitioners can also choose to opt for problems of moderate complexity which are situated along the shoreline, as it were, and I posited that these are particularly well suited to being solved by philanthropic organisations. Yet, in the initial stages of problem solving, the precise position of the problem under attack is often unclear: does it reside on high ground, is it stuck in the swamp, or is it situated somewhere in the middle? The exploration of its "proper" nature and the development of an adequate definition of the problem thus become an important part of remedial activity.

3.3 Conclusion

I have found that all problems can be reduced to a generic structure. The problem situation is made up of actors who define a problem state and envisage a future goal state, both depending on their values. It is further characterised by a barrier, which inhibits a simple transition from problem state to goal state, and the availability or a lack of relevant resources required to overcome the barrier. The problem situation itself is embedded in a broader organisational and societal environment which is usually beyond the reach of actors but essentially determines the range of available options for action as well as the prospects of success.

Social problems were defined as actual states of affairs that are perceived by a collective of observers as undesirable or threatening according to shared values or norms. These types of problems exhibit complexity, intransparency, contention and non-linear change as distinctive properties. Depending on the resources available to problem solvers, they may face four different liabilities, namely uncertainty, resistance, high costs and a lack of control. The most complex, "wicked" problems, such as poverty, terrorism or the instability of global finance, are characterised by a high level of all of these dimensions, hence they tend to overwhelm the capacities of *any* actor. For simple problems, the opposite is true. In between this continuum there are problems of moderate complexity which exhibit only one or two dominant problem dimensions. They can often be described as smaller "chunks" of much bigger problems (Ansell 2011: 87). These are the subject matter of the pragmatic model of philanthropy which is developed in this book. I hypothesize that the problems addressed in the sample cases can be characterised as innovation problems, contentious problems, resource problems or control problems, or a combination of these.

Depending on the nature of the problem under attack and the resources problem solvers command, different strategies to reduce the barrier between problem state and goal state are required. In Chapter 4, I will turn to the question of which strategies are available and what it means to match strategies with problems.

Notes

1 In some cases, problems are situated in more complex systems such as "organizational fields" (DiMaggio and Powell 1991) or socio-technical "regimes" (Kemp et al. 1998). For instance, problems of school improvement are not least caused by the embeddedness of single schools in the large and complex public school system. Under these conditions, all problem-solving attempts need to pay due attention to the demands of this environment. Hence, these problems cannot adequately be understood, addressed and solved without reference to the system, which thus constitutes an intermediary environmental level.

2 In principle, all situations are composed of an infinite number of variables. Hence, the number of *relevant* variables depends on the definition of the (problem) situation (Parsons 1968: 47–48). For instance, depending on perspective, a family of five members can be regarded as a simple system of five persons or a highly complex system of 10^{25} atoms (Ashby 1974: 98, quoted in Funke 2003: 128)

3 In the USA, 54.7 million students were enrolled in 132,183 elementary and secondary schools, whereas in Germany, 11.4 million students attended 34,538 schools (data for 2011/2012) (Thümler et al. 2014a: 6).

4 This is not to say that these are the *only* possible barriers. Rather than providing an exhaustive list, they are supposed to illustrate the multidimensional nature of social problems and to demonstrate the consequences for problem solving.

4 A Contingency Model of Problem-Solving Strategies

While the considerations above are useful to *structure the discussion* on problem solving, they do not yet provide much practical knowledge of how complex social problems can actually be *solved*. In this chapter and in Chapter 5, I will introduce and organise the available knowledge on this question in broad strokes. Once more, I will draw on research from a variety of sources such as (social) problem solving, social and socio-technical innovation as well as philanthropic and corporate strategy.

There exist three generic principles which apply to all instances of complex problem solving, namely problem adequacy or "fit", the reduction of complexity and enhanced capacity. The literature further identifies strategies and structures as the two major building blocks of problem solving. The question is, then, how they can be organised in such a way as to meet the basic principles of problem solving and to heighten the probability of success. It will be addressed in two separate steps. In this chapter, I will portray different strategic options in the language of the "innovation journey", distinguishing between exploratory, experimental and bureaucratic strategies. They apply particularly well to the cases under investigation. In Chapter 5, I will then introduce a transformative strategy which was designed to cope with systemic and "wicked" problems. This will also involve a discussion of the role of niches and networks as essential structures of problem solving.

4.1 The Nature of Problem Solving

In Chapter 3, I showed that talking about problems implies talking about solutions because actors contrast undesirable states of affairs with a supposedly more favourable alternative. In common language, activities which are supposed to transform the former into the latter are called problem solving: if the goal state has fully been realised, the problem state has literally been (dis-)solved (Thümler et al. 2014b: 214).

In the case of organised philanthropy, remedial activities are usually shaped as projects or programmes or other kinds of formal interventions. They rely on the availability of a broad set of different resources which are needed to develop, establish and sustain the intervention and also to satisfy the needs of the target group. All interventions are embedded in contexts which both enable and restrain remedial action. These elements and the relations between them are captured in Figure 4.1, which may serve as a basic tool for the analysis of all kinds of problems and problem-solving processes, be it in the field of philanthropy or beyond.

Importantly, problems in the proper sense of the term are defined as the breakdown of habitual action. Effective social problem solving thus eludes routine responses and standardised solutions; rather it involves the quest for appropriate definitions of problems and the adequate means (e.g., knowledge and techniques, skills and resources) to overcome the barrier between problem state and goal state (Simon 1962: 479; Funke 2003: 38). Hence, it always includes some degree of *novelty*.

This is why the process and outcomes of social problem solving are akin to the process and outcomes of social innovation. This latter term denotes both the search for new solutions to social problems as well as successful results of this attempt. Similar to problem solving, social innovation is a normatively charged concept. It refers to new practices which solve social problems better than existing arrangements and thus satisfy human and societal needs (Zapf 1989: 177; Moulaert et al. 2005: 1976; Howaldt and Schwarz 2010: 54–55). Hence, in what follows, the concepts of "social problem solving" and "social innovation" will be used interchangeably.

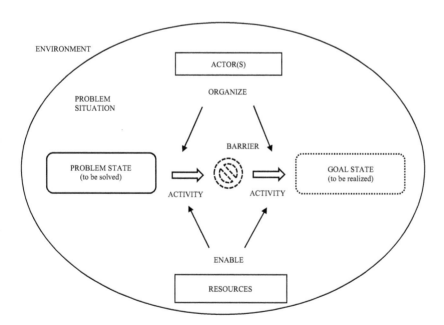

Figure 4.1   The Structure of Problem Solving[1]

However, the concept of social innovation needs to be handled with care. In practice, it is sometimes erroneously associated with creative invention through inspired individuals who leave the more arduous and trivial implementation to others. This is not what is meant here. Social innovation ranges beyond invention and essentially covers the phases of implementation, stabilisation and routinisation of new artefacts and practices (Howaldt and Schwarz 2010: 54). Importantly, just as in cases of industrial or technological innovation, this process must not be conceived as linear, orderly and predictable. Innovation processes do not resemble the pursuit of a predefined plan and they cannot be programmed. They are characterised by contingencies and deviations from plans and thus proceed in cycles and branches. This is why research portrays them as "innovation journeys" (Van de Ven et al. 2008) which resemble expeditions through unknown terrain: "when destinations are unclear and there are no preexistent goals, causal road maps are less useful. . . . Bold expeditions and even one-eyed pirates rule such seas, and voyages to India effectually end up in the Americas" (Sarasvathy 2001: 262).

This also points to the fact, that newness is not limited to the results but may also extend to the *process* of innovation (Van de Ven et al. 2008).

4.2 Principles of Problem Solving

Due to the overwhelming diversity, complexity and size of contemporary social problems, standardised recipes for problem solving are unavailable. However, there are three generic principles which can guide these processes, namely the requirements of fit, reduction of complexity and enhanced capacity. While they are distinct principles in their own right, they are also highly interdependent. What are the distinct features of the single principles, and how do they cohere?

4.2.1 *"Fit" Between Problems and Interventions*

In Chapter 1, I pointed at the broad scholarly consensus that there is not the one best approach to problem solving. Any attempt to use a standardised tool will result in "Type II" errors in terms of the application of an effective approach to an unsuitable situation (Landau and Stout 1979: 153; Hofstede 1981: 207). Rather, interventions need to be customised, that is they need to be tailored in such a way as to "fit" the constitutive properties of the particular problem situation, which depend on the objective state of affairs as well as actors, resources and the definition of the problem situation. The reason for this principle is straightforward: both social problems and interventions are highly complex phenomena. To tackle a problem in an adequate way, a variety of actors and resources have to be organised so as to effect a coherent intervention that meets the demands of the particular problem situation. Fit thus becomes a necessary condition for intervention effectiveness and organisational performance (Hofstede 1981: 207 and *passim*; Mayntz 1983: 17; Miller 1988; Snowden and Boone 2007; Ansell 2011: 90–92; Kania et al. 2014). I will demonstrate below how different types of strategies fit the requirements of different types of problem situations. Chapter 5 will extend the discussion to niches and networks as structures which are conductive to processes of innovation.

At the outset of problem solving, actors usually do not know what this requirement entails in practice, precisely which variables are relevant, and how it can be realised in varying domains of application. Hence, problem adequacy will be the result rather than the point of departure of successful processes of social innovation.

4.2.2 Reduction of Complexity

Attaining problem adequacy is all but a trivial task. For how can fit between an intervention and a complex problem situation can be achieved if the latter is blurred and characterised by dynamic change and a high level of ambiguity and intransparency? At this point, the need for a reduction of complexity comes into play. Research suggests that this requirement is important if problem solvers are to gain traction on a problem in the first place (Simon 1962; Funke 2006; Ansell 2011), for the most severe problems lack a distinctive *gestalt:* they are way too unspecific for actors to find a point of leverage. Furthermore, overly large and complex problems inhibit both the ability and the willingness to become active at all. According to Weick:

> the massive scale on which social problems are conceived often precludes innovative action because the limits of bounded rationality are exceeded and arousal is raised to dysfunctionally high levels. People often define social problems in ways that overwhelm their ability to do anything about them.
>
> (Weick 1984: 40)

In other words, it is not prudent to tackle the largest and most wicked social problems as such. They only lose their overwhelming dimensions if they are broken down into smaller "chunks" (Ansell 2011: 87) and thus become solvable or manageable in the first place. This is why Weick suggests going for "small wins" instead of revolutionary change. The term designates:

> a concrete, complete, implemented outcome of moderate importance. . . . Small wins are controllable opportunities that produce visible results. . . . Small wins often originate as solutions that single out and define as problems those specific, limited conditions for which they can serve as the complete remedy.
>
> (Weick 1984: 43)

Reduction of complexity can be achieved by means of a problem definition which demarcates the problem's boundaries and stipulates which aspects of the problem situation count as relevant, and which do not. There are different possible avenues to achieve this task. Simon (1962: 473) suggested that complex systems can be "decomposed" into constituent parts—basically the sub-units the system is made of. Accordingly, problem-solving strategies sometimes consist in reconstructing and tackling these sub-units of more complex problems. This strategy can be illustrated by the attempt to enhance the performance of single schools instead of tackling the problems of the whole school system.

Incrementalists favour a stepwise procedure. They aim at generating limited instances of progress which may add up or pave the way to larger, more encompassing solutions (Simon 1962: 472; Weick 1984: 43–44 and *passim*). For instance, an incremental strategy for school improvement might first aim at developing a programme for improving the reading and writing skills of students. If successful, it might proceed with other competencies such as maths or foreign languages or begin to advocate for policy change in order to enhance the framework conditions for better learning. According to Funke (2006: 440), another option is to focus on *essential* features of the problem. In the case of school performance, efforts might be directed at improving instruction as the core business of schools instead of addressing a multitude of potentially relevant variables, such as governance structures, leadership issues, legal requirements and the quality of school's premises. Finally, the reduction of complexity may also involve a rather limited definition of the target group (e.g., students in high poverty schools only) or the target area (e.g., a neighbourhood instead of a state) to be served (Ebrahim and Rangan 2014). Obviously, it may be prudent and even inevitable to combine some or all of these options.

At the same time, however, the reduction of complexity entails a delicate balancing act. On the one hand, interventions in highly complex, densely connected systems may evade 'chunking' strategies to some degree, because there exists a threshold for the reduction of the scope of the problem below which the requirement of problem adequacy is no longer met (Ansell 2011: 87). On the other hand, the reduction of the scale of the problem may result in overly limited 'islands of success' which remedy an insignificant part of the problem only. For instance, empirical research on school improvement has found that a considerable reduction of problem complexity and a rather moderate scale and scope of interventions tackling the 'achievement gap' are important preconditions for intervention effectiveness (Thümler et al. 2014b). Yet, programmes which meet these criteria cannot match the overall size of the challenge. This is why they have been accused of merely casting "buckets into the sea" (Greene 2005). In these cases, problem solvers will need to apply more "systemic" procedures (Ansell 2011: 87–88), which skilfully combine the demands of complexity reduction with the potential for widespread systemic change. The approach of "strategic niche management" which is introduced in the following chapter provides an answer to this challenge.

4.2.3 Enhanced Capacity

As a corollary to the above considerations, the reduction of complexity must be complemented by the principle of enhanced capacity. This has not been formulated explicitly yet, but it is implicit in much of the relevant literature. It can be seen as a response to the diagnosis that complex problems, even if reduced to chunks, tend to exceed most actors' resources, be they material, social or cultural in kind. Hence, problem-solvers need to mobilise additional resources in order to strengthen their problem-solving potential. According to the literature, networks can be regarded as a major tool to achieve this task. This is why they were introduced above as structures which are adequate to problem solving. Scholars distinguish between more instrumental *innovation networks* on the one hand and *policy networks* or advocacy coalitions on the other.

Innovation networks serve as tools for the development and implementation of solutions. They facilitate the free exchange of ideas and the collaboration of diverse autonomous actors who bring heterogeneous knowledge into direct, unmediated contact (Bruun and Sierla 2008), thus improving the flow of knowledge and enhancing learning (Powell et al. 1996; Provan and Kenis 2008; Provan and Lemaire 2012), increasing flexibility and adaptivity (Provan and Lemaire 2012), reducing fragmentation and enhancing the integration of services (Jennings and Ewalt 1998; Provan and Sebastian 1998), pooling resources and using them more effectively (Meier and O'Toole 2003). Furthermore, networks convey legitimacy (Human and Provan 2000), help to control second-order effects of programmes and support actors in finding a distinctive niche in densely populated policy areas such as welfare provision (O'Toole 1997: 47). Policy networks or advocacy coalitions, on the other hand, are essentially tools for policy change (Adam and Kriesi 2007). They are alliances among like-minded individuals and groups which are united by coherent sets of beliefs, values and interests and are supposed to build the "political muscle" necessary to "push innovations in the face of concerted resistance" (Ansell et al. 2009).

Finally, problem-solving processes may profit from a longer duration of projects or programmes. While philanthropic interventions are often set up as rather limited projects, the principle of enhanced capacity would suggest that problem solvers should be prepared to plan for decades rather than years of activity.

4.3 Processes and Strategies of Problem Solving

After these basic considerations I will now come back to the question of how social problems can be solved. In the literature, the focus is on adequate *strategies*. The discussion relies on the premise that rational problem-solving action is not random. Rather, it follows recognisable patterns of behaviour which shape the process of problem solving in important regards.

In recent years, the existence of an organisational strategy as the outcome of a formal planning process has become a hallmark of rational non-profit organisations (Hwang and Powell 2009; Ebrahim and Rangan 2010; Bromley and Powell 2012). Ideally, the term "strategy" refers to a conception that guides an organisation's behaviour by means of specifying overall goals and the means and processes required to achieve them (Moore 2000). A strategy thus answers the question of "What to do next?" (Wiltbank et al. 2006) and *how* to do it. Strategy also determines the boundaries of organisational action and thus informs actors and observers what *not* to do. Finally, it stipulates how the different operations of the organisation interact with one another to serve its overall purposes (Porter 1996). Put in evolutionary terms, the task of strategy is to direct organisational behaviour under conditions of environmental change and uncertainty. In the case of philanthropic organisations, this implies the requirement to influence and change the environment. The essence of philanthropic strategy, then, is to specify how both the organisation's assets as well as environmental conditions and developments can be harnessed and transformed in such a way as to further the organisation's goals.

4.3.1 From Planned to Contingent Strategy

In philanthropic contexts, just as in other fields of research, the term "strategy" is often associated with bureaucratic rationality. It is conceived as the equivalent of an explicit and elaborate plan oriented towards the achievement of long-term organisational goals which are treated as being fixed, specific and unambiguous. The strategy defines measures of success, specifies the process by which objectives are supposed to be attained, allocates resources and directs the coordination of activities and the monitoring of the process with the expectation of maximising returns (Nelson and Winter 1977; Mintzberg 1979a; Hayes 1985). In practice, however, "strategy" has a variety of meanings. The term refers to essentially different types of organisational behaviour, the effectiveness of which is contingent on the goals an organisation pursues and the environment in which it operates (Burns and Stalker 1961; Mintzberg 1979a; Courtney et al. 1997; Wiltbank et al. 2006; Ebrahim and Rangan 2010).

For instance, in the context of the military, conventional and insurgent strategies can be distinguished. The former are hierarchically planned and execution is supervised by central command. By contrast, the latter follow the laws of guerrilla warfare. They rely on independent field commanders who move swiftly in small groups, profit from intricate knowledge of the terrain and the support of local citizenry, and thus are able to recognise and seize opportunities quickly as they arise (Hayes 1985: 16). In a similar vein, corporate strategies are positioned along a spectrum between planned and adaptive strategies. While the former seek to position firms in the direction of envisaged trajectories of the markets they serve, the latter aim at building rapid response capacities so as to be able to follow essentially unpredictable developments on the spot (Wiltbank et al. 2006).

From a review of this literature there emerges the need for a more versatile and liberal concept of "strategy", which is more sensitive to environmental differences, embraces a wider range of alternative types of action and coheres with the results of prior research in related fields. Research suggests that rational problem solvers pursue a *contingency approach* as they develop bespoke strategies which fit the characteristic properties of the different problem situations they confront.

I have argued above that genuine problem solving always involves a degree of novelty and that processes of social problem solving are akin to processes of social innovation. Hence, in what follows I will frame the discussion on strategies in the language of the innovation journey. It also helps to see how the nature of the problem under attack may change in the process of innovation due to the remedial action of problem solvers. This, in turn, requires actors to adapt their behaviour to the new situation.

4.3.1.1 *Exploration of Unclear Problem Situations*

In the early stages of the process of social innovation, problem solvers' knowledge and understanding of the problem situation are frequently very limited. Scale and scope of the problem may be opaque, relevant stakeholders unknown and goals as vague as available options for action. In this scenario, there is neither a roadmap nor a clear goal and innovation journeys are shaped as processes of discovery. Actors are portrayed as *explorers* who cross a more or less rugged, unknown, changing and potentially even hostile problem landscape (for a more comprehensive discussion of the imagery see, e.g., Levinthal 1997; Van de Ven et al. 2008: 87–98).[2] As expeditions venture into unknown, "swampy" terrain (Hayes 1985), their goals emerge and concretise in the course of the search, and success may often consist in entirely unexpected results. Outcomes cannot be predicted with certainty and control over the search processes is low (Van de Ven et al. 2008).[3]

Navigation under these conditions of unpredictability and contingency thus requires adequate techniques. The more rugged and the less well known the territory to be crossed, the greater the need to proceed in distributed ways, for example by launching small independent groups of explorers who seek to map different parts of the terrain. Hence, these processes typically follow a "fireworks" (Braun-Thürmann 2005) or "portfolio" (Nill and Kemp 2009: 669) model: a broad and unspecific problem definition triggers search processes which are characterised by different independent paths of action. Over time they may or may not converge; some paths are given up while others are pursued further. Goals are specified in the course of the journey as innovators learn more about the field, about what is feasible and what is not (Van de Ven et al. 2008).

While explorative behaviour is the method of choice under conditions of very high uncertainty, it also entails profound disadvantages. To begin with, innovation journeys may entail particularly high costs, although they may not yet solve problems at all: some expeditions take a long time to unfold and they rely on the availability of a considerable amount of slack resources to enable the pursuit of parallel paths (McCaskey 1974; Garud and Van de Ven 1992; Van de Ven et al. 2008). Moreover, distributed innovation journeys imply coordination problems due to a shift of the locus of expertise and control from the central organisation to the multiple actors in the field. They need to continuously exchange experience and knowledge to coordinate their efforts, which is an organizationally demanding task. Finally, exploration is risky as there is no guarantee that search activities will lead to the desired goal (Van de Ven et al. 2008).

In case of success, however, problem solvers have gained a better understanding of the problem situation. They may also have learned how to decompose overly large and complex problems into less overwhelming "chunks" or clusters of problems. The resulting problem situations are of medium complexity, and they are characterised by varying degrees of uncertainty, contention, intransparency and change.[4] In what follows I will show how experimental strategies can be applied to match this new situation.

4.3.2 Problems of Medium Complexity and Experimental Strategies

Put in the language of the innovation journey, problem solvers can now formulate one goal instead of many. Although it may be somewhat provisional (with Dewey one might talk about "ends-in-view"), the definition should be sufficiently precise to guide the problem solvers through a moderately complex and stable environment in order to find a path towards the goal. In other words, actors do not yet know what works and whether the results of problem-solving action will be desirable or not. Drawing on the pragmatist discussion above, situations such as these require *search* to find feasible new courses of action. This type of strategy relies on incremental processes of trial-and-error learning. Depending on the dominant properties of the problem situation, experiments can take very different shapes.

4.3.2.1 INNOVATION PROBLEMS AND SOCIAL EXPERIMENTS

Travellers sometimes seek to achieve an uncontroversial and clear objective, yet they do not know the path leading towards the goal. It is then a rational response to sketch a provisional route and begin moving, making ad hoc corrections both to the path and to the goal as the journey proceeds. Sometimes there are different possible routes, the precise properties of which are unclear. In this situation, problem solvers may follow the different paths simultaneously under standardised conditions so as to be able to single out dead ends and to determine which one leads to the goal in the shortest time.

This imagery illustrates the fact that innovation problems are characterised by a lack of causal knowledge of how to reach organisational goals. Ideally, the ends of action are sufficiently clear and uncontroversial and alternative options for action are known, whereas the necessary problem-solving knowledge and technology are still unavailable. This is the domain of genuine social experiments which are typically conducted as randomised controlled trials (RCTs) (Campbell 1969, 1991; Banerjee and Duflo 2011). RCTs test the effects of an intervention on a group which receives the treatment and compare the results with a control group without treatment. Importantly, the members of both groups are assigned randomly. The aim is to render visible causal connections between independent and dependent variables. For these purposes, RCTs require a high degree of control over problem situation and intervention in terms of an isolation from interfering variables, for otherwise causal relations cannot reliably be established (Borman 2002: 11; Ansell and Bartenberger 2015: 6–7). RCTs have frequently but erroneously been conceived as the "gold standard" of social intervention (Ansell and Bartenberger 2015: 20). However, the discussion in this chapter shows that they are but one device in a much larger toolbox.

4.3.2.2 CONTENTIOUS PROBLEMS AND POLITICAL STRATEGIES

If the destination, the travellers or the means of transport are contested, it may be difficult to organise the innovation journey efficiently and effectively. This is the domain of political problems. They require that consensus be built so that the future journey can move safely.

Political problems are characterised by controversy and power struggles among different stakeholders who pursue incompatible interests. Contention may arise regarding the legitimacy of actors, the appropriateness of interventions or the desirability of outcomes, or other aspects of the problem situation. The discussion on philanthropic strategies has largely bracketed the contentious nature of many social problems, although it has fundamental implications for problem solvers. Compare political problems on the one hand, and problems which are of a rather uncontroversial make-up, on the other. Both types of situations function as "motors" for fundamentally different kinds of behaviour and require different types of action (Christensen 1985; Van de Ven and Poole 1995). In cases of low conflict, "teleological" modes of behaviour may proceed in iterative sequences of collaborative problem solving (Van de Ven and Poole 1995: 515–517). In the case of political problems, however, actors inhabit a "pluralistic world of colliding events, forces, or contradictory values that compete with each other for domination and control". Hence, they need to pursue "dialectical" modes of operation which terminate in a synthesis among the position of incumbents (thesis) and challengers (antithesis) of an established order (Van de Ven and Poole 1995: 515–517).

Take, for instance, the problem of undocumented migrants. Some stakeholders may argue that regularisation would solve the problem immediately and for good. Others might prefer more consequent law enforcement instead. In these cases, *political* modes of action such as moderation, negotiation, bargaining, advocacy or the organisation of protest are adequate responses. The former aim at reducing contention through the accommodation of conflicting preferences to achieve consensus and compromise (Christensen 1985: 65). Advocacy and protest strategies may aspire to gain hegemony on the issue and to either convince and marginalise or simply overrule opponents. In the case of philanthropic organisations, one would expect to find more "civil" strategies such as moderation, negotiation and bargaining as well as moderate forms of advocacy which seek to strengthen marginalised voices to allow them to be heard in the process (Christensen 1985: 68). More radical forms of advocacy and protest are the proper domain of social movements and pressure groups (e.g., Almog-Bar and Schmid 2014: 10–11).

4.3.2.3 RESOURCE PROBLEMS AND GROWTH STRATEGIES

To meet the scale and scope of social problems, problem solvers may have to build highways rather than bounded paths to enable the transport of as many passengers as possible. To cover the rising costs, they may either charge fees for their services, mobilise additional support of coalitions of public and private funders, or both. The metaphor hints at the fact that problem solvers are frequently confronted with a scarcity of material resources which inhibits their potential to match the scale and scope of social problems. This diagnosis, along with the difficulty to grow solutions to a sufficient size, has frequently been regarded as the major challenge of philanthropic action. Accordingly, achieving scale is regarded as an important indicator of the success of social sector organisations (Ebrahim and Rangan 2014; Seelos and Mair 2014).

While there are many different possible answers to this challenge, the literature on scaling is dominated by a logic of growth which relies on the mobilisation of additional resources based on supply-demand relations. Two different avenues are most prominent. The first highlights the relevance of demand. It conceives of growth as the result of the provision of attractive and highly standardised problem-solving products which create surplus value as they are marketed, distributed and sold to serve as many customers as possible, perhaps producing a monetary return, for example through user fees or cross-subsidies (Weisbrod 1998; Seelos and Mair 2014). A second, more supply-oriented version seeks to mobilise a higher amount of resources to increase outputs, for instance by means of partnerships and coalitions with public actors and their much larger assets (e.g., Frumkin 2006: 190–203; Ebrahim and Rangan 2014: 129). Of course, combinations of both are feasible, as well.

4.3.2.4 CONTROL PROBLEMS AND DIVERSE STRATEGIES

Control problems arise under different conditions, taking different shapes. Accordingly, they require the application of variable strategies, depending on the particular properties of the problem situation. Problems which are characterised by a high pace of change have attracted particular scholarly attention. These situations require "rapid response" strategies which are essentially dependent on the pre-existence of adequate operational structures and routines (Snowden and Boone 2007: 5–6; Kettl 2009).

Take the case of emergency relief organisations which are confronted with quickly unfolding crises or constantly changing security situations in highly unstable areas such as Afghanistan or Sudan. These organisations may need to intervene on an ad hoc basis, moving between distributing aid and withdrawing from an area. Hence, beyond professional knowledge and the availability of sufficient material resources, they need to acquire the dynamic capabilities necessary to respond quickly and effectively in the face of sudden and unpredictable events (Ebrahim and Rangan 2010: 26).

I have argued above that the field of school improvement is particularly prone to a lack of internal control. For instance, in a large-scale study on comprehensive school reform programmes, Rowan and Miller (2007) found that intervention effectiveness was dependent on the degree of control interventions exerted over the behaviour of teachers. In the case of the Success For All programme,[5] a tight coupling between programme requirements and teaching practice was achieved by means of the provision of standardised procedures and teaching materials, along with direct personal supervision of teacher behaviour in the classrooms. By contrast, the development of the Jacobs-Sommercamp, which sought to develop an effective summer camp programme to improve the language skills of students (Stanat et al. 2012; Beller 2014) suggests that control problems can be avoided by positioning interventions *outside* of the classroom.

Overall, however, research on control problems is rather scarce (at least what concerns a philanthropic context)—particularly as far as the risk of unintended consequences is concerned, which may cause harm among the participants of the target group or beyond.

4.3.2.5 SIMPLE PROBLEMS AND BUREAUCRATIC STRATEGIES

If experimental strategies are successful, they may result in clear goals combined with paved routes through well-known terrain. Problem solvers can now be compared with a tour operator who organises a journey to a distant destination. To achieve the task effectively and efficiently, an intricate planning process is required to take into account all relevant variables and cater to all possible circumstances. Following the acquisition of sufficiently precise knowledge of the different possible routes as well as the available means of transportation, tour operators need to weigh alternatives in terms of their individual values (comfort, speed, costs), make a decision in favour of the optimal route and vehicle, and provide adequate resources (e.g., in terms of time, costs and catering). Next time they plan the journey they learn from earlier mistakes and thus increasingly refine the travel design. As the organisation of the journey becomes more and more perfect, both effectiveness and efficiency increase as higher numbers of passengers can be transported at lower costs and fewer failures.

Tour operators are confronted with simple or tame problems which can be solved by means of professional routines, and many authors claim that these are examples of the straightforward application of bureaucratic techniques of problem solving (Rittel and Webber 1973; McCaskey 1974; Blanco 1994; Snowden and Boone 2007; Ansell 2011; Kania et al. 2014). However, if problems are defined by the breakdown of routines (Funke 2003: 25, 38) or as crises of habitual behaviour (Dewey MW 13, LW 12; Ansell 2011: 9), these cases would actually not qualify as problems at all. Hence, only a thin line can be drawn between the solution of simple problems and mere routine action.

Bureaucratic approaches seek to maximise value by means of the application of allegedly "rational" or "scientific" methods. They emphasise the importance of unambiguous and uncontentious goals as well as observable and measurable *outcomes* as the major yardstick for success. This technique further relies on the availability of reliable knowledge that specifies the causal connections between the inputs and activities on the one hand, and the desirable outcomes and broader societal impact on the other, as well as established technology which reliably transforms the problem situation into the goal situation (Lindblom 1959; Landau and Stout 1979; Mintzberg 1979a; Hofstede 1981; Christensen 1985; Blanco 1994; DiMaggio 2001; Bromley and Powell 2012).

The underlying logic has been labelled as the mode of exploitation. The concept refers to processes of "refinement, choice, production, efficiency, selection, implementation, execution" (March 1991: 71). Organisations operating in this mode create value in constant and reliable ways, enhance production and adapt to external change in incremental ways as they pursue well-known trajectories: "the essence of exploitation is the refinement and extension of existing competencies, technologies, and paradigms" (March 1991: 85).

The process leading towards effective performance is "highly ordered, neatly integrated" (Mintzberg 1979a: 67) and unfolds as follows. As a first step, actors are supposed to conduct a comprehensive analysis of the problem situation which identifies all relevant alternative options for action.

Secondly they formulate clear objectives. Based on a means-ends analysis which includes the development of scenarios of all possible outcomes which are weighed against one another, they purposefully adopt an explicit strategy in terms of an elaborate plan. This lays out how to reach both ultimate and intermediate goals and organises the relevant resources necessary for its pursuit. The strategy thus determines the further process of implementation which is constantly monitored to evaluate if goals are met, or not. In the latter case, the planning process begins anew (Lindblom 1959; Mintzberg 1979a; Hayes 1985; Blanco 1994).

The bureaucratic model seeks to achieve a high degree of *control* over the process of problem solving (for example by means of predefined milestones), of the outcomes of philanthropic action through (preferably quantitative) evaluations, and of the environment of problem solvers by means of establishing closed systems (Landau and Stout 1979; Hofstede 1981; Tsoukas 1994; Bromley and Powell 2012). The emphasis on control comes at the expense of a limited ability to address more demanding problems, though. For instance, Blanco (1994) proposed as an example the "installation of a stop sign, traffic light, or reduced speed limit to solve the problem of increased congestion on a residential street".

Generally speaking, bureaucratic strategies focus on single organisations as the major units of philanthropic action. They further have important implications regarding power and leadership. Put in military terms, bureaucratic strategies are like conventional warfare. Decision making is concentrated at the level of central command which is the locus of planning for operations on a large scale. Decisions are imposed on the organisation and enacted by the lower levels of the hierarchy based on relations of command and obedience. This is why the concept of strategic philanthropy might be attractive to the top management of philanthropic organisations.

4.4 Conclusion

In this chapter I have introduced the basic properties and principles of problem solving and discussed the different strategies which are available to actors in the face of the diversity of complex social problems. Strategies were regarded as devices to reduce the barriers between problem state and goal state. They provide orientation to actors and render philanthropic action coherent as they specify goals and organise the means to achieve them.

While bureaucratic strategies are often regarded as the paradigm of rational action, research in the social sciences overwhelmingly suggests the adoption of a contingency approach to strategy instead. In this framework, bureaucratic action is regarded as a tool for the solution of rather simple problems. It is thus situated on the boundary between genuine problem solving and straightforward professional practice. The philanthropic toolkit needs to be supplemented by explorative strategies which are supposed to provide orientation under conditions of high uncertainty. Problem solvers may further make use of experimental methods which are well suited to organise processes of search and learning.

Having outlined the contours of a contingency approach to philanthropic strategy, some shortcomings come into view, as well. Research has shown that the very possibility of enacting a particular strategy depends on the availability of adequate *structures* (Miller 1988; Ogliastri et al. 2015). In what follows I will discuss the role of social *niches* and *networks* for processes of social innovation, assuming that the requirements of problem solving can only be met if these additional analytical categories comes into play.

Notes

1 Adapted from Thümler and Bögelein (2010).
2 I owe this point to Christopher K. Ansell.
3 Not all innovation processes exhibit an exploratory phase. For instance, actors who are well acquainted with the terrain may be able to address much more bounded problems right from the beginning.
4 To be sure, problem dimensions cannot always neatly be kept apart. Problems may come in chunks or clusters, dimensions may be blurred, overlap and change depending on the phase of innovation. As a result, problem solvers will usually have to combine different types of strategies (be it synchronous or over time) to satisfy the problem-solving principle of "fit". Such combinations require diverse organisational capabilities and it may be very difficult to cultivate them all simultaneously (Gupta et al. 2006), which is what renders interventions in the field of social innovation particularly demanding.
5 SFA develops and distributes research-based programmes which focus on reading and writing skills and target children from early childhood to middle school in low-income areas in the USA.

5 The Role of Niches in Processes of (Social) Innovation

Actors who attack complex social problems frequently lack clear and consensual goals, effective remedial technologies and control over the process of implementation, all of which renders their strategies vague and may lead to a lack of orientation. How, then, can they regain both control and orientation without taking refuge in simplistic models of action?

The literature suggests that organisational performance does not rely on adequate strategy alone. Rather, the choice and implementation of strategies requires that *structural* preconditions be given. I will argue that the concept of "niches" as developed in quasi-evolutionary theories of economic and socio-technological change is particularly well suited to meet these demands. According to the literature, niches in the sense of discrete and bounded, protected and stable social spaces are of major relevance for processes of evolution in general, and for socio-technological and economic innovation in particular. They provide the prerequisites for experimental learning and may serve as *nuclei* for more comprehensive episodes of systemic change.

However, the available models cannot simply be transferred to the field of philanthropy but must be adapted to this new context. In what follows, I will introduce different perspectives on the concept of niches. They are supposed to provide the building blocks of a working concept of "philanthropic niches" that is tailored to the distinctive properties and requirements of philanthropic action.

5.1 From Strategy to Structure

Three types of structures have attracted particular scholarly attention: organisations, networks and niches. For instance, scholars have argued that a match between organisational structures and the characteristics of external environments is a precondition for organisational performance (Burns and Stalker 1961; Lawrence and Lorsch 1986). Other researchers have investigated the relation between structure and strategy and posited that the viability of particular strategies relies on the congruence with adequate organisational structures (Chandler 1962; Miller 1988). The precise relations between the different variables remain a source of contention, though.

For instance, it is unclear whether structure follows strategy (Chandler 1962), whether strategy follows structure (Bower 1986), whether a relation of reciprocity obtains between them (Mintzberg 1990) or whether the dual model is inadequate altogether, as it needs to be complemented by the environment as a third variable (Miller 1988).[1]

Innovation research has directed particular attention towards the role of networks in the development and maintenance of novel problem-solving arrangements, highlighting the relevance of networked modes of action for processes of learning to overcome cognitive uncertainty and the potential to coordinate autonomous actors outside of formal hierarchies. This is consistent with the pragmatist conviction that experimental action relies on communities of inquiry as the carriers of the innovative process. Yet, while networks increase the capacity of problem solvers, they leave open the question of how to reduce complexity and regain control of the innovation process.

In what follows I will put emphasis on the role of niches in processes of social innovation. I do so for three reasons. First, niches operate at the highest level of aggregation, that is, they necessarily comprise networks and organisational structures. Hence, they render possible the development of a framework which integrates all three elements. Second, I will argue that niches are particularly well suited to meet the demands of philanthropic organisations. Third, opposed to networks, niches have received little to no attention, both in research on non-profit impact and effectiveness. Hence, there is an urgent need to close this scholarly gap.

5.2   The Concept of Niches

In common language, "niches" designate *bounded spaces* which are more or less *stable* and thus exist over longer periods of time. They offer comfortable positions due to the *protection,* security and sustainability they provide. However, the concept may also refer to hollow or *shallow,* ossified places which points to the demanding nature of attempts to harness the concept of niches for purposes of (social) innovation research. Niches are opposed to and determined by their position vis-à-vis larger environments and can be distinguished from these due to their mostly *local* nature (Tisdell and Seidl 2004). The concept has been adopted in different academic disciplines, albeit with different meanings.

The most obvious candidate is ecology. As opposed to common language usage, ecological niches are not conceived as a habitat that is located in time and space. Drawing on Hutchinson (1957), they are defined as functions of all the conditions and resources an organism or species needs for survival and reproduction. A niche is thus to be understood in terms of a multidimensional space which describes a species' role in and relationship to all biotic and abiotic aspects of its natural environment. For instance, two different species may inhabit the very same habitat, rely on the same resources and require the same ranges of temperature. If, however, one species is nocturnal while the other is diurnal they both inhabit different ecological niches (Hutchinson 1957: 417).

These first remarks may convey a rather static image of niches. However, they have a dual face. In the literature they are also regarded as important units for processes of change. The relevance of niches for innovation processes was first acknowledged in the context of evolutionary economics which seeks to explain the emergence of new technologies as the source of change of socio-technological systems or "regimes" (e.g., Nelson and Winter 1977; Dosi 1982). Levinthal (1998) maintained that, in evolutionary terms, widespread and disruptive change cannot be explained by recourse to a single mutation. Rather, incremental developments are made possible by a combination of distinct selection criteria and abundance of resources in separate environments (Levinthal 1998: 217–221) that trigger "a divergent evolutionary path" (Levinthal 1998: 218): "after several generations of products, this may eventually result in a new product that is substantially different from the original lineage" (Schot and Geels 2007: 613).

Research in business management puts forward a third variety of niches in terms of spaces which are characterised by unsatisfied customer demands. At the same time, they provide protection from competition due to cognitive, social or spatial barriers to entry of competitors (Caves and Porter 1977; Tisdell and Seidl 2004; Schot and Geels 2007). These barriers are regarded as particularly important prerequisites for product innovation. Unless there is some degree of protection from competitors who simply copy products or services, actors lack any incentives to engage in expensive processes of research and development (Tisdell and Seidl 2004: 128). Scholars further distinguish between market niches, which refer to smaller shares of a broader market, served by specialised products, and emerging niche markets created through the development of new products (Pepall 1992). Either way, they are created and seized by means of a "niching strategy" which includes the task to "identify a segment (or demand pocket) that . . . has structural characteristics allowing high returns. The firm then invests in building its position in this segment" (Porter 1980: 269).

Yet, this is not to say that these segments *are* the niches, for the conception relies on a constructivist ontology: niches are both found and made. They are "out there" because they involve populations and resources which exist in time and space. But they are also *made* as firms or entrepreneurs develop new organisations, technologies or products in order to meet customers' demands in unique ways or to create entirely new markets (Porter 1980; Geels 2002; Tisdell and Seidl 2004; Santos and Eisenhardt 2009; Schot and Geels 2007). Niches, then, must be conceived as a function of customers and their resources, firms and their products, as well as a firm's competitive advantages over its competitors (Tisdell and Seidl 2004: 122).

5.3 Transformation Research and Strategic Niche Management

The concept of niches in terms of societal spaces which are conductive to innovation has received most attention in quasi-evolutionary theories of socio-technological change. They play a particularly prominent role in research on technological transformation processes. Building on a combination of the above-mentioned conceptions of niches, they are credited with high transformative potential as they play a crucial role in processes of radical systemic innovation. An important strand of this research is based on the description, analysis and explanation of processes of radical socio-technological innovation such as the transition from sailing boats to steam ships (Geels 2002). Scholarship is motivated by the question of how conventional technological systems can be altered in favour of more sustainable alternatives, regardless of high levels of inertia, path-dependence and lock-in. The insights of transformation research have resulted in the development of the approach of strategic niche management (SNM). It seeks to provide an answer to the question of how dominant technological "regimes" can be changed (Kemp et al. 1998). The concept signifies complex arrangements of infrastructure and organisations, techniques and knowledge, actors in different positions and functions, as well as the norms, practices, vocabularies and motives which shape their behaviour. They constitute the foundation of any technological system from which innovations deviate to more or less degrees. Take as an example Kemp et al.'s (1998) analysis of the automobile industry. This is based on a "dominant design" which evolved during a phase of intense development activities in the period 1890–1920. It includes, among others, a combustion engine, a metal frame and a steering wheel (Kemp et al. 1998: 178) and it has not been essentially modified since then. Based on this design, a complex socio-technological system has emerged, including a large physical infrastructure (such as automobile factories, large networks of petrol stations and garages, along with experts who know how to repair them), millions of cars, a comprehensive legal regulation and institutionalised ideas both of manufacturers and clients of how a "real" car must look.

Systems like these develop a high degree of inertia for the following reasons. First, their complex components have been synchronised over long periods of time. Hence, the diversity of different components means that they mutually stabilise each other and thus create path dependencies which cannot easily be changed:

> What we have is not a set of factors that act separately as a containment force, but a structure of interrelated factors that feed back upon one another, the combined influence of which gives rise to inertia and specific patterns in the direction of technological change.
>
> (Kemp et al. (1998: 181)

Second, complex systems evade planned interventions because they evolve dynamically due to social and technological change. However, this development does not follow predictable rules and "does not aim through target-oriented and linear ways towards enhanced functionalities. Rather, it can be compared to the growth of yeast" (Ilten 2009: 16, my translation).

Third, even if regimes suffer from fundamental problems, the development of alternatives remains difficult. New technologies such as electric cars cannot easily be introduced and established because the set-up of the necessary infrastructure is expensive and risky. Innovations face powerful opposition by incumbent industries and suffer from uncertainty regarding reliability and functionality and the question of which new problems may be caused by the broad diffusion of new technologies (Kemp et al. 1998; Schot and Geels 2008).

5.3.1 The Role of Niches for Processes of Regime Change

In sum, radical innovators face all the challenges which are characteristic of wicked problems. How, then, can they be successful in the long term, regardless of the high stability of incumbent regimes on the one hand, and the low certainty and predictability of new technologies on the other? Recall that, according to evolutionary economics, fundamental change cannot come about in a single creative event. Neither does it rely on the inspiration of a gifted entrepreneur. Rather, systemic transformations emerge incrementally and in the course of experimental processes which unfold over long periods of time. Innovation must be conceived as a minor deviation from a dominant path which leads to the emergence of radically divergent arrangements, given that the new direction is pursued for long periods of time. Research further maintains that the transformation does not follow a coherent masterplan. Rather, it is dependent on the highly complex, co-evolutionary and co-constructed development of a diverse and heterogeneous set of technologies, user preferences, cognitive frameworks, technical skills, public regulations and markets themselves, the results of which may, over time, converge to a new proto-regime as a viable alternative to the incumbent system (Dosi 1982; Schot and Geels 2007: 616).

The problem is that, under prevailing market conditions, new technologies are the less viable the more they deviate from conventional standards. In their infancy, they are simply not robust enough to compete with established products. The concept of protective *niches* suggests a pragmatic response to these problems. A niche is defined as a discrete and bounded space in which an emerging innovation is protected from prevailing selection mechanisms as long as it cannot compete and survive under mainstream conditions (Kemp et al. 1998: 273; Schot and Geels 2007: 615; Verheul and Vergragt 1995: 320). Niches may operate inside or outside of dominant regimes (Schot and Geels 2007) and they open up a space for experimentation and learning. Over time, the novel technology becomes more competitive as its performance increases, supportive networks expand and as it is increasingly well adapted to environmental demands. In the case of success, it may migrate into the regime or even transform it, and protection can be reduced or removed. Niches thus have a triple function. They provide protection against selection pressures of the environment; they allow for both the freedom and the control necessary to develop new arrangements experimentally; and thus they can become sources of the transformation of incumbent regimes (Schot and Geels 2007; Verheul and Vergragt 1995; Smith and Raven 2012). Just as in the case of ecology or economics, an innovative niche cannot be *reduced* to its inhabitants or to the environment in which it exists. Rather, the concept designates a specific configuration of protective space (including networked actors, technologies, experimental processes, available resources) and its boundaries vis-à-vis the wider societal environment.

Niches, thus conceived, have a number of important advantages. To begin with, they facilitate *learning* processes as they provide the bounded space necessary for the generation of causal knowledge. As opposed to large-scale programmes, "they are less costly and more conducive to modification and change" (Kemp et al. 2001: 293–294). Learning takes place in incremental processes of experimentation and bricolage with a heterogeneous set of material, social and cognitive resources. This includes:

> learning about problems and how they may be overcome, how the technology may be integrated into the existing system, for what users the technology is attractive, for what purposes the technology may be used, how it may be sold, and so on.
>
> (Kemp et al. 2001: 293)

Hence, niches are regarded as the adequate organisational form to both organise and cope with non-linear developments as they allow the parallel exploration of the nature of problems and potential solutions (Geels and Raven 2006; Seyfang and Smith 2007; Schot and Geels 2008).

Niches have the further advantage of creating *variation:* as they are bounded experimental spaces rather than large and complex programmes, a multitude of different experiments may be created and nurtured, which is why, at least initially, efforts may "go in all kinds of directions" (Geels 2002: 1262). Yet, variation is not blind, as in Darwinian evolution. Transformation research follows a more Lamarckian paradigm, assuming that actors strategically aim at developing products which are fit enough to survive in a market environment. They thus attempt to anticipate the future course of selection, also trying to shape the selection process itself by lobbying for subsidies, programmes or other types of support: "variation comes subsequently pre-packaged in the right direction" (Schot and Geels 2007: 614–615; 2008: 539).

Niches also serve as *demonstration sites* which provide tangible examples of innovative approaches, prove the viability and effectiveness of a new technology (Kemp et al. 1998; Seyfang and Smith 2007) and help to formulate and substantiate promises regarding the future effectiveness and performance of novel artefacts or practices. If these claims are accepted by outside actors and sponsors, they are transformed into *expectations* which rely on the shared assumption that the new technologies "will become important for realizing particular societal and collective goals in the future" (Schot and Geels 2008: 539). Expectations promise the solution of shortcomings of incumbent technologies and regimes, guide the further development of niche technologies, serve as self-fulfilling prophecies and help to mobilise constituency and support (Kemp et al. 1998; Geels and Raven 2006).

At the same time, niches are an effective format to *stabilise* inchoate approaches over long periods of time. Because their size is limited, they are comparatively easy to sustain. Niches help to bridge the "valley of death" of innovations and to sustain new technologies until they are sufficiently robust for market entry (Schot and Geels 2008: 538). Finally, the establishment of innovative niches may depend on the willingness of powerful actors in the field to accept or ignore deviations from the norm. Bounded experiments may make it easier to remain below the radar of potential opponents (Thümler 2015).

5.3.2 The Process of Innovation

More comprehensive processes of transformation require a dynamic development of niches in quantitative and qualitative regards: over time, new and more diverse local activities accumulate in processes of co-evolution which are increasingly well aligned. Some of them may exhibit high rates of growth: depending on developmental stage, niche actors may be merely local bricoleurs or develop significant size. Parallel to this, a qualitative development occurs. This leads to more functional technologies, increased knowledge on conditions of application, cheaper and more reliable technologies of production, etc. Single niche activities thus cumulate into a sub- or proto-system, which is regarded as a precondition for a more comprehensive transformation of the dominant regime (Geels 2002).[2] This interplay is illustrated by Figure 5.1.

However, even the best performing niche practices transform into the dominant regime only if environmental conditions are favourable, particularly in the case of systemic crises. These may be triggered by internal conflicts, but, more often, they are caused by disruptive events on a societal (macro) level, called the "landscape" (Geels 2002: 1262). The energy transition in Germany following the nuclear accident at Fukushima is a particularly dramatic example of this constellation. In the niche of renewable energy which had developed over decades, a working alternative to nuclear power and fossil energies had emerged. However, a fundamental crisis was still required to destabilise the incumbent regime and trigger the transformation in the first place. Yet, the opposite may occur, just as well: "Actors construct market or technological niches to get the world under control, but these newly created niches can become utterly useless as a result of unexpected new developments elsewhere" (Schot and Geels 2007: 619).

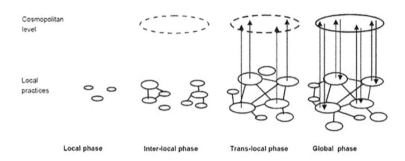

Figure 5.1 Local and Global Dynamics in Transformation Processes
Source: Geels and Deuten (2006: 269).

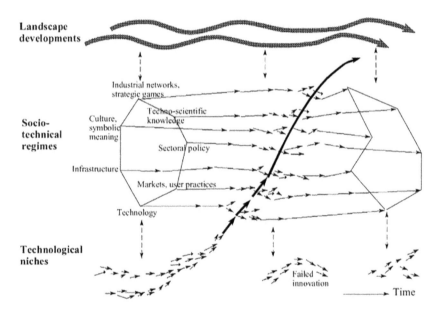

Figure 5.2 Multilevel-Perspective of Technological Transformation
Source: Geels (2002: 1263).

Figure 5.2 illustrates the interplay between niches, regimes and land-scape.[3] It demonstrates that niche technologies can only migrate into the regime in the case of *windows of opportunity* due to instability at the levels of landscape and regime and thus influence both of them.

Consistent with this, research emphasises the length of innovation processes: to be successful, "innovation journeys need to be sustained for long periods of time, often decades rather than years" (Geels et al. 2008: 524).

Yet, at the same time, the essential uncertainty of niching processes even under favourable conditions is highlighted. Success is by no means guaranteed as new practices may not come up to prior expectations. Changing environments may render effective new practices unviable and windows of opportunity may not open up (Kemp et al. 1998).

5.3.3 The Actors, Networks and Strategies of Niche Management

Strategic niche management emphasizes that the establishment and development of niches is an essentially collaborative endeavour that depends on the engagement of a diverse set of committed and networked organisations or individuals. It thus favours a multi-actor perspective rather than focusing on single organisations or markets (Geels et al. 2008: 524).

Many local experiments are created and sustained organically and from the bottom up by small entrepreneurs, NGOs, grassroots groups or activists, or other actors at the periphery of established fields. Yet, niche activities may also be strategically initiated and supported in a rather top-down fashion by governments, large corporations or research institutes (Seyfang and Smith 2007; Verheul and Vergragt 1995; Schot and Geels 2008: 538–539). Intermediary actors such as professional societies, business platforms or NGOs play an important role on a global, that is, cross-project level (Geels and Deuten 2006).

Regardless of the uncertainty inherent in niche processes, these diverse actors invest a wide array of resources based on a common problem definition and the motivation not only to criticise dominant regimes but to create viable alternatives. They share the assumption that the emerging new practices or technologies "will become important for realizing particular societal and collective goals in the future" (Schot and Geels 2008: 539) because of their superior potential to solve or alleviate the social problems they address (Kemp et al. 2001: 290; Verheul and Vergragt 1995).

5.3.4 The Role of Networks

In discussions on adequate strategies under conditions of complexity, the subjects of remedial action are conceived as alliances of collaborating organisations and/or individuals. Problem-solving tasks are distributed over a variety of different actors, which is why the effects of interventions are less easily attributable. Rather, goals and strategies are co-produced, implementation is collective and the emphasis on control and planning gives way to an emphasis on learning (Heifetz et al. 2004; Kania and Kramer 2011; Kania et al. 2014).

The literature also observes a shift of the locus of power that goes along with lower degrees of predictability and a heightened need for adaptive and dynamic capabilities. For instance, in the case of corporate strategy, centralised planning departments lose their dominant position in favour of a stronger role for line managers and regional offices (Hofstede 1981: 199; Grant 2003: 512, 514).

Accordingly, scholars of technology transitions assign high relevance to the connection of diverse actors in heterogeneous *networks* (Kemp et al. 1998; Geels and Raven 2006; Caniëls and Romijn 2008; Schot and Geels 2007; Verheul and Vergragt 1995; Geels et al. 2008; Schot and Geels 2008). They relate the failure of niche projects to overly narrow networks. The exclusion of outsiders proved to be detrimental to learning, whereas the inability to involve regime actors resulted in a lack of resources (Schot and Geels 2008).

At the local level, networks of organisational and individual actors are regarded as the major carriers of innovation. They support the niche process through the provision of resources such as money, time and staff, knowledge and skills. At the same time, the close interaction between the members of the network renders possible those intense learning processes which are characteristic and constitutive for innovative niches as they generate highly concrete, problem-specific knowledge (Geels and Deuten 2006).

Networks further play an important role on a global niche level. Yet, these are composed of different kinds of actors and their contribution is of a different nature. Globally networked actors and, in particular, intermediary organisations facilitate the exchange of information as they generate more abstract, situation-independent knowledge which may circulate among distributed local niche actors. They aggregate "sticky" local knowledge to generic lessons learned, build infrastructure to store and exchange knowledge, and, based on these abilities, coordinate local action and thus play a central role in the global development of a niche (Geels and Deuten 2006). Furthermore, they may help address the specific challenges local experiments face, such as the provision of resources, the effectiveness of management and the diffusion of results in case of success (Seyfang and Smith 2007; Hargreaves et al. 2013). Actors on the global level also contribute to an emerging sense of community as they facilitate the development of overarching narratives which help single and possibly isolated actors to regard themselves as members of a community and participants in a common project (Geels and Deuten 2006; Raven and Geels 2010). Finally, networks have an essentially *political* dimension. For instance, Schot and Geels (2008) found that the networks' members protect the niche against external interventions. Smith and Raven point at the relevance of narratives which put forward promises of niche technologies, emphasise problems and contradictions of the prevailing regime and thus justify demands for support by mainstream actors (Smith and Raven 2012: 1032–1033).

5.3.5 Varieties of Niche Management

The *management* of niches is essentially determined by the fact that new systems can neither be planned in advance nor steered in a predefined direction, because they lack clear and consensual, let alone quantified, objectives (Kemp et al. 2001: 280). What is more, potential solutions will rely on the reconfiguration of a broad set of heterogeneous elements, the particular nature and properties of which are unclear in the early stages of the process as some of them are still under construction while others may only emerge in the future. The challenge of SNM, then, is to harness and modulate rather than steer and direct a wide and heterogeneous variety of constantly emerging and evolving activities. A niche manager needs to conceive of her- or himself as an enabling "catalyst rather than a regulator . . . [who] facilitates—rather than forges—change in a new direction" (Kemp et al. 1998: 191–192).

Three major elements of niche management have been identified in the literature, namely the *establishment* of niches (Kemp et al. 1998; 2001), their sustained *protection and support* (Smith and Raven 2012: 1026–1032) and the decision on when to *breakdown protection* and open up the niche (Kemp et al. 1998; 2001).

In the beginning, actors constitute a niche through a collaborative act as they choose a technology and a mode of protection. The further existence of the niche depends on the sustained willingness to maintain support. It ends when support is withdrawn and protection is removed as the niche either fails to meet the expectations of niche actors, or successfully migrates into the regime (Kemp et al. 2001). Importantly, the creation and maintenance of a niche involves a genuinely:

> protective space [which] is constructed through a form of *boundary work* in which global networks develop a repertoire of narratives . . . to key, resourceful audiences in the wider social world, and rendered credible (or not) by drawing upon local network experiences. . . . The question then becomes one of how that boundary between niche context and content is negotiated and transformed productively over time.
>
> (Smith and Raven 2012: 1032)

Niche protection is provided by means of shielding, nurturing and empowerment (Smith and Raven 2012). *Shielding* aims at the suspension of institutionalised pressures for routinised "correct" action and conventional selection mechanisms. There are two ways to achieve this. *Passive protection* is obtained if niches are positioned in favourable environments, for example at the periphery of fields, in geographically separate areas, or in spaces in which the innovation's disadvantages are less problematic (examples include the military, where costs play a less important role, or societal milieus in which alternative values and cultures prevail. For instance, environmentalists may be willing to pay higher prices or accept lower performance if services or commodities are regarded as more just or "green") (Kemp et al. 2001: 290; Smith and Raven 2012: 1027; Seyfang and Longhurst 2013: 883). *Active protection* refers to all types of deliberate attempts to shield niches. These include favourable frameworks set by policymakers such as tax exemption, subsidies or quotas on the one hand, as well as private and civil society activities like direct funding, incubation efforts or cooperatives on the other (Smith and Raven 2012: 2017). Protection also needs to be provided against actors who "will actively try to undermine niches and disrupt their space for development" (Smith and Raven 2012: 1026), for instance through the creation of supportive networks (Kemp et al. 1998).

Niches are *nurtured* if actors provide resources with the intention to deepen the processes of learning and broaden niche growth and expansion. Nurturing in terms of cognitive work occurs if actors trigger and sustain experimental learning processes, or if intermediary actors facilitate interaction among local actors and support the generation, consolidation and distribution of context-free knowledge. Cognitive nurturing also includes the articulation of the expected potential returns on new technologies. Nurturing in terms of management refers to all those processes which seek to enhance management capacity and skills or to generate and stabilise supportive networks as vehicles for learning and for building constituency (Kemp et al. 1998; 2001; Deuten 2003; Geels and Deuten 2006; Seyfang and Smith 2007; Smith and Raven 2012; Seyfang and Longhurst 2013).

Niches are *empowered* by activities which either seek to make the niche innovation "fit and conform" with incumbent regimes in order to pave the way for entry in a system that remains more or less unaltered otherwise, or to "stretch and transform" the environment to the effect of destabilising regimes, for example by pointing out and exploiting weaknesses or tensions of prevailing technologies (Smith and Raven 2012: 1030). To the degree that niches are created and designed to alter the behaviour of regime actors through the modification of norms, cognitive standards or organisational routines, they are inherently *political* projects, which are dependent on the ability to apply the instruments of collective political action (Smith and Raven 2012: 1031).

Finally, niche management also includes the decision for the end of protection in the case of success, or termination in case of failure. Opposed to conventional philanthropic interventions in the form of projects, SNM emphasises the long-time horizons required for radical change. Scholars have a clear preference for small and long-term rather than large and rapid processes: "Learning is far more important than achieving high sales. . . . There is often more to be learned from a program lasting 10 years than a short program of 5 years that costs twice as much" (Kemp et al. 2001: 293–294).

Determining the right timing for the end of protection is obviously a difficult task and a major challenge of niche management. It implies the risk of picking the wrong approach and staying on course for too long to the effect of channelling considerable resources into an infertile or ossified niche, or to remove protection too early and risk the loss of all prior investments.

5.4 Niche Management at the Grassroots

SNM suggests how complex, distributed and controversial innovation journeys can be realised in *technological* domains, but it is not intended for use in philanthropic contexts and does not cover processes of social innovation. However, scholars acknowledge that a wide range of actors, including technology users, non-profit organisations or community groups, may establish, manage or support niches (Kemp et al. 1998: 188–189; Schot and Geels 2008). Moreover, the analytical framework of SNM has already been used for the investigation of sustainability innovations through civil society actors at the grassroots level, which suggests that it may be transferred to a philanthropic context, as well.

This literature has highlighted important areas of overlap. Both in technology and in grassroots innovation, protected niches serve as important sites of experimental learning. Both rely on well-functioning and sufficiently resourced intermediary organisations as well as the existence of effective networks (both formal and informal and on local and global levels) (Geels and Deuten 2006; Seyfang and Smith 2007; Seyfang and Longhurst 2013; Hargreaves et al. 2013).

However, there are also a number of important differences that need to be acknowledged. To begin with, *actors* and their *motives* diverge fundamentally. While the empirical studies underlying SNM have a strong focus on for-profit firms, civil society innovation is driven by a diverse range of non-profit organisations, cooperatives, activists, voluntary associations or community groups, which are often highly embedded in and committed to the welfare of local environments (Seyfang and Smith 2007: 591). Opposed to conventional innovators who are motivated by the desire to generate profits, civil society actors are often oriented towards a broad range of alternative values and cultures. Some of them regard niches as instruments for escapism rather than experimentalism or transformation (Seyfang and Smith 2007: 592).

Second, research on SNM mainly addresses very broad social problems and is concerned with path-breaking change processes aiming at regime transformation.[4] By contrast, civil society innovators often pursue much more modest *aims*. They do not necessarily seek to alter or replace the incumbent regime, but rather to create parallel systems (Seyfang and Longhurst 2013: 888) or to provide services in order to satisfy unmet social needs on local or regional levels (Seyfang and Smith 2007: 591–593). Hence, Seyfang and Smith (2007: 593) distinguish between "simple niches" which do not seek regime change, but are assigned intrinsic value, and "strategic niches" which are designed with the intention to effect broader societal transformation. While the latter represent the collective attempt to transform "not simply the market choices available, but sometimes the entire market system itself" (Seyfang and Smith 2007: 595), the former rather seek to complement existing arrangements. They aim at creating jobs, providing training to develop professional and other skills, improving access to services and thus fostering personal growth, health, civic engagement and a flourishing and coherent community, with the overarching goal to "improve the quality of life in local communities" (Seyfang and Smith 2007: 593). But even *if* civil society actors seek to trigger more widespread and more fundamental change, they do not necessarily target a particular system. Sometimes, they address multiple regimes or no specific regime at all (Seyfang and Longhurst 2013: 888).

Third, civil society actors operate in divergent *environments*. Technology innovation focuses on markets and subscribes to their logics, that is, the need to develop standardised products which are supposed to generate financial surplus. By contrast, civil society innovation is situated in non-market, civil society arenas or in the social economy, with an emphasis on non-monetary, social or environmental returns (Seyfang and Longhurst 2013). This has important implications in terms of sustainability, as the two types of niches rely on different resource bases. While technology innovations are fuelled by public subsidies and the generation of commercial income, civil society actors draw on a heterogeneous set of alternative and often quite fragmented sources of funding such as grants, volunteering or mutual exchanges, which are often poorly tailored to the demands of sustainability experiments:

> Funding programmes are often short-term, frequently linked to constraining targets, bureaucracy and requirements, and leave little room for core development. . . . Frameworks for funding are often imposed by funders, rather than responding to recipients' development. Grassroots innovations can fall between the interstices of traditional social, economic and environmental issue boundaries.
>
> (Seyfang and Smith 2007: 596)

Not least due to this reason, the resource base of grassroots experiments is frequently unstable and precarious:

> Experience suggests initiatives spend 90% of their time simply surviving, and only 10% developing the activity. . . . This has implications for niche survival. First, they fail to develop robustness and resilience. . . . Second, short-lived initiatives frequently leave no formally documented institutional learning.
>
> (Seyfang and Smith 2007: 596)

Finally, commercial concepts of innovation subscribe to *expansion* as a major mechanism to influence or replace regimes, whereas civil society actors are sometimes highly critical of the very notion of growth. This is not to say that civil society niches do not grow at all—research has found that they may alter prevailing regimes though the mechanisms of replication, scaling up and translation (Seyfang and Haxeltine 2012), which are quite familiar in philanthropic contexts. However, the heterogeneous and fragmented field of civil society experiments may just as frequently conflict with growth-oriented logics (Hargreaves et al. 2013) and interventions which aim at the scaling up of grassroots innovations may be inappropriate or even outright detrimental to their cause (Seyfang and Smith 2007: 599).

5.5   From Grassroots to Philanthropic Innovation

Research shows that the approach of SNM can be adapted to the particular requirements of grassroots action and makes suggestions as to how this can be done. Many of these lessons can easily be transferred to philanthropic actors. For instance, as non-profit organisations, they are not motivated by commercial interests, either. Moreover, funding is often of a very moderate scale and activities fall more into the incremental than the disruptive domain. Finally and possibly most importantly, just like grassroots actors, they are not confined to market environments but operate in a very wide range of arenas. Hence, conventional notions of growth may not always be applicable. In case they are, an alternative model of growth might be needed.

However, there are also important differences. The organisations in my sample are inhabitants of a distinctly philanthropic world. This is particularly true in the case of the four foundations in my sample. They are neither complete insiders nor outsiders in the fields in which they engage; neither established members of the professional orthodoxy nor actors at the periphery. This is why they may be well positioned to foster innovation in terms of moderate and system-sustaining reforms, whereas they are unlikely to go for disruptive change.

Second, they do not necessarily address sustainability transitions but cover many other fields of society, as well. While Foundation Interkultur is the exception to the rule, the other three organisations are clearly not examples of sustainability experiments at the grassroots. This is not a problem as such, since research predicts that the approach of SNM should be transferrable to other societal sectors, such as health or education. However, systems like these will probably differ from energy or transportation and the consequences for niche management are unclear (Nill and Kemp 2009: 678; Seyfang and Longhurst 2013: 888).

Third, the literature provides no answer to the question of how, precisely, solutions to problems are created, that is, how a tight coupling between means and ends comes about, and how it can be explained. Finally, research in the context of SNM tends to presuppose rather than substantiate the *value* created by niching processes.

Hence, there is a clear need to match the propositions of SNM against my empirical cases, the overarching intention being to develop the outlines of a conception of "philanthropic niches" which is tailor-made for the purpose of both the explanation and the design of effective philanthropic interventions.

5.6 Conclusion

I argued in Chapter 4 that research on adequate problem-solving *strategies* needs to be complemented by an investigation of the *structures* which play a role in processes of social innovation. Networks and niches are of major instrumental and explanatory importance in this regard. The approach of strategic niche management was introduced as a framework which integrates both. In this context, niches are defined as protected and bounded social spaces of some permanence which provide the necessary leeway for experimental action. They are populated by actors who are organised in different types of networks and pursue varying strategies to explore and exploit new problem-solving arrangements. Niches, thus conceived, have a number of evident advantages. They are compatible with a quasi-evolutionary perspective as they enable processes of learning and adaptation to external environments, while, at the same time, being credited with transformative potential. Moreover, niching satisfies the basic requirements of problem solving. Due to their bounded nature, they serve as instruments for the reduction of complexity. At the same time, they are versatile enough to facilitate the implementation of experimental strategies, exploit unexpected opportunities and thus help satisfy the requirement of strategic fit. To the degree that innovative niches are based on networks, they also help to mobilise additional resources. Finally, niches are particularly well suited to serve as the building blocks for an alternative account of meaningful growth in the third sector.

At the same time, this conception raises a host of different questions. In which ways are philanthropic niches similar to the niches of SNM and how do they differ? How and why are boundaries drawn, protected and stabilised, and what role do processes of growth play? What types of niches are there and how can they be managed in practice? These questions can only be answered by reference to my case studies, to which I shall now turn.

Notes

1 There is consensus, however, that the different variables are not to be conceived as static entities. Strategies, structures and environments may change. In either case, a change in one variable should induce a change in others (Amburgey and Dacin 1994).
2 Importantly, this framework also suggests an alternative model of growth, which is not confined to a single product, a single organisation and a linear process of diffusion, but is systemic, distributed and non-linear in nature. Opposed to top-down programmes, niche actors are more sensitive to local problems and demands, they know "what works in their localities, and what matters to local people" (Seyfang and Smith 2007: 593–594). The approach thus may help to solve problems of sticky knowledge and heterogeneity of demands.
3 The Figure may falsely suggest a linear development, assuming that once practices have migrated, their integration into the system remains stable. Research on educational innovation has shown that the adoption of a new approach does not necessarily result in permanent adoption. There are also cases of "tentative" integration, important parts of which may be reversed after some time. This

observation shows that, while niches need not necessarily be sustained in perpetuity, they must not be dissolved too early. They require protection until permanent and irreversible establishment in the regime has occurred (Thümler 2015: 57).

4 However, transformation research increasingly investigates alternative types and pathways of innovation, such as the incorporation of new practices to the effect of a reconfiguration rather than a transformation of regimes (Schot and Geels 2008).

Part II
Case Studies

6 The Chance: Opening the Doors to the Labour Market for Disadvantaged Youth

The Chance Foundation[1] was established in 1999 as a spending-down trust by a private founder. It does not rely on the interest of its endowment, but the whole asset may be spent for operative purposes. The organisation operates in six cantons in eastern Switzerland. It supports adolescents aged 15 to 22 who have problems finding an apprenticeship or drop out of vocational training. The Chance helps them to enter training, graduate and successfully manage the transition into the labour market. Both the trainees and the firms in which they work and learn are offered comprehensive, intense and tailor-made support throughout the whole process until the participating youths have found a permanent position. The organisation has a consistent success rate of above 80 per cent for graduation and 90 per cent for employment. The Chance employs eight staff in its headquarters in Rheineck and in regional offices. It operates on an annual budget of around CHF1.2 million (The Chance 2012, 2013, 2014a, 2015a).

6.1 Societal Background and Process Leading to the Establishment of The Chance

In Switzerland, vocational training is provided through a dual programme of apprenticeship which combines practical training in firms with more theoretical learning modules in vocational schools. This system is widely regarded as an effective way to manage the transition from school to the labour market. Yet, in the late 1990s, youth unemployment was on the rise. Each year, around 10 per cent of young people were not able to find a regular apprenticeship, particularly those who had problems in school or dropped out altogether. Yet, untrained workers found it increasingly difficult to get regular employment and they had to work in precarious jobs instead or rely on public welfare. At the same time, firms faced difficulties finding qualified staff. These developments had negative consequences for the social security systems and the economy. Most importantly, though, they caused dramatic individual problems for the adolescents themselves (Bethmann 2014; Thümler and Nelles 2015).

According to The Chance, the problems they tackle are due to the fact that the requirements of companies have become more and more demanding, which is reflected in increasingly ambitious vocational training curricula, even in those programmes which were designed for low achievers. The accelerating speed and complexity of professional life tends to overwhelm both youth and their parents. Foundation staff said:

> Take, for instance, a carpet layer. There used to be ten different types of floor cloth, three different types of glue. Today, we have 100 different types of cloth, 30 different glues. How am I supposed to keep them all in mind. Then there is the pace of work, which must be finished in due time.[2]

On the other hand, an increasing number of adolescents struggle to meet even low standards. This is explained by unstable and dysfunctional families on the one hand, and the migrant backgrounds of families on the other. Either way, parents cannot adequately support their children (Bethmann 2014: 80). The situation is aggravated by problems on an individual level such as a lack of personal discipline and resilience in times of difficulties: "they have developed their flight behaviour, of course. To evade when things become concrete, not to react".

When The Chance was established, both the public system and firms were unable to cope with these problems effectively. The public authorities did not yet provide systematic and individualised support and most small to medium-sized enterprises lacked the capacities necessary to intervene in case of problems (Bethmann 2014: 67).

As a result, a growing discrepancy between the demands and provisions of the system of vocational training and the competencies and capabilities of adolescents was perceived. To meet these challenges and to develop and provide a private remedy to a public problem, The Chance was founded in 1999.

6.2 The Chance Foundation

The Chance Foundation started its operations in 2000. It was founded by a successful businessman who knew the aforementioned problems first-hand. The organisation is based in eastern Switzerland with its headquarters in the city of Rheineck/St Gallen. As of 2014 it operated in six cantons[3] plus Liechtenstein. It supports 336 youths, drawing on a network of 227 participating firms. The Foundation maintains that its services are in high and continuous demand and they constantly receive more applicants than they can handle (The Chance 2014a, 2015a), although the organisation does not actively recruit or advertise its services.

According to the Foundation, the situation for disadvantaged youth is characterised by multiple barriers which inhibit a successful transition into the labour market: the need to find an adequate trainee position, to remain in the programme regardless of possible problems, to graduate successfully and to find employment in the regular job market. The organisation aims to help the adolescents they support to overcome all of these barriers. Organisational objectives are defined in quantitative terms. For those who begin vocational training, the Foundation's board has set a success rate of 80 per cent for graduation and 90 per cent for transition. These targets have constantly been exceeded in recent years (Bethmann 2014; Thümler and Nelles 2015).

The Chance relates this success to the fact that it addresses *all* the barriers mentioned above, which is their signature strength and characteristic. Furthermore, it emphasises the importance of its freedom and independence from public regulation, which allows it to operate a highly tailor-made programme, plus the capability to adapt flexibly to changing circumstances. The programme is based on a close and long-term mentoring approach which combines emotional and practical support with clear expectations vis-à-vis the trainees to become active themselves, to confront problems and to persist in times of crisis. This core solution is complemented by a number of accompanying activities and arrangements. Additional efforts include the "translation" of official information on vocational training into readable language, the publication of around 100 easy-to-read leaflets on existing training programmes, advocacy for and support of the development of new programmes to suit better the demands and abilities of their trainees, for example though a shift in focus from theory to more practical competencies.

6.2.1 Approach

The basic approach was developed by the first two employees and the process operates as follows. The first contact with The Chance is made by parents or relatives, friends, firms, members of public administrations or the youths themselves—usually when they drop out of training or are confronted with severe problems during vocational training or search for a trainee position.

If a youth is accepted, his or her strengths, resources and interests are determined by means of a standardised test. Based on this diagnosis, employment options are explored to identify jobs in which he or she can best combine and make use of his or her capabilities. This reflects an important principle of the organisation's work.

The trainees are then assigned the task of finding an appropriate firm on their own (regardless of the question of whether the company has free positions or not). The Chance requires them to come compile a list of suitable companies and does not become active unless this task is completed. Once this is the case they help to make contact with the firms.

After a position is found, further support rests on two pillars: a mentoring and coaching programme which is tailor-made to meet the individual demands of participants. If necessary, they receive intense, close and sustained support. It begins with vocational training and lasts until trainees have successfully managed their transition into the labour market. If necessary, support is also provided to the participating firms to help solve problems throughout the whole training period (The Chance 2015a; Thümler and Nelles 2015).

6.2.2 Operating Policy

The Chance's approach is characterised by a tailor-made and comprehensive arrangement for their participants that seeks to "channel" them into, through and out of apprenticeship. On the one hand, it is oriented towards the interests, strengths and resources of the youth to make vocational training as satisfying as possible. Help is offered whenever necessary, particularly in times of crises, and with the intention not to overwhelm adolescents with problems they cannot handle on their own. The advantage for the trainee was described as follows. In the programme "I am not left alone, I always get answers, I always have a contact person, I do not need to be ashamed".

On the other hand, trainees are expected to conform to the rules and mobilise reasonable efforts of their own from the very beginning. They need to meet generic and individual rules and targets, including frequent reports or phone calls, as well as the participation in additional support and training sessions. For instance, youths who perform weakly in the vocational school must visit the school's homework tutoring regularly and for as long as necessary. In the event that they don't comply, The Chance has the option of imposing sanctions. If participants repeatedly leave trainee positions or commit crimes, they are either excluded from the programme or it is left pending, with a later decision on whether to exit or continue being deferred (Bethmann 2014: 67–68). Foundation staff described this dual function as the need to:

> accompany youths through these hard times, to keep catching them, to be confident in them, to tell them that they will successfully graduate, too, and not letting them down and to keep pulling them up, to not letting them slip and sometimes doggedly sticking with them, to persevere in awkward situations.

A similar approach of continuous and flexible support combined with clear demands is also practised vis-à-vis their partner firms: The Chance helps them if problems occur, but also intervenes if companies do not support the youths adequately but exploit them as cheap labour or treat them in prejudiced or unfair ways (The Chance 2013). Finally, this regime may also include interventions into the families of participating youth in cases of domestic violence and sexual abuse.

6.2.3 Organisational Structure and Governance

The organisation is characterised by a high degree of independence on the one hand, and by close links to its environment on the other. Staff and documents suggest that organisational independence grants the necessary freedom to address flexibly and coherently all the potential barriers on the path from school to regular labour (The Chance 2013), which is regarded as a major comparative advantage vis-à-vis the fragmented competencies of public authorities. One of the members of staff said:

> I do not have to enroll somebody somewhere and then wait for acceptance. . . . Weeks pass and I have the job, now he should go and I would have to wait for the OK. During this period of time the adolescent disappears, doesn't take me seriously anymore. I can react much faster than I would if I had to wait for the verdict.

What is more, the governance of the Foundation also includes independence vis-à-vis the founder himself. Beyond presiding over the board, he refrained from becoming active himself, leaving the development of the approach and the operations to the experts instead.

On the other hand, organisational autonomy is complemented by a large and dense network. This comprises a multitude of public and private actors, who work with the mentored youth, their families and their instructors in the centre. Moreover, The Chance cooperates with career counselling, vocational schools and authorities as well as social welfare offices, regional employment bureaus, youth advocates and the like. On the corporate side, the Foundation currently cooperates with 227 firms (The Chance 2014a). Since its establishment, a network of roughly 850 companies has emerged.

The relevance of regional embeddedness became manifest as the organisation applied for massive support from a programme to support initiatives fighting youth unemployment, which was created and run by a Swiss bank. As a precondition for funding, the bank required The Chance to scale up its programme to cover all of Switzerland. However, the Foundation refused to do so, pointing at a lack of local networks and knowledge as major conditions for the success of its work. In the end, support was granted based on the agreement to expand to the two neighbouring cantons of Graubünden and Glarus only (Bethmann 2014: 70).

6.2.4 Organisational Development

The Chance started operations in 2000 in the four cantons of St Gallen, Appenzell Inner- and Außerrhoden and Thurgau, beginning with a pilot project which supported 30 youths in the field of logistics. While the organisation's goal was clear right from the beginning and remained stable over time, almost all elements of the initial approach changed. To begin with, the founder's original idea was to focus on the very first step of the transition phase only, helping weak students to find appropriate trainee positions. Staff said: "in the beginning we clearly wanted to offer teenagers with a weak school performance an opportunity to find a training position, to go through, and to graduate". But it soon became evident that additional support was needed:

> The point of departure was merely the search for employment and this has increasingly changed over time . . . because we have seen where the gaps are, where the youths have difficulties, how many times they drop out of training. So mentoring was added. This is even our main strength, the mentoring.

What is more, the exclusive focus on logistics was soon given up. As time passed it became clear that teenagers had much broader interests and, hence, required a wider range of different vocations.

The number of participants varied considerably over time. Initially, the board aimed at a number of 20–30 youths only, but success triggered a phase of quick growth to 50, then 100 trainees. In 2003, 171 youths participated in 143 firms. By the end of 2010, the programme reached 309 participants in 184 companies. In 2014, 336 youths in 227 firms were supported (The Chance 2010, 2014a).

At the same time, the target group changed as well. In the beginning, The Chance would not accept students from upper secondary schools. Today, these formal limitations have been dropped and the existence of a personal problem has become the most important selection criterion.

More importantly, staff reported that the need of trainees for support has increased, which has resulted in many failures and dropouts:

> the project has changed in the sense that we suddenly got much more difficult adolescents than in the beginning. Which meant that all of a sudden the support activities strongly increased and this has led to near collapse.

The recruiting process had to be changed as well. In the beginning, The Chance recruited in schools directly. But after a while, the teachers sent all problematic students to the organisation, which overwhelmed its capacity:

> it began so rapidly, it almost cracked in the beginning . . . It almost burst at the seams, due to the reason that students were captured . . . already in school . . . and in every class there is someone and then it adds up.

Today, the public authorities are more active and offer more support in schools. Hence, participants are usually recruited in the period after graduation from school or during an active apprenticeship.

These developments resulted in the very intense mentoring programme that is practised today, which favours intensity of support and chances for success over quantitative expansion, and thus set limits to the possible rate of growth:

> this is maybe the biggest change the Chance has undergone. . . . Mentoring work has become much more intense. And we simply need time for this, which means that we cannot admit so many people anymore.

Finally, the Foundation became active beyond the programme itself. It noticed that increasingly demanding academic curricula posed problems for the members of its target group. The organisation thus helped to develop additional support programmes in schools as well as new types of vocational training for youths with less academic and more practical strengths. Their programmes are shorter and more practically oriented in order to help participants to get into contact with firms and labour early on and thus facilitate entry into the labour market. After graduation in these programmes, youths can enrol in more specific and more demanding follow-up training (Bethmann 2014; Thümler and Nelles 2015).

6.2.5 Budget and Staff

As of 2014, The Chance employs eight staff in its headquarters in Rheineck and in regional offices. It operates on an overall budget of CHF1.29 million (The Chance 2014a). All its employees are experienced practitioners in the field, usually former teachers in vocational schools. The first head of the Foundation used to be the director of a vocational school in the region and the second employee, a former teacher, was regarded as a "luminary" in the field. All employees can thus draw on extensive experience, substantial professional know-how and large personal networks. Furthermore, they are required to be able to "talk in the language" of adolescents so as to be able to build a robust working relationship with them.

The Chance was founded as a spending-down trust, endowed with assets of CHF4.2 million. This circumstance reflects the founder's convictions that the organisation need not exist in perpetuity but only as long as there is a clear societal need, and that it is impossible to predict future problems reliably (Bethmann 2014: 66). Today, assets of CHF3.0 million remain. These funds are supposed to be kept as a reserve to make sure that all participants may finish training even in the case of a complete loss of funding. Hence, the organisation is now dependent on additional and continuous fundraising or other sources of income (The Chance 2014a; Thümler and Nelles 2015).

For most of its time, The Chance was entirely independent of public funding. This abstinence was explained by the need to safeguard its independence, which was seen as a precondition of effective performance. The organisation chose to fundraise among private funders instead. According to Foundation staff, this private funding was favoured over public support as it was more based on trust and less on control. In recent years, a large single grant from a Swiss bank paid the bulk of the budget. Additional funding was provided by foundations, corporations and private donors.

However, this approach was confronted with a systematic problem. Foundation staff reported that private donors and, in particular, foundations prefer limited projects as vehicles for their funding, and do not wish to make long-term commitments. Hence, it became clear that the Foundation needed to mobilise public funding as well. In 2014, the organisation co-created the association Check Your Chance with five other partner organisations in the context of the above-mentioned national initiative against youth unemployment. They are all active in different regions of Switzerland and, hence, are not competitors, even if some degree of overlap may occur. They all pursue similar aims, if based on different approaches. The platform is headed by the president of the Swiss Employers' Association. It conducts its own fundraising activities, the results of which are distributed according to a key which relies on the size of the single organisations. Importantly, Check Your Chance managed to sign an agreement with the State Secretariat for Economic Affairs for the period 2015–2020 which grants up to CHF1.0 million of public funding for the purposes of the prevention of youth unemployment, based on the requirement that two-thirds of private funding be raised in addition (The Chance 2015b). What is more, the association has also developed into a powerful learning tool. According to senior staff of The Chance, collaboration is characterised by a high degree of mutual trust, and the other members have become important sources of advice who are consulted in case of problems.

In 2014, after 14 years of operation, The Chance developed its first formal strategy. This comprises five fields of focus, namely communication, regional development, finance and budgets, continuous development, and cooperation. The focus is clearly put on: the necessity to generate new and stable sources of income, for instance through communication of the Foundation's unique competencies and achievements; partnerships with and funding through public actors to reflect better the advantages that the organisation generates for local communities; and the reorganisation of its programme in modules, some of which are free of charge, while others must be paid for (The Chance 2014b).

6.3 The Societal Environment

In a favourable overall economic situation, the problem of youth unemployment has decreased. However, the number of youths in demand of additional support has increased. Hence, regardless of societal change, the demand for the services of The Chance has remained high and stable.

As Switzerland's welfare regime can be qualified as liberal, private contributions to the solution of public problems are regarded as neither unexpected nor illegitimate—at least in principle—and no major overt criticism of the Foundation's work has been observed (Bethmann 2014: 79).

In practice, however, The Chance was eyed with suspicion by established actors at least in the beginning. The organisation was perceived as an illegitimate intruder into an established field and as a potential competitor. According to our interviewees, this changed as soon as it turned out that there is actually no competition among the different actors, but rather a relationship of functional differentiation. Today, The Chance collaborates closely with public authorities who approach it frequently and proactively if they have problems with youths they cannot handle themselves. Foundation staff said:

> they have noticed that we neither interfere nor take their work but we really step in when they are finished because they work in their offices and not outside on the front. And when their consultation work has been done, their options are finished . . . then I may receive an email.

6.4 Success and Failure

In organisational terms, success consists in the fact that the organisation has become part of the established cantonal infrastructure and is viewed as a legitimate actor by other stakeholders in the field, as well as by the public. This is reflected by the fact that The Chance has received a number of awards, for example the second prize in the Carl Bertelsmann Award in 2005, issued by the German Bertelsmann Foundation. However, unlike other foundations, publicity seems to play only a minor role in the organisation's motivation. Its founder said: "we are not there to receive awards—we are doing an important job" (The Chance 2014a: 6). Furthermore, organisational success is frequently expressed in terms of costs saved. The Chance has expenses of about CHF3,000 per trainee a year whereas the costs of trainees who abort vocational training without follow-up employment is approximately CHF10,000 per year (Fritschi et al. 2009: 1). According to foundation staff, this figure may become much higher over a lifetime:

> When I say that an adolescent costs 2500 to 3000 francs per year, a social outcast, who needs to be supported for . . . 20 to 60 years by welfare, costs much more than one million, that's a fact. We give a lot to the state with these 3000, 6000 or 9000 [francs]. That used to be our fight with public bureaucracies in the beginning, that they did not want that and did not realize that.

Most importantly, success can also be expressed in terms of numbers of graduates and employees. In the period 2000–2014, The Chance mentored 1,443 participants, with a constant graduation rate of around 85 per cent (against an 80 per cent target) and an employment rate of around 95 per cent (against a 90 per cent target). In 2014, 76 mentees graduated successfully (88.4 per cent), while ten failed. Of those who graduated successfully, 58 obtained a regular job while 11 chose to enter continuous professional training (90.8 per cent).[4] Seven graduates have not yet found a job (The Chance 2012, 2013, 2014a). Judging from its own indicators, The Chance has been continuously very successful over a long period of time.

The positive effects of the programme have been confirmed by a scientific evaluation in the context of the aforementioned program against youth unemployment. The authors conclude: "the evaluation shows that all six programmes are effective and should be sustained. . . . The costs of less than CHF5,000 per person per year are worthwhile" (Neuenschwander 2014: 31, my translation).

However, The Chance also experiences failure on the individual level, as there are constantly dropouts and youths who do not graduate successfully. Foundation staff said: "we have to cope with setbacks, too. . . . This is hard to admit each time, we are so sorry for the adolescent. . . . There are youths for whom our system fails. They cannot be placed".

Finally, The Chance has been credited with help in cases of domestic violence and sexual abuse, the creation of new apprenticeship positions, a diffusion of parts of its approach to other organisations as well as the redesign of apprenticeship programmes and curricula, and the establishment of tutoring systems in vocational schools (Bethmann 2014: 81–82). However, the actual effectiveness of these interventions cannot be substantiated based on the available data.

These rather comprehensive activities are summarised in Bethmann's diagnosis that "the success of The Chance [consists] in actively building an environment where young adolescents with problems are given a chance to develop a career according to the skills they possess" (Bethmann 2014: 69).

6.5 Social Impact

The impact of The Chance resides primarily on an individual level. It is of a broad and comprehensive nature that is not limited to the number of certificates or contracts. However, it is characteristic of social service programmes that social impact can be determined rather reliably and in quantitative terms by means of using the numbers of certificates and contracts as "proxies" (Anthony and Herzlinger 1975: 141), assuming that those who have successfully graduated and found a job have much better opportunities to become autonomous in economic terms and to have a higher level of job satisfaction if compared to those who fail. Furthermore, they are less likely to become unemployed, consume drugs or commit crimes later in their lives, which is obviously desirable in societal terms (Bethmann 2014: 81).

Further impact can be hypothesised on a broader societal level. As firms gain qualified staff they might not have found otherwise, they become more productive and pay higher taxes, and so do their employees. If unemployment is reduced, so are the expenses of the welfare state. Both developments ease the strain on public budgets.

What is more, The Chance's rates of success and failure equal or even exceed those of "ordinary" participants in regular vocational training (Bethmann 2014: 80–81). The Chance thus successfully contributes to closing the achievement gap between advantaged and disadvantaged youth and helps to make society more just. Yet, effects such as these are obviously very hard to determine with precision.

Notes

1 In German: Die Chance: Stiftung für Berufspraxis in der Ostschweiz (The Chance: Foundation for Vocational Practice in Eastern Switzerland).
2 All interviews are translated by the author.
3 The two Appenzell, Glarus, Graubünden, St Gallen and Thurgau.
4 Foundation staff claim that numbers are actually higher as some youths do not need a formal mentoring but some "nudging" only. They are supported on an informal basis and not included in these numbers.

7 Foundation Interkultur and the Intercultural Garden Movement: Catalysing Emerging Practice at the Grassroots

The German Foundation Interkultur was founded in 2003 by its parent organisation, Foundation anstiftung & ertomis, to support a new type of urban "intercultural" gardening. It aimed at fostering the qualitative and quantitative growth of these gardens through a wide range of means such as financial funding, networking, generating and disseminating of knowledge, advice and advocacy. While the organisation itself has been reintegrated as a department into the Foundation anstiftung, its approach has continually been pursued and refined by the latter. Since its creation, the number of intercultural gardens has grown massively. The Foundation's database lists 452 urban community gardens in Germany as of July 2015, about half of them explicitly calling themselves intercultural, and the movement has diversified into a broad range of additional practices such as "neighbourhood" or "guerrilla" gardening.

7.1 Background: The Intercultural Garden Movement

In Germany, just as in other European countries, urban gardens have a long tradition. For centuries they played an important role in the food supply of urban populations, particularly during times of crisis (Cockrall-King 2012). However, in recent decades they have been considered a rather peripheral niche issue, and their public image has been shaped by the highly regulated culture of allotment gardens. In recent years, new varieties of urban gardening have seen a surge of growth, along with an increase in societal recognition and public attention.

Intercultural gardens are part of this broader development. The prototype for this new form of gardening (initially called "international gardens") emerged in 1996 in the German city of Göttingen through the initiative of Bosnian refugee women. They perceived the loss of gardens in their home countries as a major loss of quality of life: "at home we had our gardens. That's what we missed the most. We so much wanted to have gardens in Germany as well" (Krüger 2010: 2). Hence, together with other migrants, they set out to obtain and cultivate their own piece of land. The first garden was created by families from Afghanistan, Bosnia, Ethiopia, Germany, Iran, Iraq and Kurdistan (Müller 2002: 16). This soon found early adopters in other German cities and has triggered widespread and growing interest ever since. The garden was perceived as a highly promising novel model which created a wide spectrum of different advantages for the participants involved, from enhanced quality of life and intercultural contacts to language learning and better integration into German society. Still in existence, this first garden has considerably developed in size and received numerous awards (Internationale Gärten 2015).

Generally speaking, intercultural gardens oriented towards the original template are collective grassroots activities. They are set up on patches of urban land by local activists and gardeners. Most of them are managed by volunteers while some also employ staff paid by municipal funds. All gardens have the following basic purposes: to provide gardeners with access to their own piece of land, to enable them to own the means of production and become productive in sustainable ways and to provide open, non-commercial space for communication and exchange among a diverse group of participants. Gardeners particularly stress the first two aspects, pointing to the improved quality of life provided by gardening and the opportunities it affords for personal engagement. The Foundation also puts emphasis on the third aspect, that is, the idea that a democratic society needs free and non-commercial space for participation and integration.

The gardeners themselves often have diverse ethnic backgrounds. However, the attribute "intercultural" is not limited to the issues of migration or ethnicity. The idea is rather to convene members of diverse societal groups who would not otherwise meet and communicate. The communicative potential is further enhanced through connections to the surrounding neighbourhoods:

> in very many gardens, schools or kindergartens have a patch of land, or . . . facilities for handicapped people. . . . A lot of them organize . . . small workshops or organize parties. . . . And everywhere neighbours are always invited, as well.[1]

7.2 Foundation Interkultur and Foundation anstiftung

The Foundation Interkultur was founded in 2003 as a semi-independent operating body of the charitable Foundation anstiftung which seeks to foster sustainable lifestyles and to develop alternative models of societal welfare by means of investigating and supporting "commons, do-it-yourself and sustainable regionalization" (Baier and Müller n.d.; anstiftung 2015). Set up in 1982, the Foundation anstiftung currently works with an operating budget of EUR1.3 million and employs a staff of ten, plus three persons in the management team (anstiftung 2015a).

The Foundation anstiftung first pursued an approach based on action research. It initiated and ran its own projects, such as houses of active work, which were (self-) critically studied to reflect on and learn from developments in practice. However, over time the organisation realised that its own projects required too much capacity—it proved to be more prudent to support the developments of others and to enhance the momentum of emerging innovative practices (Baier and Müller n.d.: 3). Foundation staff concluded as a major lesson learned that philanthropic organisations "cannot purposefully initiate societal change", but are better advised to "go with the flow" (Baier and Müller n.d.: 3–4).

Foundation Interkultur always operated in close proximity to the parent organisation. It was located in the same premises in Munich, and funding was provided and staff were employed by the Foundation anstiftung. At the same time, the newly created charity enjoyed a high degree of independence due to its independent leadership; a staff of eight persons, equivalent to 3.5 full-time positions (Krüger 2010: 1); an annual budget of approximately 25 per cent of the overall budget of the Foundation anstiftung (over the last ten years), with an increase to approximately 50 per cent as of 2007.

The aim of Foundation Interkultur was to foster a new understanding and innovative models of societal integration, with a major focus on the support of the intercultural garden movement. Its creation was motivated by the assumption that a single-issue organisation would considerably facilitate this task. While it always remained closely related to its parent organisation, Interkultur was different in two important respects. First, another governance structure was purposefully chosen. While anstiftung was based on a direct democratic structure, with all employees having a say in important decisions, Interkultur opted for a more hierarchical model with a managing director and a board at its top. The intention was to be more flexible and to increase the speed of organisational decision making in order to be able to cope with the rapid pace of developments in the field. Second, Interkultur put more emphasis on participation in discourse, both in terms of scholarly research and theory as well as broader societal debates.

Today, Foundation Interkultur has ceased to exist as an independent body as it has been reintegrated as a department into its parent organisation. According to Foundation staff, this decision was motivated by mainly administrative reasons. While the semi-independent organisational form was regarded as a successful and effective means to foster its mission, it also proved to be difficult to administer in the long run. For instance, problems occurred with the tax authorities as the arrangement did not fit their conventional templates. However, its particular forms of governance and operations were adopted by the Foundation anstiftung. Senior staff described this process in terms of the relationship between a small "submarine" and its larger home base. The vessel cruises freely for a limited period of time to collect new experiences which can then be incorporated into the parent organisation upon return.

7.2.1 Operating Policy

The approach of Foundation Interkultur was described by an interviewee as the provision of a platform for existing activities in order to "unfold power which already exists". Accordingly, the Foundation did not develop its own solutions to societal problems but rather sought to identify and support promising practice at a grassroots level. Senior Foundation staff said:

> Participation is . . . absolutely a success factor for our work. We have this praxeology-driven approach, as Pierre Bourdieu now puts it. That means that we learn from practice and practice is a model for the Foundation's work. We are not oriented towards grassroots democracy, that is not the case. But taking societal practice seriously, I believe this is a success factor.

Consistent with this approach, the Foundation described its role in terms of concepts such as "mentor", "moderator", "facilitator" and "mediator" which accompanies, supports and shapes ongoing societal processes rather than inventing them. For these purposes, it employed a hybrid operational model which included both financial grants and operating activities.

The funding approach was characterised in terms of low thresholds and high degrees of trust rather than bureaucracy and control. Staff claimed that the support of practitioners is only possible if these requirements are met and if the Foundation accepts "conflicts, problems and failure" as necessary components of the local learning process (Baier and Müller n.d.: 2). In particular, the Foundation sought to provide easy access to support and accepted almost all requests for funding. Staff said: "when somebody has approached us to open up a garden and submitted a proposal [they have all been] integrated into the network without inspection, as it were".

This policy has been confirmed by the local gardeners, who regarded it as an important virtue of the Foundation's work. One interviewee said that if a proposal is submitted "you can rather assume that they do it. . . . This is crazy today, how much time is wasted in proposals".

7.2.2 The Problem

The Foundation's engagement was based on a dual motivation. Its parent organisation regards a lack of public spaces as a threat to democracy. It also strongly supports the emergence of sustainable lifestyles. These commitments were shared by Foundation Interkultur. Senior staff said that "public space is important and needs to be defended and created in the first place, so that people have an opportunity for participation. . . . This is the project per se". But there was also a much more concrete rationale. The creation of Foundation Interkultur was preceded by an established record of collaboration between the gardeners in Göttingen and the Foundation anstiftung. The new garden was regarded as promising and innovative practice and supported by direct funding and research, which included the publication of the book *Wurzeln schlagen in der Fremde* (*Taking Roots in Foreign Land*) (Müller 2002). The publication triggered an immediate surge ("a deluge") of interest and demand for advice, support and information by local public administrations, religious communities, gardening and migrant initiatives.

However, there existed no infrastructure to satisfy these demands. Gardens are operated by volunteers who lack the time, energy and commitment to engage beyond the local level. Neither the Foundation nor the gardens had the necessary resources to cope with this situation, which overwhelmed the capacities of both.

At the same time, the events were regarded as an indicator of enormous and highly promising potential. For while single gardens are not expensive at all, they have a high reach which is not even limited to gardening as such. Rather, they also contribute to neighbourhood development and thus further the very basic values of civic participation and the availability of public space that were so central to the Foundation's mission. Foundation staff said that in this situation "it was clear: wow! This is a treasure. How can we pick it up and shape it?". The process that led to the establishment of Foundation Interkultur seems to have emerged rather organically from these considerations: "there were long discussions about whether we can do this in the present structure. . . . But it didn't really feel so good".

As the template for intercultural gardens had already emerged in Göttingen, it was quite clear how an answer to the above-mentioned problems might appear. Moreover, obstacles to creating, developing and retaining existing gardens are rather low. Activists report that it may take considerable time to find appropriate premises, but once this has been achieved, the initiation of a garden requires only basic financial resources and a moderate level of knowledge about administrative procedures. Hence, the most important barrier was the low overall number of gardens in Germany and the lack of support for existing sites.

For these reasons, the newly created Foundation set out to help create as many gardens as possible and to enhance the quality of gardening for all interested participants, without specifying goals in detail, let alone in quantitative terms. By these means, the Foundation aimed at creating a multitude of spaces for collective engagement and participation.

7.2.3 Operations

The Foundation pursued a multi-level, multi-instrumental approach which combined a broad diversity of means to help establish new gardens, support existing gardens and practitioners, make good practice visible and create a favourable environment. It drew on a broad organisational toolkit which contained the following elements:

- Financial support of up to EUR5,000 for the establishment of gardens.
- The creation of networks at national, regional and local levels. Annual meetings for all the network members are organised as opportunities

for mutual encounters and learning. Financial support is provided to
the gardeners who participate.

- Documentation and dissemination of local experience and practice
which might be of relevance for the members of the network. For this
purpose, the Foundation searches for particularly successful practice
through its own observation and accompanying research. The resulting information is distributed through publications and workshops.
Examples include knowledge on the equipment necessary to start a
garden or workshops on the breeding of seeds, but also the provision of more administrative best practice, e.g., exemplary tenancy
statutes.
- Information and advocacy to enhance visibility, voice and legitimacy of
intercultural gardens. The Foundation hosts a website, maintains contact with the media and organises public relation activities. Staff give
speeches. In terms of advocacy, the Foundation lobbies for gardens in
politically precarious situations: "because otherwise there is the danger
that you don't have a political lobby, and . . . with a single garden . . . it
can happen quickly that a house needs to be built on the very ground of
your garden".

    In what can be regarded as a successful instance of framing, the
Foundation claims to have invented the label of "intercultural gardens"
which helps to communicate the nature and virtues of the model. All of
these activities are further supposed to motivate and strengthen gardeners and to build a sense of community (Baier and Müller n.d.: 2).
- The Foundation reflects and theorises on the practice of urban gardening and related activities. Beginning with *Wurzeln schlagen in der
Fremde,* the potential meanings and ramifications of the emerging practice have been explored in a series of publications. These discuss the relevance of urban gardening practices for a broad range of macro-issues
such as ecology and climate change, migration, refugees and integration, economization and alternatives to neo-liberal capitalism as well
as societal inequality and the exclusion of precarious groups (Müller
2002, 2012).
- The Foundation provides own advice and makes accessible external
consulting services for gardens in the process of being founded as well as
for experienced gardeners. Beyond that, it mediates in cases of conflict.
- The Foundation conducts research projects of its own and it supports
diploma theses on intercultural gardens (for an overview of completed
theses, see anstiftung 2015a).
- The Foundation runs its own practice projects such as the "bee project" which develops, accompanies and documents activities to keep bee
hives in intercultural gardens.

Today, the Foundation anstiftung continues to employ these instruments.
Since 2008, operations are organised by a rather informal strategy which

is updated on an annual basis. It mostly reflects on past experiences and sketches a short schedule for the year ahead, but explicitly abstains from formulating a detailed plan with milestones or quantitative goals (anstiftung 2015b).

7.2.4 The Societal Environment

Both Foundation Interkultur and the Foundation anstiftung have largely operated in a highly positive and supportive environment. In Germany, (urban) gardening is perceived as a friendly and uncontroversial issue which has become a broad societal trend in recent years. Similar movements have emerged in many other countries, such as the UK and the USA, mobilising additional visibility and credibility for domestic actors. Foundation staff said that:

> you can perform great public relations work for years and everybody keeps thinking: "What the hell do they want with their gardens?" And suddenly Michelle Obama . . . creates a garden in Washington. . . . Suddenly there is something which . . . takes off and broadens and thus simply makes more and more voices resound.

Moreover, Germany has increasingly become a country of immigration. While this diagnosis has been subject to considerable controversy for decades, it is increasingly regarded as a given fact by policymakers, most political parties and the public. This development has led to a heightened attention towards gardens as a feasible means to foster integration and has raised their image as being societally relevant and not merely a private hobby. In this context, Foundation staff talked about a "negative success factor" due to a high degree of helplessness vis-à-vis problems with migrants and migration:

> All sorts of things have failed. You didn't care for ages and suddenly you try language courses and somehow that doesn't work either. . . . Then you say: Well, who are those people anyway? . . . Where could there be common ground?

The gardens are also associated with other important issues such as climate change (community gardens are seen as a carbon dioxide-neutral way of production and consumption), capitalism after the financial crisis (through their focus on immaterial values and on non-commercial public spaces) and an increasing interest in practices of self-repair and do-it-yourself.

Probably due to a mixture of these factors, the political parties and the general public are largely sympathetic or at least indifferent to the cause of intercultural gardens. Only a small amount of criticism has been reported, mostly by the organisations of traditional gardeners such as the Association of Allotment Gardens (Kleingartenverband). There have also been local instances of right-wing protest.

7.3 Success and Failure

Intercultural gardens have experienced a rapid period of growth, and the original template has been copied in a multitude of places. The database of the Foundation anstiftung lists 435 intercultural gardens in Germany as of April 2015. Beyond intercultural gardens, a variety of related other practices such as "urban", "community", "guerrilla" or "roof top" gardening have evolved, all of which leads to the perception of a dynamic "little movement". Foundation staff added that "there is no end in sight. . . . Ever more garden projects are emerging. I think that we are right in the middle of it".

Intercultural gardens have further attracted a high level of visibility. Gardeners reported a heightened legitimacy and reputation of these forms of gardening which may to a large extent be due to the new conceptual and organisational frame provided by the Foundation. They said:

> all of a sudden it has been held in such a high esteem. Yes, all of a sudden there is a framework to which it is attached in proper form. We are a member of Foundation Interkultur. There are intercultural gardens all over Germany, everybody has heard about it. And there is a book about it and there is knowledge on these gardens' effects. [. . .] [A]ll of a sudden that was a wholly different lobby, a wholly different outward effect . . . I think that the . . . respect . . . simply has increased since this Foundation came into being, as a framework for us.

Gardeners also reported an increased legitimacy of previously precarious, conflict-ridden situations due to public support by senior politicians that was triggered by increased public awareness for the relevance of intercultural gardens.

7.4 Social Impact

The motivation to create social impact played an important role for the Foundation. Senior staff said: "to unfold impact is a major leitmotif of our work. . . . It always has been. . . . In regard to the gardens we noticed early on that it is very easy to generate impact". Yet, the precise nature of these effects cannot be captured easily. Beyond the mere numbers of newly established gardens, evidence for the Foundation's impact is difficult to assess. Interviewees' assessments of the value of intercultural gardens revolve around an enhanced quality of life due to the availability of beautiful space, experiences of intercultural contact and communication as well as the opportunity for purposeful and self-reliant activity. Interviewees repeatedly stressed that gardens satisfy the fundamental needs of adults and children alike, which range beyond mere gardening. Hence, some of them are active in winter time, as well: "they come, wait and see if somebody else joins them, and that amounts to a lot of quality of life; that's very important".

These remarks may hold true for the situation of poor and excluded people in general, and migrants in particular. For instance, gardens were described as an "oasis" for people who suffer from bad housing conditions. They were also associated with alternative types of wealth and welfare based on ample resources such as crops, knowledge, competencies and time (Baier and Müller n.d.: 7). Gardens were conceived as a valuable source of positive feedback for migrants who kept "having the experience that their knowledge and skills are no longer required in the . . . host society. . . . No one cares, everything is worthless". And all of a sudden their knowledge is relevant for their fellow gardeners, the media and public authorities: "you experience yourself as someone who also has knowledge which is in demand, thus, a revaluation occurs".

It is further related to a transfer between the situation of plants and one's own situation, combined with aesthetic experience: "the plants I know from home, from my childhood, they grow here, too. So I can grow here, as well". Moreover, gardens support mutual learning and a culture of self-help as gardeners need to support each other and to cope with conflicts constructively. While not every gardener seeks and appreciates contact to other and different neighbours, many of them value this aspect highly:

> The impact is that we learn to cope with other people of a different ethnic origin. The work with the plants is what connects us. So there is a basis for a good exchange. . . . That is, the one learns from the other, from his or her culture. So we practise being tolerant, that's extremely important.

I conclude that the effects of intercultural gardens need to be framed in very broad ways. It is the combination of the "activation of all the senses" and the mobilisation of "material, spiritual, aesthetic [and] cultural" (Baier and Müller n.d.: 3) resources by means of do-it-yourself production, intercultural communication, self-help and cooperation which gives rise to an impression of a "context of meaning which covers the gardens".

Beyond these more immediate impacts, some examples of the improvement and revitalization of the neighbourhoods of gardens have also been reported. These positive effects are made possible by the fact that gardens do not foster integration based on planned designs, but in organic ways, through the creation of room for personal engagement. Hence, Foundation staff described its most important achievement in terms of the "creation of spaces. I find this so important at the present time, to have that. And it is achievable and it is inexpensive and it is feasible almost everywhere, and so many people get infected by it".

All these effects are obviously hard to determine with precision, let alone in quantitative terms, and assessments are based on anecdotal evidence only. The same qualification applies to the attribution of effects to the activities of Foundation Interkultur and the Foundation anstiftung. While all interviewees credit them with a positive influence on both individual gardens and the movement as a whole, the impact cannot be assessed more precisely or reliably due to the indirect nature of the chosen approach. Finally, the Foundation anstiftung does not attempt to determine its contributions by means of formal evaluations. However, they support students in writing theses which seek to explore processes like those described above on a case study basis.

Note

1 All interviews are translated by the author.

8 The Nuffield Foundation and the Nuffield Council on Bioethics: Organising the Provision of Non-Partisan Expertise

The Nuffield Council on Bioethics was established in 1991 by the UK-based Nuffield Foundation. The Council addresses ethical problems which arise due to advancements in the biosciences. It is composed of 21 members from relevant academic disciplines, together with others from, for example, industry and the media. They identify upcoming problems, open questions, commission working groups that explore the chosen issues in depth, and publish reports with recommendations for practitioners and policymakers. Beyond that, the Council seeks to further the public discussion on bioethics, for instance by means of educational materials for young people. Its work is coordinated and facilitated by a secretariat of 11 staff. The organisation operates on an annual budget of around GBP760,000. Since 1994, the Council has been funded by a coalition of three partner organisations, including the founding Nuffield Foundation, the Medical Research Council and the Wellcome Trust (Nuffield Council 2013).

8.1 The Nuffield Foundation

The Nuffield Foundation is a UK-based charitable trust. It was established in 1943 by William Morris (Lord Nuffield), the founder of Morris Motors. The Foundation is the largest of a diverse set of organisations created by Lord Nuffield to serve a range of different issues, from health and farming to the armed forces (Nuffield Foundation 2015).

Its mission is to contribute to improvements in society and to further the advancement of social well-being, particularly by means of high-quality scientific research and innovation in education and social policy (Nuffield Foundation 2015). To further these aims, it mainly supports research "that's going to make a difference" (Foundation staff), but it also conducts programmes of its own targeted at advancing social change. In addition to grant-making and its own projects, the Foundation also operates as a convenor. For instance, in 2007 it organised 400 meetings involving some 7,000 participants. Finally, it seeks to increase the capacity of research, for example by supporting young scientists in the early stages of their careers

(Thümler 2010). Against this background, the Nuffield Council represents a rather atypical kind of work.

In particular, the Foundation targets "areas where government cannot, will not, or should not" (Thümler 2010: 1104) become active, for instance in those cases in which it is a stakeholder in the problems or is part of what is being studied. The Foundation thus seeks to position itself in a "small-but-interesting" niche in which its unique competences are best made use of.

8.1.1 Operating Policy

The Foundation describes itself—especially in relation to the Council—as a strategic and enabling funder. It provides the Council with medium-term funding and a set of parameters within which to work, but respects its independence in relation to the details of the work it undertakes and the conclusions it draws. At the same time, it is very much and increasingly interested in the wider impact of the Council's activities. Today, the funding of the Council is reviewed only every five years. Senior staff[1] reported that the Foundation encourages the Council to think long term instead of seeking quick fixes, which is seen as a major advantage compared to the field of politics.

8.1.2 Societal Background

The roots of the Nuffield Council date back to the 1980s. In those early days of medical ethics and bioethics, medical experts began to realize that technological progress was giving rise to new ethical questions which extended far beyond the boundaries of the Hippocratic oath. For instance, attempts to map the human genome raised both fears and questions of the implications of the new knowledge (Nuffield Foundation 2011: 3). However, due to a lack of institutionalised spaces for systematic discussion, they could only be dealt with on an improvised ad hoc basis. For these reasons, the first ethics committees were set up in universities and hospitals to explore the new problems more coherently, and demands for a national bioethics committee were raised (Lock 1990). One of the Foundation's trustees, a practising clinician, was actively involved in these developments and convinced the organisation to take up the issue and investigate it in more depth. As a result, the Foundation decided to fund a "smallish" number of projects, including the training and funding of "early people", thus creating a first, if modest, track record in the field.

Parallel to and independently of the developments in the Foundation, scientists approached the Thatcher government with a proposal to create a public unit supposed to explore issues in the field of bioethics. However, the government refused to become active in this. As a result and due to personal contacts, researchers turned to the Foundation to apply for support, which was granted in 1990.

8.2 The Process Leading to the Council's Establishment

At that point, it was not clear how an instrument required to address the new problems effectively would have to look. Hence, the Foundation hired a staff of two and issued a preparatory process which lasted one year and resulted in the creation of the Council. In this early phase, neither the precise shape nor the viability of the future Council were entirely clear to the Foundation. Senior Foundation staff said that they didn't think about establishing a formal UK bioethics commission right from the beginning, but rather followed a tentative and incremental approach to find out what works in instrumental and political regards. For this reason, the Council was funded on an annual "and almost on a case-by-case basis" in the first years, as "the decision to continue it wasn't a done deal. So when it was set up, it wasn't 'Well, we'll run this in perpetuity.' It was 'We'll run it for three years and see what happens'". This cautious approach was also due to the fact that the new body faced the scepticism of established stakeholders in the field who "didn't necessarily see this as something that an upstart body like Nuffield should do".

Hence, during these early stages, the most important task of both the Foundation and the Council was to carve out a legitimate niche among a multitude of established stakeholders inside the governmental as well as the scientific world: "there was a lot of diplomacy and politics". In particular, clear boundaries needed to be drawn vis-à-vis the domain of clinical ethics, which is the responsibility of the medical profession. The Council's terms of reference were drawn up explicitly to recognise this distinction; and they determine its purpose as follows: "to identify and define ethical questions raised by recent advances in biological and medical research in order to respond to, and to anticipate, public concern". Senior Foundation staff underlined the relevance of this: "that was part of the early politics, because the . . . medical bodies would have been very unhappy . . . about some third party pronouncing on clinical ethics".

Interviewees further emphasised the role of the Council's leadership in this process. For instance, the first chairman was a retired Permanent Secretary of the Health Department who was frequently described as very competent and well connected in the field. As he also was "extremely good" in political terms, he helped "steer us through". Moreover, the organisation appointed the president of the Royal College of Physicians to the Council, which proved to be a very influential sign toward the professional community in terms of the legitimacy of the newly founded body.

8.3 The Nuffield Council on Bioethics

The Council was established by the Nuffield Foundation in 1991 and is still housed in the Foundation's headquarters. Since 1994, it has been funded by a coalition of three partner organisations, including the Nuffield Foundation, the Medical Research Council and the Wellcome Trust.

Right from the beginning, the Council was designed for the purpose of identifying, discussing and responding to new, relevant and urgent ethical problems and dilemmas which arise due to developments in the biological sciences and technologies, and in biomedicine. It seeks to provide these services continuously and long term, as well as in rational, secular and thorough ways, excluding any vested interests as far as possible.

This it does mainly by means of identifying relevant upcoming topics and by commissioning a "working party", that is, a group of 7 to 13 experts. It is supposed to prepare a report which explores the chosen issue in depth over a period of around 18 months and to make recommendations to practitioners and policymakers.

The process relies on methods which seek to guarantee a high quality of results, including objective feedback through peer review and comments through stakeholders who are "critical or even hostile" to the Council's work. The Council also aims at broadening the input it receives by means of written submissions, consultations and workshops with members of the public.

Since 1993, 28 reports have been published. The first report was entitled *Genetic Screening: Ethical Issues*. Since then, the Council has covered a broad range of issues such as health care in developing countries (1999, 2002, 2005), animal-to-human transplantation (1996), genetically modified crops (1999), animal research (2005) and children and clinical research (2015), to name only these.[2]

8.3.1 Organisational Structure and Independence

The Council is currently composed of 21 members. It used to be a mainly scientific body of experts from the relevant academic disciplines, in particular the (social) sciences, medicine, philosophy and law. Today, this policy has changed and the Council convenes a broader range of stakeholders. Increasingly, the focus on scholars and scientists has been relaxed, and it now also includes representatives from professional or patient's organisations and lay members. Gender balance also plays a role in the composition of the Council.

The Council thus aspires to join together a wide variety of different interests and positions. Senior staff described its role in terms of "bridge-builder, convenor, [and] translator". However, the Council is not a representative body and it does not seek to integrate *all* possible interests. In particular, the churches are not automatically or formally involved in the Council's bodies. This policy is justified with the argument that, while a wide range of the most relevant topics and interests must be considered, it is impossible to cover *all* possible interests without losing focus and the chance of arriving at consensual outcomes.

Although it lacks an autonomous legal status, the Council is characterised by a considerable degree of independence from external influence, be it governmental, professional or corporate interests (Nuffield Foundation 2011: 3). A similar diagnosis holds true for the members of the Council who become active in their own right as they do not serve as representatives of the organisations they come from (Leat 2008: 5). All interviewees underlined the importance of this arrangement. One member of a funding organisation said:

> It is a strange example for us. Usually we fund in order to get government or someone else to take over. . . . In this case we very much don't want government involved. It is very important that the Council is independent of government. We don't want politicians driving the UK research agenda.

In important respects the Council's work is self-governed, based on a cooperative structure. While its chair is selected by the funding partners, it is in charge of all other decisions on membership. Its members decide on the future work programme, review the quality of reports and are responsible for the organisation's management. The more operational work is conducted by different subgroups. The above-mentioned "working parties" explore the issue under scrutiny in depth and prepare the Council's reports. A "future work" subgroup explores potential future topics, the "council membership" subgroup recommends on future members, the "educational advisory" subgroup conducts activities to engage young people in informed debates on bioethics and the "management and risk" subgroup is responsible for business management. The Council's work and the subgroups are coordinated and facilitated by a secretariat, which is also responsible for the follow-up process of reports, collaboration with other organisations, communication and smaller projects. The structure of the Council's work is displayed in Figure 8.1.

The Council is a member of an international community of national councils on bioethics and part of a much broader network of similar bodies which examine related questions, particularly in the field of medical and research ethics. In this environment, the Council's independence is allegedly "a source of envy" as it results in a privileged position in the political arena which sets it apart from all other similar European councils.

The Council and its funders describe this autonomous position as a prerequisite for the validity and objectivity of its results due to the freedom from governmental influence or political preferences. Moreover, it is credited with a number of other advantages, such as the opportunity to choose its members based on competency instead of proportional regional, societal and political representation. Finally, it supposedly enables the Council to venture on contentious terrain such as clinical research in developing countries.

However, independence also implies trade-offs. In particular, several interviewees argued that a private Council lacks the authority of a public body

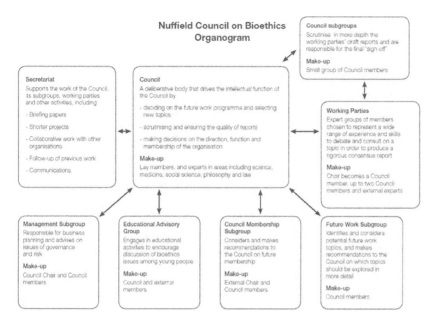

Figure 8.1 Organogram of Nuffield Council
Source: Nuffield Council (2012: 8).

which makes it easier for policymakers to ignore the results. Moreover, it may lead to elitism and a lack of responsiveness to public concerns, as well as to organisational inertia. Finally, funders diagnosed a "slight tension" arising when the Council chose not to investigate topics favoured by them.

8.3.2 Recent Developments

As of 2011, the Council has adopted a new policy of strategy development and implementation. As a first step, a review of its work was conducted in 2011/2012. This suggested that the Council should revise its membership criteria in order to reflect better the wider concerns of society, pursue a more rigorous approach to topic selection, engage a broader audience by more flexible means and become more transparent by evaluating its work. The suggestions were taken up in the *Strategic Plan 2012–2016*. It outlines how the Council will increase the diversity of contributors and create additional input opportunities (Nuffield Council 2012). This more inclusive process is illustrated by Figure 8.2.

The Council now aims at communicating to a broader range of audiences beyond expert and political communities by means of a wider range of avenues, including electronic and social media formats. This reflects an

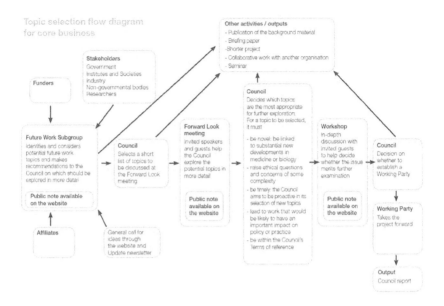

Figure 8.2   Topic Selection Flow Diagram for Core Business
Source: Nuffield Council (2012: 10).

increasing view that bioethics should not remain an issue for experts only—particularly given the fact that, as biotechnologies become more pervasive, everybody might be affected by these developments. The Council further seeks to respond to the increasing globalisation of science and a faster pace of change through work in partnerships and (international) networks. Finally, it formulates "clear success/outcome evaluation measures and procedures for reporting these", including "key outcome measures concerning quality, reach, impact, and value for money" (Nuffield Council 2012: 13) and aims to create the governance and management structures necessary to enable and support these new tasks.

Before the end of the period covered by the Strategic Plan 2012–2016, a stakeholder review was commissioned, which sought to trace implementation success based on a perception study among major stakeholders (Martin et al. 2015). This investigates the progress that has been made against the strategic objectives and makes suggestions which are relevant for the preparation of the follow-up strategy.

The sequence from strategy development and implementation to evaluation is supposed to become standard operating procedure. This decision was motivated by the funders' demand that the Council be more explicit about the nature and scale of the value it creates. According to the Council's senior staff, they suggested evaluating the attainment of objectives in more reliable ways in order to be able to determine better the ultimate "return of their investments" in terms of organisational impact and effectiveness. Council staff themselves underlined the importance of determining and demonstrating the outcomes of their work in terms of real world effects to justify the Council's continued existence.

8.3.3 Budget and Staff

The annual budget has increased from GBP69,898 in 1992 to GBP760,000 as of 2013 (Nuffield Council 2000; 2013). All funders described the amount as moderate, agreeing that "funding wasn't a particular problem; it wasn't terribly expensive to start with, and it still isn't". This is not least due to the fact that all members of the Council and contributors to the working parties provide their services for free (Nuffield Foundation 2011).

The major share of the budget goes to the secretariat. This started off with two employees only; today it employs a team of 11 staff members. It has constantly pursued a policy to hire highly competent and experienced staff. For instance, its first director was formerly a senior official in the Treasury.

Today, funding has to be renewed every five years. Two of the funders reported that the length of support is unusual as they prefer to fund limited specific projects. This exception was justified by the Council's strong track record and, again, the need for independence. This is also regarded as a requirement of its subject matter: "we are engaged in an activity that is about shaping the way that things are managed on a societal level. And that's . . . really a farsighted activity".

8.3.4 Environment

According to Foundation staff, the Council was set up in a dynamically evolving societal environment. Interest in medical ethics was on the rise in the 1990s and attempts were made to institutionalise the discussion of new issues. However, the field was not as crowded as it is today since no formal academic or public bodies had been established then and competition was low. In retrospect, Foundation staff judged that it became active at the early stages of a very consequential process, with "most developed countries having national bioethics commissions of various kinds" today.

Over time, there have been recurrent discussions on the necessity to establish a national Bioethics Council in the UK, as well. Some actors, and particularly the churches, may still be in favour of a statutorily established national bioethics commission which would have to include people from all points of view, and the Council has been criticised for not including such stakeholders. However, these discussions seem to be muted and today Foundation staff describe the environment as "very favourable and responsive". This may be not least due to the fact that the scientific community has now "embraced the notion of self-examination and . . . critical ethical examination of its work. Ten years ago, that was rather different, because . . . there was a fear that ethics was about stopping scientific development".

The Council lacks direct competitors and makes sure that it does not threaten the position of other actors (Leat 2008: 8–9). Yet, in recent years there has been a proliferation of new centres in universities which cover overlapping terrain. As a result, a key role for the Council has been to establish itself as a trusted, independent and authoritative arbiter among those different voices. The organisation seems to be widely regarded as a credible, competent and legitimate institution (Martin et al. 2015), although its members are not democratically elected (Leat 2008: 3). At the same time, it also faces a number of fundamental challenges due to an accelerating pace of environmental change which is characterised by heightened degrees of complexity. Developments are no longer limited to bounded, single technologies but converge in clusters of different types of innovation. For instance problems of "big data" in biotechnology are caused by the interplay of advances in information technology, health technology, genomics and information policy. This raises the question of whether singular working parties are still the adequate format for coping with the problems in the field or if they need to be balanced with programmes which scan the field in more continuous ways.

This is complemented by a drive towards internationalisation in terms of a faster global exchange of technologies, which challenges the adequacy of an exclusively national framework for ethical debate. Council staff reported that these developments go along with a growing demand for policy advice. As the government has reduced its own capacities in the years of economic austerity, it has become more reliant on external advice, which points at a potentially increasing relevance for the Council. Under these circumstances, senior staff found it "very difficult to find certainty or arrive at a stable position" and welcomed the newly adopted strategic process as an opportunity to respond systematically to the need to "locate yourself" in the middle of these developments.

8.4 Success and Failure

After an early unstable phase of exploration and constitution during which the Council was regarded with some degree of scepticism and possibly even suspicion by members of the scientific and medical community, it is now successfully established as a key player in its field of activity. Its reports and recommendations circulate widely and they have frequently been regarded as "influential" in the field (Wikipedia 2015). The Nuffield Foundation used to regard the Council as one of its most successful activities, and another funder literally referred to it as "a joy and a jewel". No major failures or shortcomings were reported, with the difficulty of establishing access to broader audiences as the one important exception. Interviewees frequently reported that the Council's success was dependent on the high quality of its work which is based on an established network and a solid reputation among professional experts and policymakers, both of which would be much harder to achieve vis-à-vis the general public. These impressions are confirmed by a review of the 2003 report on *Pharmacogenetics* (Corrigan 2005) as well as the recent stakeholder review (Martin et al. 2015).

8.5 Social Impact

The social impact of a research and advisory body such as the Nuffield Council is obviously hard to determine and Foundation staff acknowledged that "there are very few definitive things". Evidence circles largely around the level of output. For instance, stakeholders' demand for the Council's reports is indicated by "the number of reports they've produced, the number of downloads, numbers of copies sold, numbers of citations, and so on". The Council tracks media coverage (e.g., broadcast interviews or print articles), web statistics, presentations at conferences, consultations and academic citations in its annual reports (Nuffield Council 2013; Martin et al. 2015).

When it comes to more concrete outcomes, however, mostly anecdotal evidence is available. The current stakeholder review found that the Council had "significant direct impact with UK policymakers on specific issues. It has also had a demonstrable, though more indirect impact on academic researchers, funders, the public, international and the private sector" (Martin et al. 2015: 3).

Foundation staff suggested as an "unusually clear example" the 2006 report on *Critical Care Decisions in Fetal and Neonatal Medicine: Ethical Issues,* which focuses on the treatment of very premature babies. According to their observations it was uniformly welcomed by the relevant medical associations and incorporated in the British National Formulary as well as the guidelines to the members of the British Neuroscience Association and the Royal College of Paediatrics and Child Health.

The stakeholder review (Martin et al. 2015) highlights the 2012 report on *Novel Techniques for the Prevention of Mitochondrial DNA Disorders: An Ethical Review* as a prominent example:

> Several policymakers believe that this report had a direct and significant impact on the government's decision to allow mitochondrial pre-placement. A media stakeholder commented that it would be difficult to identify a debate about mitochondria replacement where the Nuffield Council on Bioethics was not mentioned.
>
> (Martin et al. 2015: 26)

The reports themselves receive most public and scientific attention. However, the level of demand for the Council's products varies, and while some reports attracted a high level of attention, others were more regarded as a useful compendium. Beyond a dissemination of reports, governmental demand for advice was also regarded as an indicator of influence. Occasionally the Council may also play a role as an agenda setter "in research, one of the most creative parts is . . . looking for questions that are both . . . timely and important and relevant but also answerable. . . . And I think that's an area where they have actually been successful".

Finally, the fact that the Council's reports and recommendations are based on impartial, high-quality research may be regarded as an instance of value creation as well, since, under these conditions, "people are much more likely to take it seriously and regard that as a good in itself". For these reasons, funders said that the Council's social impact may be of a rather abstract, fundamental and long-term type as it "contributes to creating a framework for policy development that has got farsighted benefits to science and society".

Notes

1 All the quotes refer to *former* members of staff. They can't be presumed to reflect the current position of the Foundation.
2 For a complete list see http://nuffieldbioethics.org/publications/.

9 The Joseph Rowntree Charitable Trust and the Campaign for Freedom of Information: Campaigning for Access to Files

The Campaign for the Freedom of Information (CFoI) is a UK-based, not-for-profit advocacy organisation. Its main aim used to be the enactment of a comprehensive Freedom of Information Act in the UK. For this purpose, the CFoI built a broad coalition of different partners and a large informal cross-party network, conducted research on similar legislation in other countries and lobbied for a change of law. The process from first activities in 1984 until the Act was brought into full force in 2005 lasted 21 years. The Freedom of Information Act (FOIA) grants any person, anywhere, access to information held by government and public authorities. After it came into force, the character of the CFoI changed. It now focuses on defending the Act against attempts to restrict it as well as on improving its use (CFoI 2015). From 1989 through to the present, the CFoI has almost continuously been supported by the Joseph Rowntree Charitable Trust (JRCT).

9.1 The Foundation

The JRCT is a philanthropic organisation that was founded in 1904 by Joseph Rowntree, the co-founder of the confectionary firm Rowntree & Co., as part of a family of three charities.[1] The headquarters of the UK-based organisation are located in York. It employs 12 staff (10 full-time equivalents). In rough figures, the organisation currently spends GBP6 million on grants and GBP1 million on running the organisation.

The Trust is strongly influenced by the Quaker background of its founder. Today, some senior staff and all trustees are Quakers. Its objective is to create a fairer, more just and peaceful society by means of "supporting people who address the root causes of conflict and injustice" (JRCT 2015). To achieve these aims, the Trust pursues an advocacy approach: most initiatives seek to change policy. Since charities in the UK are not allowed to fund political campaigns or parties, the JRCT often works "at the boundaries of charity law" (Davies 2004: 283).

Historically, the Trust has exclusively pursued a grant-giving approach, funding activities in the UK and Ireland.[2] Beyond that, grantees have received additional operational support such as media training, legal advice and IT courses.

9.1.1 Funding Policy

The approach pursued by JRCT exhibits a number of distinctive elements. To begin with, the work is organised into five programmes which comprise a portfolio of different organisations and individuals working on similar broadly defined problems. However, grantees do not necessarily work in similar ways or directions. Senior Foundation staff said:

> we do fund people who take different approaches to the same issue. And I have had one occasion when someone has come to me and said, how can you be funding me if you're funding them, because everything that I'm doing they're countering.

Secondly, the Trust claims that it does not seek to exercise undue control over the work of its recipients but leaves a lot of room for manoeuvre. It abstains from organising the funding process in overly planned ways, such as the setting of milestones and a close monitoring of progress. Senior Foundation staff said: "we're not into the climate of setting targets and performance monitoring in a way. We're more about providing and offering core support to people and organizations that we feel are contributing to the aims that we have". This may be due to the fact that the Foundation expects change and failure to be part of the process. Hence, grantees are not only asked for progress and success, they are supposed to report "changes to the objectives" and "least successful objectives" (CFoI 2007). Consistent with its policy of "strengthening the hands of others", the Trust claims to play the role of a critical friend who becomes active as an enabler in the background rather than intervening in the process or seeking visibility itself: "we would see our role as kind of being an engine house behind the scenes rather than taking the profile".

Finally, the organisation pursues a policy of long-term, yet flexible, collaboration over extended periods of time, which is described in terms of "taking the long view" and as "work done in faith", because in the field of policy-oriented reform, initiatives often take a lot of time to unfold whereas the chances of success are often hard to assess. While grants are awarded for a period of up to three years, the Trust often makes repeat grants to the same organisation. While sustained support over 26 years (as in the case of CFoI) is unusual, it is not unique. Importantly, the Trust supported the CFoI, even in times of lack of progress, despite the fact that it was impossible to know if it would ever be able to achieve its goals. This steadfast approach was combined with adaptability to changing circumstances. For instance, after the FOIA had been introduced into Parliament, the Trust had urged the CFoI to seek new sources of funding through training and consultancy in order to become more independent. When it turned out, however, that the FOIA's implementation would be delayed for four years, the CFoI was encouraged to return to campaigning. This flexibility allowed the CFoI to "adapt our work to changing circumstances, in the knowledge that so long as this is justified by the interests of the issue, the Trust is likely to encourage us in this path".

9.1.2 Background, Development and Status Quo

Prior to the decision to fund the CFoI, the JRCT became alert to developments following the second re-election of the Thatcher government in 1987. The Trust generally diagnosed an increasing culture of secrecy on behalf of the government, accompanied by a general lack of trust in public authorities and of opportunities for the participation of citizens. These developments were seen as an outright threat to democracy and it was concluded that a "sort of a revolution" was needed to change this.

At the same time, the organisation profited from a massive increase in resources due to the sale of the Rowntree Company, of which the Trust held a share of stocks, to Nestlé in 1988. This made additional action possible (List 2009: 2).

9.1.3 Process

While charities in the UK are not allowed to fund political campaigns or parties, they are allowed to support politically relevant research. The Foundation therefore "decided to support projects seeking to explain the causes of democratic decline, outline possible remedies and disseminate findings widely" (Davies 2004: 276). In 1988 it commissioned a mapping study that sought organisations, individuals and ideas which might help to further these broad purposes, the CFoI being one of them. The organisation was highlighted as being particularly professional, successful and skilled in building cross-party support (Swailes 1988: 5). The report reconfirmed that the Trust's concerns were widely shared among progressive practitioners and academics. Its author also found that "there were a lot of different organizations. A lot of them picking away at sort of single-issue bits of the problem" and thus recommended the creation of a more encompassing grant-making programme with the overall purpose of sustaining and reinvigorating democracy. More precisely, the researcher suggested:

> develop[ing] a broad but cohesive strategy sifting and refining the many strands . . . identifying projects at both the "elite, opinion-former" level, and at the grassroots; sponsoring policy-orientated research and the dissemination of such research. . . . Particularly important would be to combine short-term achievable aims on a small scale with the much longer term activity aimed at changing the climate of opinion.
>
> (Swailes 1988: 11)

As a direct result of this, a programme named "The Democratic Process and the Abuse of Power" was initiated in 1989, with the CFoI as one of its initial grantees. Thus, a very long partnership emerged (although it was by no means expected to be that long). The Foundation was engaged as a funder only, with the CFoI acting as an independent operating body.

9.2 The Campaign for Freedom of Information

The CFoI is a London-based, not-for-profit organisation that was founded in 1984 and still exists today. Its mission used to be campaigning for the introduction of an FOIA in the UK, based on its own independent research. For these purposes, the CFoI combined "the characteristics of pressure group and think tank" (Davies 2004: 277). Today, its role is to "advise the public on using the Act, encourage good practice, provide training for freedom of information (FOI) requesters and public authorities and try to improve how the Act works" (CFoI 2015).

9.2.1 Resources

The CFoI is run by a small team of two staff. Its director has worked with the organisation since its beginning in 1984 and has headed it since 1987. He was consistently characterised by our interview partners as a "very determined, very committed" person and credited with outstanding personal skills.

The CFoI operates on an annual budget of GBP100,000 (CFoI 2015). It has received funding from a broad variety of sources, the most important being the Consumers' Association, which paid the salary of the CFoI's director (and thus funded the non-charitable campaigning work), and the JRCT. Other funders include the Allen Lane Foundation and the Nuffield Foundation. Surprisingly, the CFoI did not receive substantial contributions from the media as one of its major beneficiaries, although media firms contributed through fees for training courses (List 2009: 12).

The JRCT has been funding the CFoI for 26 years, beginning in 1989. According to the Trust's database, 13 grants have been awarded since 1989, totalling GBP1.09 million. The most recent grant award was made in December 2013 (all figures of 2016). The largest grant was made in 2000, the year the FOIA was introduced in Parliament, in order to strengthen the CFoI's work at a crucial moment (List 2009: 5–6). In the first years, the Trust exclusively supported the CFoI's research activities due to the already mentioned legal restrictions on charitable work. As of the period from 2000 to 2002, however, the grant's purpose changed from the support of research to the funding of core activities (List 2009: 6), which was made possible by a change in charitable law. Funding has been almost completely continuous with only short gaps and has been made every year since 1989, except for 2002. The gaps occurred when the CFoI had enough funding from other sources. In sum, the Trust has been the CFoI's most loyal funder. Without this support, it would probably not have been able to operate for such a long period of time.

The financial resources have constituted the Trust's major contribution (List 2009: 5). Beyond that, its network may occasionally have been helpful. For instance, in 2001, Joseph Rowntree Reform Trust board member, MP Archy Kirkwood, introduced an FOI bill to Parliament which had been drafted by the CFoI (List 2009). Furthermore, the researcher who conducted the mapping study for the Trust later served as a director of the Allen Lane Foundation which also supported the CFoI (List 2009: 6).

Regardless of this long history of support, the CFoI's current financial situation seems to be far from stable. Although it operates on a very limited budget, it lacks reliable sources of funding (CFoI 2015). Given that the organisation is unequivocally judged as outstandingly competent and successful, and also assuming that it keeps playing an important function in the field, it is surprising that it does not attract more substantial and continuous funding. This impression is supported by Foundation staff. With hindsight, the Trust self-critically concluded that it would have been better to provide the CFoI with more slack resources so that it might become more resilient.

9.2.2 The Problem

In 1984, FOI laws had been implemented in a number of different countries, including the USA, Canada and Australia, but not in the UK. The CFoI regarded the lack of a comprehensive freedom of information legislation in the UK as a political problem of particular importance and aimed at the development and enactment of a comprehensive FOIA.

In the UK, a first attempt at introducing FOI legislation had failed due to a complex set of barriers. To begin with, it faced political resistance from the conservative Thatcher government. Yet, while the oppositional Labour party was much more sympathetic to this cause at that time, the CFoI's director saw a rather fundamental problem. While a party in opposition would favour freedom of information, they would regard it as a threat once they came into office. Moreover, he observed a political culture of secrecy which caused government and civil servants to regard the classification of information as the natural state of affairs. Although journalists seemed to be natural allies, the campaign faced a lack of interest as long as concrete advantages to the media were unclear. Finally, the interest on the side of the public was low and FOI was generally regarded as a leftist theme of little political or practical relevance. The challenge was, then, to change this climate of opinion and to build sufficient political and public support to overcome political resistance.

9.2.3 The Strategy

The experience of early failure led the CFoI to adopt an incremental advocacy strategy to attain its goals. This was based on the generation of networks and knowledge as key components. The overall idea was to develop momentum for a change in legislation by working with opposition parties, assuming that only *new* governments are sympathetic to the issue, since, when once in office, enthusiasm quickly wanes.

The incremental character of the strategy is expressed in the accumulation of small and rather easy wins in the early years. For instance, in 1987, 1988 and 1990 the campaign successfully drafted and supported bills granting citizens the right to access personal data such as social work and housing records (Access to Personal Files Act) and medical files (Access to Medical Reports Act; Access to Health Records Act). Another bill provided access to information on organisations breaching environmental protection and safety laws (Environment and Safety Information Act) (CFoI 2015).[3]

However, attempts to introduce more comprehensive bills were defeated in 1988 and 1992 (CFoI 2015), which shows that the CFoI needed to combine perseverance with a good deal of resilience against failure. The idea was to create an:

> organisation that just dedicates itself to a now achievable aim and does so over a period of years, so then after it is defeated once, it comes back again, it's defeated twice, it comes back again. Finally, you're building up the evidence, you're building up the support.

The Foundation regarded this procedure as a major factor of success. One of the interviewees said:

> I think the other strength they had was . . . realizing that you could bite off chunks of this in different areas, like medical records. . . . And, gradually, you could get to the point where you've then got a government who was prepared to even consider it. You could say: Well, hang on, look, we've got freedom of information in half-a-dozen areas, you cannot say we won't do it as a principle. So, I think it was that strategy that was largely responsible for the success.

The political nature of the problem called for an advocacy approach which aimed at building sufficiently strong constituency and consensus to bring FOI legislation through Parliament. The major instruments to achieve this were the coalition of supporting organisations which ramified into a large and heterogeneous informal network of supporters that addressed politicians, civil servants and journalists. The organisation pursued a cross-party approach which would explicitly include representatives of almost all parties, following the principle of "maximizing support" across political preferences and societal fields.

Beyond that, the CFoI awarded an annual prize to individuals, organisations and public authorities who had made significant contributions to their cause. In 1996 Tony Blair, then still an ordinary MP, presented the awards and made a strong public commitment to the issue (CFoI 2015). Combined with research and dissemination activities, the campaign succeeded in "building up . . . a cadre of professionals to see the value in . . . open government".

Finally, the long-term horizon opened up the opportunity for continuous learning and dissemination of knowledge. The CFoI conducted a comprehensive research programme to learn about the experiences with FOI legislation in other countries. It was supposed to generate arguments for the discussion with opponents and for the creation of a better proposal.

In the period between 2000 and 2005, that is before the Act came into force, the CFoI also took part in other organisations' training events for public authorities, to help them prepare to implement the Act properly.

This overall approach was supposed to create enough momentum to achieve the original goals in case a window of opportunity opened up. Senior staff said: "our objective was to have the bill ready which showed what it would look like, so that we would say, these are the problems and these are how you answer them".

9.2.4 The Process

The phase of small wins lasted from 1987 through to 1997. In that year, a Labour government was elected, the new minister responsible for Freedom and Information being acquainted with the CFoI network. Preparatory activities were taken up soon after and a white paper entitled "Your Right to Know" was published that made suggestions for a very advanced and comprehensive FOI bill (Freedom of Information Unit 1998). However, after a change in ministerial responsibilities, the draft was considerably watered down until it was considered "shockingly" weak both by the CFoI and the Foundation, which caused the CFoI to lobby for improvements. While Davies (2004: 278) assumed that this might have resulted in some "minor concessions", the CFoI maintains that changes were substantial. Either way, the FOIA finally passed in an improved version in November 2000. However, implementation was postponed for four more years (CFoI 2015). This created an experience of failure that was described as "very demoralizing" by a member of the CFoI. Yet, the organisation made use of the remaining time by preparing media and civil servants for the proper use of the bill. On 1 January 2005 the Act finally came into force; it:

> gives any person a right of access to information held by over 100,000 public bodies. The bodies are required to respond within 20 working days. The time frame can be extended to allow for consideration of release on public-interest test grounds as long as it is within a time period that is deemed "reasonable in the circumstances". There are no fees for requests which cost less than GBP600 for central government bodies or GBP450 for local authorities.
>
> (Banisar 2006: 154–5)

Moreover, in 2002 Scotland adopted a more substantial FOIA, which was strongly influenced by Labour's original white paper and, thus, the ideas developed by the CFoI (Davies 2004: 278). This came into full force in 2005.

However, it soon became clear that constant political attempts to revoke the Act necessitated a constant engagement to defend it. For instance, in 2006, only two years after its enactment, an amendment to the bill was introduced intending to protect the correspondence of MPs from disclosure (CFoI 2015). While, through the efforts of the CFOI and a network of partners, these attempts were defeated, the episode documents the frailty of contentious achievements like these, which need to be constantly protected. This diagnosis, in turn, underlines the importance of a long-term perspective and the readiness to support causes like FOI without a time limit (Ellis 2012; List 2009). At the same time, it became clear that both requesters and civil servants needed continuous training to make best use of the new law. As a result of these events, the role of the CFoI changed. Today, it also provides open and in-house training for civil servants/public authorities, media and other campaigners to acquaint them with FOI issues. The aim of these activities is twofold. In the case of public authorities it is to help them learn about important new decisions of the Information Commissioner and Tribunal. In the case of campaigners and journalists, the CFoI seeks to help them make effective use of the Act. Senior staff summed up these activities as follows: "I think we've got mixed roles now. I think we're there to help defend it, we're there to help promote it".

Noticing the need for permanent support, the Foundation urged the organisation to diversify its sources of income and to place more emphasis on own-income generation by means of training for both requesters and their civil service counterparts.

9.3 Environment

Success would probably not have been possible without the profound change of the social and political environment that occurred during the long partnership between the CFoI and the JRCT. Initiated in 1989 during Margaret Thatcher's third term in office, it saw a continuous change of governments who took different positions on FOI issues. At the same time, FOI legislation diffused widely in the Western world. The United States had taken the lead as early as 1966, Scandinavian and Commonwealth countries such as Australia, New Zealand and Canada passed laws in the 1970s and 1980s, and the EU made it obligatory as of 2005 (European Union 2003).

While there have always been other organisations working on issues related to the FOI such as JRCT long-term grantees Democratic Audit at the London School of Economics and the Constitution Unit at the University College London, the CFoI claims that there have been no other lobbyists. This has changed in recent years as some websites and blogs have emerged who support the cause of FOI as well (List 2009: 12).

In particular, the role of the media vis-à-vis FOI legislation seems to have changed. While, in the early days, low media interest was reported (with the exception of the newspaper *The Guardian*), this attitude changed "once the FOIA was enacted and the media began to reap its benefits with headline stories based on information released under the Act" (List 2009: 11). One interviewee said: "it used to be a small leftist theme of little relevance. Now it has become mainstream". What is more: "the media are now using the Act, they now understand it's really in their own interest to protect this Act, which they didn't have before. Before . . . they didn't know which benefit they'd get from it".

Beyond that, a "solid constituency of information users and honest-dealing public sector professionals has developed" (List 2009: 11), who make use of the Act and who can be mobilised in case of attacks (List 2009). In sum, the societal environment is mostly favourable as FoI legislation is in an advanced process of institutionalisation.

9.4 Success and Failure

In retrospect, Foundation staff concluded that, while no "revolution occurred" due to the programme, the problem itself seemed less threatening as well. One of our interviewees concluded: "looking back at it, perhaps we overreacted—but it all looked quite scary at the time".

In 2002 the Trust commissioned an internal evaluation on the Power and Responsibility programme, the successor to the Democracy programme. It reviewed the whole programme and looked at specific areas in more detail. Overall, a comparatively high level of programme impact was diagnosed, yet evidence for these claims is rather anecdotal, which may be explained by the very nature of a long-term and rather indirect approach toward funding. Hence, the question of programme effectiveness must remain open in this case study.[4] At the same time, however, the author regarded the CFoI as a major case of success and perceived the Trust's persistent support of the organisation as an important reason for why these achievements were possible in the first place (Ellis 2012).

While the law and the corresponding procedures and costs are not without critics, it seems plausible to assume that the CFoI and its allies have succeeded in establishing a complex infrastructure of legal regulations, political and civil society constituency, trained civil servants as well as informed media and the broader public. This includes an information commissioner who oversees the use of the Act as well as an information tribunal to decide on contentious cases (Banisar 2006: 155). All of these elements, taken together, have contributed to a well-functioning system which is in constant and high demand.

9.5 Social Impact

The number of requests to central government bodies has increased from 2006 to 2013 by 6 per cent each year. In 2013 a total of 51,696 requests were received, in 2014 the rate dropped to 46,806. Of requests received,

91 per cent either received a response within the statutory deadline of 20 days or were subject to a permitted deadline extension (Ministry of Justice 2014).

Based on disclosed information in the media, a variety of information has been released on a wide range of issues such as the UK's role in the Iraq war, the lobbying efforts of Prince Charles and of multinational corporations, the safety of nuclear plants as well as the expenses of public officials, and many others (Ellis 2012; List 2009).

When it comes to an overall assessment of the role of the CFoI in these developments, it is obviously very difficult to make causal attributions. The Foundation certainly regards the funding of the CFoI as an outstandingly effective investment. An evaluation concluded that the CFoI would not have been able to survive without the Trust's continuous support. Due to a lack of other funders or campaigners, the FOIA might not have come about (Ellis 2012).

It is also possible that, sooner or later, the UK would have adopted some type of FOI legislation anyway, as did the majority of EU countries. However, in such an hypothetical alternative scenario it would not have been *this* law, as, according to the CFoI, politicians would have preferred a much weaker version. Hence, the campaign can most certainly be credited with accelerating the adoption, and enhancing the quality, of legislation. What is more, the CFoI also takes care of its results and seeks to preserve and enhance the Act. In 2004, Davies assumed that, once it was implemented, "the Campaign could have a vital role in testing the legislation . . . and in building a culture in which people exercise their rights" (Davies 2004: 278). In retrospect, this prognosis seems to be correct. In other words, while the enactment of an FOIA as such might possibly have occurred otherwise (although the opposite may also be true), the time of implementation, the quality of the legislation and the intensity of its use can certainly be regarded as major achievements of the CFoI and, hence, the supporting Foundation.

Notes

1 The other two are the Joseph Rowntree Foundation, which funds social policy research and development, and the Joseph Rowntree Housing Trust which provides social housing. A fourth organisation created by Joseph Rowntree, the Joseph Rowntree Reform Trust, is a non-charitable political body aiming at social reform. They are among the most prominent policy-oriented, non-profit organisations in the UK, pursuing different but largely complementary styles of work (Leat 2005).
2 Interviewees have reported that this might have changed recently in favour of a more proactive stance in case the trust sees the need to take initiative, albeit with the qualification that they "tend only to act when people say to us, . . . you are well placed to do that".
3 For the history of freedom of information in the UK, see www.cfoi.org.uk/about-foi/history-of-freedom-of-information-in-the-uk/.
4 The author of the evaluation further concluded that the Trust should retain its basic operational approach. At the same time, the author expressed concerns that it might spread its resources too thin and suggested making more use of the JRCT's extensive knowledge and networks.

Part III
Analysis

10 From Exploration to Exploitation: The Pragmatic Model of Action in Philanthropic Practice

As a first step of the analysis I will discuss the questions of if and how the pragmatist framework as introduced in Chapter 2 of this study can meaningfully be applied to my four cases. According to pragmatism, intelligent social action is motivated by the immediate perception of a serious problem which cannot be remedied by means of habitual behaviour. This triggers a process of inquiry, which is conducted by collectives rather than individuals. A problematic situation requires actors to abandon routinized behaviour in favour of a phase of experimental learning in which emerging hypotheses and novel practices are confronted with situational reality. Experimental strategies are pursued as long as uncertainty and instability prevails. In the case of success, this phase generates new solutions to the problem under attack which sediment in enhanced and more task-adequate collective and individual habits.

10.1 Actors

The foundations under investigation do not operate in isolation. Rather, they are active in—or in-between—distinct societal fields which are characterised by particular institutional orders and logics (Friedland and Alford 1991; Thornton and Ocasio 2008), namely the capitalist market and the bureaucratic state (The Chance); civil society and science (Foundation Interkultur); science, the state and, increasingly, democracy (the Nuffield Foundation); and democracy and the state (The Joseph Rowntree Charitable Trust and the Campaign for Freedom of Information). Accordingly, they are oriented towards the values, stakeholders and methods of operation of the sectors in which they are embedded. This is mirrored in the composition of organisational staff.

Foundation Interkultur is characterised by its explicit orientation towards grassroots practices and activists; it prefers bottom-up approaches and supports local self-help initiatives. At the same time, however, it is strongly influenced by its founder's preference for a style of social intervention that is based on a research perspective (*"forschender Blick"*). The organisation thus employs staff with academic and grassroots backgrounds. Both the Nuffield Foundation and its Council subscribe to scholarly standards and conventions of academic investigation. In the beginning, they targeted mainly academic and public policy audiences. The Council's composition reflects this division of labour. While the Council itself is largely made up of academics, the secretariat employs staff with a background in public administration; its managing director is a former senior civil servant. Rowntree intends to change or influence public policy. Not being an operating foundation, the Trust relies on activist organisations such as the Campaign for Freedom of Information (CFoI) which reaches out to public policymakers. The Chance is best characterised as a hybrid organisation which inhabits the terrain between the system of public vocational training and commercial firms. It thus exhibits both entrepreneurial values, as well as the values of public administration. The board is composed of members with a business background while the organisation recruits experienced practitioners such as headmasters and teachers in public vocational schools.

This introductory diagnosis is important for the following reason. Although the foundations in my sample play an important role in initiating, resourcing or realising interventions, they never determine, tackle and solve problems on their own. In all cases, initiatives are created and maintained collectively and through the interplay with members of the organisational environment. Value is co-produced in a complex process which is driven by a multitude of distributed organisations (other foundations or non-profit organisations, public bureaucracies, corporate firms) and individual actors, most of whom are independent of the foundation. Collaborations take place at different stages of the programme and on different levels, from local to national. The partners perform very diverse functions and provide different competencies and resources and thus complement those capacities and abilities that foundations lack. For instance, Foundation Interkultur reached out to activists who autonomously created and ran the intercultural gardens. The Chance relies both on the collaboration with firms who provide trainee positions as well as on the active participation of the trainees themselves. The Nuffield Foundation is dependent on the contributions of experts who staff the Council and the working parties, while the CFoI's success depended on support by politicians and civil servants. Hence, neither case can meaningfully be analysed if only the foundation or the organisation it funds, let alone a solitary, inspired and visionary social entrepreneur, is put in focus.

Yet, it would be equally wrong to assume that all actors perform largely equal roles, and that outstanding individuals or organisations have no role to play in this framework. On the contrary, neither of the cases would have been possible without the foundation's initiative; furthermore some philanthropic organisations play a dominant role in the networks which were created to serve as their working instruments. In addition, interviewees frequently emphasised the importance of the founding directors of organisations, who were perceived as outstandingly experienced, competent and motivated. In the cases of the Nuffield Foundation and The Chance, they also had long professional track records in their fields. These persons were regarded as being of particular relevance in the first stages of innovation due to their superior knowledge of the field, their large personal networks and their organisational and political skills. For instance, Rowntree staff emphasised the relevance of the CFoI's director and his "particular qualities". He was consistently described as very "bright", "passionate", "determined" and "committed". One interviewee pointed at the Trust's principle of "supporting all sorts of inspirational individuals. And I think the Trust has always felt a bit that way about" him.

These findings are consistent with Miller's (1988) diagnosis that innovation is dependent on the availability of experienced experts and technocrats, but it also points at the relevance of senior staff with entrepreneurial skills, that is, the ability to operate beyond the confines of their own sector, to create new organisational forms and products and to mobilise support by external stakeholders and to suppress or evade opposition.

In sum, the data discourage heroic pictures of philanthropic action in splendid isolation. They support arguments against single organisations as the unit of analysis if social impact and effectiveness of philanthropic organisations are the dependent variables. Instead, they corroborate the pragmatist emphasis on the collective and networked nature of social problem solving, if not without leaving room for a more prominent role of distinguished organisations, skilled experts and committed entrepreneurial leaders.

10.2 Habits and Problems

The pragmatist model further predicts that intelligent actors choose social problems as a point of departure for what they do. The perception of problems interrupts routinised organisational action and leads to new courses of action. Hence, the resulting activities are characterised as "problem-oriented" or "problem-driven" (Ansell 2011: 84; Andrews et al. 2013; Thümler et al. 2014b: 218).

10.2.1 Change of Habits

The analysis of my sample cases confirms these propositions. Organisational behaviour was always triggered by the perception of concrete problems which arose out of practice in a particular societal field or subsystem. The perception, choice and definition of problems clearly reflected the different preferences and values of organisations and the environments in which they were embedded. Problems were never tackled by means of standard operating procedures, in the context of established organisational structures and by the usual instruments, such as single grants or projects. Rather, the problem perception led to a modification of organisational routines or even the creation of new organisations.

In the case of The Chance, both the founder and the first managing director knew the problems very well due to their own professional backgrounds. While the founder chose to invest his own wealth to create the Foundation, the director quit his job as headmaster of a vocational school. Both aimed at tackling the problem of disadvantaged youths transiting into the labour market in innovative ways, which, in their opinion, would have been impossible in the context of established institutions. The activities of Foundation Interkultur were triggered by the inability to cope with the surge of interest in the first migrant gardening initiative, which created an impression of excessive demands, described by Foundation staff in the words "Help, we cannot cope with this any more". This led to the creation of a single-purpose organisation which aimed to foster the emerging movement by new organisational means. The Nuffield Foundation reacted to calls from the field of biomedicine and established the Council as a specialised instrument of inquiry, which was not the standard operating procedure for a scientific foundation. Just like many other members of the progressive milieu in the UK, Rowntree was alarmed by the re-election of the Thatcher government and the possible future consequences of this event. As a response it created a new programme to tackle a very broad and opaque problem in new and systematic ways.

10.2.2 Types of Problems

I reported above that the literature consensually regards a reduction of complexity as a major prerequisite for successful problem solving. However, an overly strong limitation of scale and scope may result in societal irrelevance. Consistent with these assumptions, the foundations neither chose to attack tiny and simple problems, nor overly large and complex "wicked" problems (with the exception of Rowntree), but instead smaller chunks of much larger societal problems.

For instance, Foundation Interkultur addressed broad purposes such as the integration of migrants and a lack of space for free and non-commercial exchange, yet it did so by supporting intercultural gardens as a highly specific organisational form. As the Foundation could draw on an existing and uncontentious model, the challenge was largely to help diffuse it as widely as possible. Processes of growth frequently suffer from a lack of resources. However, intercultural gardens cannot simply be "bought". Their establishment and diffusion essentially relies on the autonomous initiative of widely distributed gardeners. Under these conditions, the Foundation primarily faced a control problem.

By contrast, The Chance addressed the wide field of youth unemployment by choosing a comparatively small target group in a limited geographical area. Yet, to do this effectively, the organisation had to develop an effective programme as a first step. In a similar vein, the Nuffield Foundation reduced the broad ethical problems related to technological, scientific and, in particular, medical progress as it focused exclusively on the exploration of the issue of bioethics. However, the Foundation needed to invent and establish a suitable organisational form to serve these purposes. In both cases, the new activities were eyed with suspicion by the established stakeholders in the field, but the focus on clearly bounded terrain helped to avoid competition or even active resistance. Furthermore, it limited the amount of resources necessary to establish and maintain the programme. Hence, both organisations were primarily confronted with an innovation problem. In the case of The Chance, organisational growth resulted in a lack of resources which became dominant only later in the process. Yet, it remained manageable because of the regionally bounded character of the activity.

Rowntree addressed a culture of secrecy on behalf of the government along with a lack of trust in public authorities and poor opportunities for citizen participation. This was a very broad, diffuse and highly contentious "wicked" problem, which exhibited all the problem dimensions to high degrees. While the available data are not very comprehensive, they suggest that, overall, the chosen approach either failed or did not yield conclusive results. In hindsight, Foundation staff concluded that the first activities were based on a problem definition which turned out to be wrong. Success proved to be dependent on the support of a single organisation such as the CFoI, which tackled a much smaller, better defined and more bounded chunk of the overall problem. As the CFoI chose to advocate for legislation which had already been implemented in a number of other countries, it could draw on extensive knowledge and experience. It further profited from the advantage that legal change requires a single formal act instead of resource-intensive processes of growth. Furthermore, the infrastructure necessary to sustain the freedom of information (FOI) system was built and sustained by the state. However, as an FOI law was unpopular among a majority of politicians and civil servants, and as the CFoI had no direct influence over the political process, it was confronted with a major political and control problem.

These results can best be classified by recourse to Schön's (1987) diagnosis that problem solvers must choose between high ground and swamp. In my sample cases, funders' decisions are clear. Rowntree's democracy programme descended into the swamp and came back with the CFoI as its major achievement. But the CFoI and all other programmes populate the shoreline between high ground and swamp where the ground is shaky and the feet become wet but where risks are still manageable and uncertainty is bounded. In this intermediary zone they found and tackled problems of medium size and concern, as it were. I infer that these are privileged candidates for philanthropic organisations aiming to make a social impact by solving social problems.

10.2.3 Origins of Problems and Solutions

This diagnosis entails the question of where these manageable problems come from and how they are defined. Above I demonstrated that actors are embedded in professional and institutional contexts. This circumstance is particularly relevant for the recognition and definition of problems, for, at least in principle, endowed foundations do not have an obligation to address specific problems, but they are free to choose and, sometimes, do not address problems at all (Alberg-Seberich and Meibom 2009; Thümler et al. 2014b: 213). Yet, even if they *do* choose problems as a point of departure for their activities, they might either act arbitrarily and in isolation, or else conduct strategic planning efforts. In the case of The Chance, the former motivation may actually have played a role, although shaped by the founder's immediate professional experience. The established foundations, however, displayed a different pattern of action. The problem was recognised, defined and addressed in distributed and collective processes which included serendipitous elements and emerged out of close contact with the social and professional communities in which foundations operated.

For instance, Rowntree responded to an atmosphere of political crisis prevalent in the progressive circles in the UK but certainly not shared by the majority of citizens who had just re-elected the Thatcher government. The recognition of the problem and the call for action, the decision to take action, the exploration of options and suggestions for a funding strategy, the adoption of a strategy, including funding of the CFoI, and the actual work done by the campaign all involved different actors on different hierarchical and functional levels, inside as well as outside the Foundation. The activities of Foundation Interkultur emerged organically out of the constant contact and interaction with grassroots' and migrants' groups. The problems which triggered the emergence of the first intercultural garden were formulated by migrants themselves, and the model solution was developed by them. In the case of the Nuffield Foundation, the problem of bioethics was first perceived by a trustee who was a member of the medical community, and it was finally taken up after the government refused to become active and experts turned to the Foundation for help.

From this I infer that, consistent with pragmatist assumptions, problem-orientation is a common property of effective philanthropic action. What is more, foundations address profound problems experienced in concrete problem situations which trigger "real and living" doubt (Peirce 2011 [1877]). Rather than formal procedures it is the close embeddedness of foundations in distinct communities that enables them to perceive problems in the first place and to become responsive to social needs. The ability to detect emerging or unsolved problems due to close contact with practice in particular fields can similarly be regarded as the ability to recognise windows of opportunity. This provides both the motivation and the rationale for foundations to become active, as well as the sources of legitimacy to operate in environments which are often densely populated by other established actors and their programmes which might otherwise crowd out philanthropic action.

Yet, the embeddedness of foundations and their responsiveness to the concerns of particular communities does not come without strings attached.

Except for The Chance (which was committed to a limited geographical area, though), none of the foundations tackled a widely known and broadly agreed upon societal problem. Instead, they responded to new and emerging problem perceptions, the importance of which was limited to a distinct social community. As a result of this, solutions may be characterised as being of "middle range" in scale as well as in relevance. They are not marginal, but nor do they cause major societal change or "disruption". Rather, they are perceived as significant by a particular segment of society populated by the foundation, its grantees and target groups, stakeholders and external observers.

10.3 Versatile Strategies

Drawing on pragmatist theory and an established tradition of scholarly research on problem solving and innovation, I proposed earlier that successful solutions to complex social problems rely on the adoption of variable strategies, whereas bureaucratic modes of operation alone are not conducive to problem solving. The following analysis seeks to show how actors made use of different strategies depending on the properties of the problem situation they confronted.

10.3.1 Exploration and Discovery

Exploration in the proper sense of the term happens in highly opaque problem situations in which both a definition of the very nature of the problem and its possible remedies are unavailable. Under these conditions, actors seek to gain general orientation in terms of an overview of the field and feasible courses of action. Rowntree is a good example of such an explorative approach. This included the combination of a mapping exercise which considered different potential avenues of activity and a rather conventional portfolio of grants which allowed the Trust to pursue different possible paths over a long period of time. Due to the opaque nature of the problem, it was impossible to formulate a strategy based on clear and explicit goals, and there was neither a logic model nor much control over a highly distributed and contentious process. Under these circumstances, funding of the CFoI could only be based on trust, not on control. An external partner said: "they would never have known there was some chance of success, but they've supported things which have even remotely chances of success". One of the Trustees added that, under these circumstances:

> you aren't doing good unless you're backing failure, because you don't know which are the winners. . . . [This] could have been a flop, and, therefore, you wouldn't have gone on for 20 years with it. But it seemed as if we were getting somewhere, we were getting a bit further and getting a bit further.

In a similar vein, Davies claimed that the Trust:

> cannot be credited with spotting a window of opportunity for reform in the late 1980s. When the democracy programme was established, its goal was to curb perceived Thatcherite excesses. The Trust did not anticipate a reforming Labour government ten years later. . . . The timing of the democracy programme and some of its positive outcomes were serendipitous; they were more the result of a principled investment in the talents of individuals and organisations than a hunch about the future.
>
> (Davies 2004: 283)

10.3.2 *Experimentation and Search*

Once the overwhelming size of the problem had successfully been reduced to a manageable degree, or if actors had sufficient prior knowledge and understanding of the problem situation anyway, the sample organisations employed *experimental* strategies. They relied on trial-and-error processes which reflect the risks and uncertainty inherent in problem solving. Neither of them employed a formal strategy. But, compared with explorative behaviour, they were directed by a better understanding of targets and ideas of how to achieve them.

For instance, the early work of The Chance was based on an operating model which required major corrections. In the beginning, staff were required to check the mailbox early in the morning in case the head of the Foundation had decided to change important operational rules overnight. The necessary creation of a new and effective organisational arrangement was achieved through a learning process that was based on ongoing sequences of trial and error. This process generated causal knowledge, reduced uncertainty and thus created a coherent and effective programme. As a result, the original approach was transformed into what has now become the organisation's operating core.

The development of the Nuffield Council followed a largely similar pattern, as it was not based on an established model and the events did not follow a coherent plan. After a short exploratory phase, the Foundation developed a new practice by means of a design experiment. As opposed to The Chance, interviewees here stressed that goals were imprecise at the beginning. The process included the generation of new knowledge and the reduction of uncertainty regarding the new organisational form. Senior Foundation staff said:

> The question about how it would manifest itself took some time, . . . maybe a year. And there would have been other options. I mean, one could have had a break into conferences or funded an academic department, or whatever. So I don't think the decision to form the Council was a sort of shoo-in.

By contrast, Foundation Interkultur chose a fundamentally different approach. It became active only in a later stage of the process of innovation, when an uncontentious and effective model solution was available. Yet, the organisation still faced the problem of how to grow intercultural gardens. The same can be said for the intercultural gardens themselves. While interviewees reported a diversity of benefits, the precise process towards individual or collective advantage cannot be predicted or programmed in any targeted way. Hence, the goals of Foundation Interkultur are rather vague. Instead of a plan based on causal knowledge, the strategy lists and organises a broad portfolio of methods and activities which reflect past experiences and which are supposed to be carried out in the future. No monitoring or formal evaluation is conducted. This approach bears close resemblance to the toolkit of intermediate actors as discussed in the context of strategic niche management. It is based on the assumption that actors can neither plan nor exert direct influence over dynamic processes of niche establishment and development. The best they can do is to support and modulate social dynamics which occur regardless of organised action.

The CFoI chose to tackle a complex, yet much more limited, problem that included both political and control dimensions. The organisation could draw on existing models of legislation and did not face a growth problem. The CFoI had clear ideas about its goals and the means to achieve them. It pursued an incremental advocacy strategy supposed to create pieces of successful legislation in less contentious fields and build constituency—particularly so in the Labour Party, but also among Conservatives and civil servants who were sympathetic to its cause—thus to prepare the ground for an enactment of the law after a change in government. This approach was regarded as highly coherent and convincing by Foundation staff:

> one of the things that really struck me about the campaign . . . was that they were actually, really saying: "Well, this is how the world is and we can change this". . . . But they had a really strategic view of how they were going to get to where they wanted to be.

However, as a political outsider, the CFoI had no control over the process whatsoever. It thus had to work for a very long period of time to change the climate of opinion among decision makers. Similar to Foundation Interkultur, the CFoI made extensive use of the SNM toolkit. For instance, it organised its own research process to learn more about foreign experiences with FOI legislation in order to enhance its arguments and to fit its proposals better to the particular requirements in the UK. Regardless of its strategic outlook, a high degree of risk, uncertainty and fallibility was inherent in this approach. The according need for experimental behaviour is reflected in an episode which was reported by senior staff. When the organisation needed to hire a lawyer to help draft an FOI bill, the head of the organisation chose the only (foreign) candidate who admitted that he gave false answers to some of his questions during the job interview, whereas all other applicants (of British origin) denied being wrong. Referring to the latter, our interviewee resumed: "you can't work with somebody like that in these circumstances".

Surprisingly, the experimental repertoire of action is strikingly similar in all the four cases, although they exhibit different *dominant* problem dimensions. For instance, the CFoI focuses more on advocacy to overcome contention and less on the generation of causal knowledge, such as The Chance does. Nevertheless, both facilitate learning processes, advocate or practice diplomacy in cases of actual or potential contention, mobilise resources to sustain and/or grow operations, and try to gain control over the problem situation. This observation can be explained with the messy and non-transparent nature of social problems: different problem dimensions come in interdependent clusters in all the cases, regardless of the degree of complexity reduction. Hence, in practice it seems to be impossible to tailor social problems in such a way as to generate neatly bounded uni- or bi-dimensional problem definitions which can be tackled by the corresponding types of action. By corollary, I infer that experimental action is equivalent with hybrid or "dirty" strategies which address most or all of the problem dimensions. In the event of success, this type of action will reduce uncertainty and contention, enhance control and enable processes of growth, simultaneously.

10.3.3 Bureaucracy and Exploitation

In each case, the experimental period was followed by a more stable phase, during which the focus of action changed. Organisations no longer concentrated on developmental processes and rather sought to preserve their achievements, to exploit the newly mastered habits and, sometimes, to grow operations. This stage was characterised by an increase in the characteristics and elements of bureaucratic models such as the existence of formal strategies[1] (The Chance, Interkultur and Nuffield Council), clear goals (Nuffield Council) and causal knowledge as well as increased control over the process of production (The Chance).

Furthermore, it included processes of standardisation and formalisation: the phase of exploitation relied on routinised organisational processes in every case. An organisational routine is defined as "a repetitive, recognizable pattern of interdependent actions, involving multiple actors" (Feldman and Pentland 2003: 96). The turn towards organisational routines is reflected in a change of emphasis: processes of search, learning, variation and change are not turned off but reduced, and more standardised operating procedures prevail. This is consistent with organisational research which regards routines as "the primary means by which organizations accomplish much of what they do" (Feldman and Pentland 2003: 94). They are regarded as important tools for the preservation of organisational experiences as well as the means for cognitive efficiency and the reduction of complexity (Feldman and Pentland 2003: 97). While the term has frequently been used in a rather pejorative way as the mindless execution of standardised patterns of action (Feldman and Pentland 2003; Cohen 2007), routines have also been conceived as the organisational equivalent of habits in the pragmatist sense of the term. These are not to be equated with the mechanical performance of particular acts but rather with the execution of a masterful technique (Cohen 2007: 777–779), which may eventually become a source of new change processes (Feldman and Pentland 2003).

This diagnosis clearly applies to The Chance. After a phase of intense development activities, the operations of The Chance became much more routinised and stable. They relied on an evidence-based model which constantly met its own, quantified goals. As of 2014, the organisation adopted a formal strategy for the first time, which focused largely on future opportunities to stabilise and increase the budget. At the same time, it did not seek further growth and planned to retain its regional character.

The Nuffield Council established a stable operating model, as well. What is more, as of 2012 it adopted a new steering model, intended to facilitate a better adaptation to changing environments and to allow for more control over organisational processes and outcomes. This is based on five-year strategic plans, followed by a subsequent evaluation of implementation success. Future funding is supposed to be informed by the outcomes of strategy and evaluation. Regarding growth, this issue does not seem to be particularly well suited or applicable in meaningful ways to an organisation which is based on scientific logic and the generation of knowledge and ideas.

Foundation Interkultur is an example of a particularly interesting variety of standardisation by which the "experimental arm" of the Foundation anstiftung has been reintegrated into its parent organisation. While the organisation itself has not been maintained, the newly established operational model has been adopted as a template for the entire organisation of origin. It keeps supporting urban gardens in the ways Foundation Interkultur did, but also transformed its governance structure and its operations in other fields of activity. As of 2008, the operations of the Foundation anstiftung are being guided by an informal strategy. However, goals still remain vague and the written strategy is very different from a roadmap or a plan which specifies operations in more detail.

Of all the organisations in my sample, Foundation Interkultur/Foundation anstiftung fitted the bureaucratic model the least well; senior staff certainly and explicitly reject its logic.

In the case of the CFoI, an important shift in operations can be diagnosed since the adoption of the FOI legislation in 2005. While the CFoI used to be a challenger of legal orthodoxy, it has now become an incumbent of legally protected rights. Hence, campaigning capacity is now directed at defending rather than establishing the law. Furthermore, a large share of its activities is now invested in the incremental enhancement of the system of FOI in the UK, particularly by means of providing training for those who request it and civil servants who operate the system.

For the CFoI, growth is no issue and probably never has been. The law has met a high level of demand right from the beginning and keeps attracting high and stable numbers of inquiries. Senior staff reported that the organisation is concerned not to overwhelm the system and to keep the number of requests stable, because an increase in numbers might raise public concerns and criticism regarding the costs of the system. Hence, the CFoI aims more at enhancing the quality of the system rather than increasing its size.

10.3.4 A Combination of Strategies

It is certain that the cases do not support a linear phase model based on the straightforward transition from one mode to the other. Neither are the different strategies irreconcilable. Rather, I find that the distinct dimensions may occur in parallel, or even in recursive loops, which is strongly supported by research on organisational innovation and learning (Landau and Stout 1979; March 1991; Braun-Thürmann 2005; Gupta et al. 2006; Van de Ven et al. 2008).

For instance, in a case such as The Chance, exploitation played a role in the early, experimental stages of organisational development and the distinction between both was more a matter of emphasis. Moreover, as predicted by the pragmatic model, new social or organisational problems emerge during the phase of stability which requires new processes of learning. Depending on the nature of the problem, this may take place in the confines of the present organisational trajectory, or it may require new phases of exploration or experimentation. For instance, The Chance kept refining its working model by means of incremental improvements. As the organisation did not rely on the interests of its endowment, and as the high demand for its services led to a phase of expansion, it soon faced a resource problem. Although the dimension of growth was limited to a medium level due to the organisation's regional scope and a limited number of participants, The Chance had to mobilise a reliable and increasing flow of resources. While it was clear how the result of this process was supposed to look in *figures,* the *means* leading towards the aim were unknown. The problem was tackled by rather conventional fundraising efforts, but also with the creation of "Check Your Chance", a national association of six similar organisations fighting youth unemployment which mobilised support by economic elites and successfully lobbied for public subsidies. Yet, although new private and public sources of income could be tapped, the financial situation remains volatile and the organisation can probably not be regarded as resilient to future crises. The new strategy of 2014 can be regarded as a tool to cope with these challenges in systematic ways as its major focus is on the exploration of all potential sources of additional income.

In between the last and the forthcoming strategies, the Nuffield Council observes new challenges, as well. Senior staff reported major changes in the organisation's environment. These are related to the increasing complexity, speed and globalisation of technological and policy developments, which make it more and more difficult to cover those processes by means of established procedures. While no coherent answer to these challenges has yet been put forward, the organisation might ultimately have to question the successfully established operating model, which would require a new phase of exploration or experimentation to pursue new organisational trajectories.

10.4 Conclusion

In sum, I find that the pragmatist model applies to my cases, if with some amendments. Problem-solving action is always triggered by the immediate perception of a problematic situation which is sometimes quite vague and which arises out of confrontation with practice, not as the outcome of formal strategy development processes. In cases of highly opaque problem situations, the issue is further explored in such a way as to make it more bounded and tractable and to enhance understanding. The result is a rather clear problem definition in terms of a "chunk" of broader societal problems. It serves as a point of orientation for the further course of behaviour which can thus be characterised as problem-driven or problem-oriented. This process further includes recognition of the inadequacy of existing organisational routines. As a response, actors employ diverse strategies which are labelled "experimental" to designate the inherent causal and normative uncertainty they face and to emphasise those elements of action which are adequate for the exploration of unknown terrain and the establishment of causal knowledge, rather than the organisation of a voyage based on established routes and fixed timetables.

The above discussion thus clarifies the aspects in which exploratory and experimental strategies differ from bureaucratic models of action; but it also demonstrates how they all can be reconciled: there is no strict cleavage between bureaucracy, exploration and experimentation but rather a continuum which unfolds between both ends of the spectrum. If successful, experimental behaviour results in novel organisational habits supposed to exploit the newly established arrangements in such a way as to produce the desired effects permanently and reliably. However, organisations still need to retain innovative capacity in case they are confronted with new problems: the ability to find the right balance between exploitation and exploration is essential for sustainability and future effectiveness.

Importantly, *all* interventions exhibit an early phase during which an effective model solution is generated, followed by the stabilisation of the newfound solution as well as different degrees and dimensions of growth.

However, not every organisation developed a model of action on its own. There occurs a division of labour which draws on prior development activities on a local level (Interkultur) or abroad (CFoI). Yet, in these cases, philanthropic organisations exhibited intense activities to refine the model (Interkultur) or to adapt it to a new environment (CFoI). I infer that it is most important *that* these requirements are met, rather than *when* it is the case or by *whom* it is carried out. Finally, growth is not much of a problematic issue. While all programmes exhibit processes of diffusion and expansion, this happens easily and, in the case of the CFoI, almost as a by-product of the intervention. Growth does not seem to have been perceived as a major organisational challenge in either case.

These findings contrast sharply with conventional philanthropic practice, with its preference for hierarchical decision making, control over developmental processes, neglect of sustainability issues and an emphasis on the problem of growth. Seen from a pragmatist perspective, bureaucratic approaches to philanthropy commit three fallacies. First, they fail to acknowledge the high degree of uncertainty and the lack of control which is characteristic of the developmental stage of innovation. Second, they disregard the necessity to exploit newly established arrangements long term. Third, they underestimate the need to keep balancing exploitation and exploration once the new arrangement has been established.

Yet, while the analysis has thus clarified the actors, strategies and processes which are relevant for the solution of problems, it has left open the question of how the *nature* of the value created can be described and explained: what kind of social impact has been generated as a result of these interventions, and why? I will now turn to a closer scrutiny of these questions which are obviously essential for a study on social impact and innovation.

Note

1 However, instead of being a sign of a step towards a logic of exploitation, the increasing use of formal or informal strategies might also be due to a change in societal expectations of how a rational non-profit organisation must behave.

11 Explanations for Social Impact: The Door-Opener Mechanism

Pragmatism posits that the creation of value consists in personal and societal *growth,* understood as the increasing capability to solve problems in intelligent ways, which results in better and more adequate habits. According to this perspective, impact may occur at the individual, community and societal levels. It denotes a complex and multidimensional state of affairs of some stability which is highly dependent on the original problem situation and cannot easily be summarised or standardised, let alone quantified. In the case of philanthropic organisations, this entails the important qualification that *other* peoples' problems are solved, and not one's own. However, recall Dewey's assertion that happiness cannot simply be *given* to recipients in need. The question is, then, how impact looks in practice and how it can be generated by philanthropic parties.

In the case of Foundation Interkultur/Foundation anstiftung, intercultural gardens seek to create advantage on a predominantly individual level as they respond to a wide diversity of human needs. They are created with the intention of establishing a favourable environment which facilitates the joyful perception of natural beauty as well as desirable habits such as intercultural communication, and even contributes to the repair of severed ways of life. The emphasis on gardens as non-commercial spaces for the encounter and exchange of people of different social origin as well as the high number of gardens may also point towards favourable effects on the community and even at the societal level. Obviously, the precise outcomes of processes like these cannot be defined, described, forecast or planned in detailed ways. Instead, the effects of gardens are frequently expressed in metaphorical terms. For instance, one interviewee commented on a fellow gardener: "since he has got the garden and comes out with the children, the children grow. Now they grow at last".

At first glance, The Chance is a much more straightforward case. The available data suggest that the organisation succeeds in helping disadvantaged youths to graduate and find permanent jobs, and these objectives can even be quantified. Yet, the numbers do not equal the value created, but serve as proxies only. What is more, successful graduation and transition rates are not the only dimensions of value created. Impact is rather expressed in complex and qualitative terms such as the ability to become economically independent, to develop more stable personal routines, to persist in challenging situations and to solve new problems on one's own. Senior staff said:

> In my opinion, success happens when someone manages to take his life into his own hands after the training and really succeeds in pursuing his aims and [if he] achieves a certain autonomy and does not rely on help . . . then the aim has completely been met.

A different diagnosis applies in the case of the Nuffield Foundation. While quantitative outputs in terms of citations or downloads can be measured, they do not represent the value created at all. Characteristic for the generation of knowledge and ideas, impact cannot be determined reliably because, while both travel easily, they may be transformed beyond recognition in the course of the journey. Moreover, attribution problems are pervasive in multi-actor environments and effects may be delayed. Unlike Interkultur and The Chance, it would be almost impossible, and probably even meaningless, to determine impact at an individual level. Positive effects are rather to be sought in the domain of public policy and, with limitations, academic research. In case of success, professional debates become richer and better informed as they draw on independent, sound, coherent and reliable information and advice. Enhanced professional practices and public regulations may be the result.

Similarly, the value created by advocacy organisations such as the Campaign for Freedom of Information occurs at the societal and not (save in exceptional cases) at the individual level. Again, requests for the release of governmental information and responses can be measured quantitatively. But value is produced as individuals make use of access to governmental files; thus society as a whole becomes somewhat more transparent.

In sum, the pragmatist assumption is confirmed as all cases seek to generate broad and multidimensional advantages which, in turn, rely on a complex set of enhanced practices of members of the target groups, be they disadvantaged youths, public policymakers, urban gardeners or journalists. These advantages cannot be provided directly in any of these cases. Rather, all organisations aim at generating *opportunities* for their target groups. Individual or societal welfare is enhanced only if they are grasped.

Importantly, all these organisations seek to produce benefits *continuously* and based on new, more adequate and stable *habits and structures*. Moreover, they rely on conscious decisions and the permanent willingness of members of the target groups and other stakeholders to engage in the common endeavour. The pragmatist approach thus stands in sharp contrast to techniques such as "nudging" which seek to induce a desired behaviour, for example the choice of healthy food or favourable pension schemes, by means of the design of decision architectures which facilitate desired and discourage unwelcome decisions (Thaler and Sunstein 2008). This is not at all the case here. All programmes rely on the autonomous and informed choice of the members of the target group, and not on mechanisms which operate behind their backs. They aspire to solve complex and persistent problems through the establishment of better habits which work in permanent rather than punctual ways and result in the attainment of multiple, rather than single, objectives. The pragmatic approach thus suggests an alternative means to secure compliance to interventions and helps to find answers to a major problem of intervention design, namely the need to overcome multiple rather than single barriers, induce complex and ongoing changes of behaviour rather than a single act, and achieve diverse rather than simple targets (Weaver 2014: 250–251).

However, the discussion up to this point did not specify precisely *how* these demanding outcomes are achieved. This rather vague conception of social impact might raise the sceptical question as to *whether* value has been created at all. Furthermore, it is not always clear if the actions of philanthropic organisations were the *cause* of desired effects. The above descriptions might still be overly idiosyncratic to the particular problem situations which are addressed in my cases and, hence, not very helpful for orienting other philanthropic actors in different situations. As long as the relationship between inputs and outcomes is merely anecdotal, there remains a black box at the very centre of this study, as it were, which weakens the argument and results in a lack of practical knowledge. Hence, there is also the need to provide an explanation of *why* an impact has come about.

I conclude that, as a next step, the nature of "impact" needs to be specified in more generic ways. Furthermore, an explanation of why impact happened in the first place needs to be provided. I will proceed with a discussion of the kind of answer that would be required to satisfy potential sceptics.

11.1 The Door-Opener Mechanism

While I have shown in Chapter 4 that experimental behaviour is conducive to the generation of new organisational routines, these need not necessarily constitute effective solutions to bounded social problems. After all, the manifest possibility of failure is a constitutive feature of experiments. The resulting arrangements might as well fail to establish effective solutions and/ or to achieve this persistently and reliably. What is more, even if beneficial change can be observed it might not necessarily be causally related to the new organisational practices. The *explanatory* value of the identification of different factors which account for the creation of new practice thus remains limited.

According to the literature, new routines can only count as solutions to social problems if they successfully establish a *tight coupling* between organisational means and ends, that is, if organisational activities are causally linked to the desired outcomes (Bromley and Powell 2012: 14 and *passim*). The essence of tight coupling can be expressed in terms of a direct relation between two elements A and B by which A causally produces B.[1] For instance, tight coupling obtains in the case of an actor who purposefully switches on the light by means of pressing the light switch or of a soldier who reliably obeys the commands of his superiors. However, in the case of philanthropic interventions, the relationship between A and B is usually not immediate and simple, but dependent on intermediate processes. Hence, Seelos and Mair (2014) further demanded that the relationship of tight coupling between organisational means and ends be analysed in terms of the identification of generative social *mechanisms* which account for the regular and attributable creation of value.

In what follows I will argue that the identification of a social mechanism helps to reconstruct the required connection. It helps to understand the *type* of value which is created, *why* it is created in the first place, *how* it comes about and why it is created on a *regular* and not simply contingent basis. The identification of a mechanism thus considerably advances the understanding of the nature of the impact created by philanthropic action and it substantiates the claim *that* impact has occurred in the first place (Hedström and Swedberg 1998: 9). I will further argue that all four cases essentially rely on the same type of mechanism, albeit triggered in different ways.

11.1.1 The Role of Mechanisms

It has frequently been argued that mechanisms are important building blocks of scientific theories in general (Bunge 2004), and of theories in the social sciences in particular (Merton 1968). In discussions on the relevance of mechanisms for organisational research, their role in the establishment of managerial *control* is particularly highlighted (Tsoukas 1994; Bunge 2004; Davis and Marquis 2005; Weber 2006).

Mechanisms serve as the "nuts and bolts, cogs and wheels" Elster (1989: 3) of sociological inquiry as they *explain* regularities of social life by means of a specification of the cause-effect relationships between inputs and outcomes. They do so by means of the reconstruction of those structures and processes which produce the explanandum (Hedström and Swedberg 1998; Stinchcombe 1991; Tilly 2001; Mayntz 2004).

Importantly, mechanisms provide a particular type of explanation, because they are situated between mere working hypotheses on the one hand, and generic social laws on the other (Hedström and Swedberg 1998: 6). Mechanism-based theorising proceeds beyond the identification of idiosyncratic patterns of events as its results are applicable to phenomena which may occur in a variety of different situations (Bornmann 2010: 31). However, unlike laws, they do not necessitate outcomes. Rather, they are only activated if particular conditions obtain (Mayntz 2004).

Drawing on Coleman, mechanisms have thus been characterised as "sometimes-true-theories" (Stinchcombe 1991: 375) as they stipulate what an object endowed "with particular causal capabilities" (Tsoukas 1994: 290) is "capable of doing in the appropriate set of circumstances" (Tsoukas 1989: 553). For these reasons, mechanisms possess an intermediary degree of generality only, and their predictive capacity is limited (Elster 1989: 6–10). Due to these limitations, mechanisms have also been characterised as "bits of theory" (Stinchcombe 1991: 367) as opposed to more comprehensive social theories on a higher level of which they may be a part. Accordingly, their primary purpose is often to contribute to the coherence, accuracy or parsimony of these larger bodies of theory (Stinchcombe 1991: 367; Weber 2006: 121).

Mechanism-based research is further distinguished from the detection and analysis of *correlations* between inputs and outcomes since the mere diagnosis of a regularity between variables does not provide an explanation of why it occurs and thus renders the intermediate structures and processes a black box. The task of mechanism-based research, then, is to open up the black box and to reconstruct those structures and processes, which, through their interaction, tend to produce the correlation, given that necessary conditions prevail (Hedström and Swedberg 1998: 9; Elster 1989: 4–5; Mayntz 2004: 240; Bornmann 2010: 30–31). Hence, Hedström and Swedberg have proposed conceiving a mechanism as:

a systematic relationship between two entities, say *I* and *O*. In order to explain the relationship between them we search for a mechanism, *M*, which is such that on the occurrence of the cause or input, *I*, it generates the effect or outcome, *O*.

(Hedström and Swedberg 1998: 7, italics in the original)

These claims obviously rest on the assumption that inputs and outcomes are not directly coupled, but linked through a set of elements. Mechanisms thus further designate: "a set of interacting parts—an assembly of elements producing an effect not inherent in any one of them. A mechanism is . . . about . . . the wheelwork or agency by which an effect is produced" (Hernes 1998: 74).

Furthermore, if mechanisms do not operate like social laws but under certain conditions only, research needs to specify these and their interplay with the mechanism and show "*how,* by what intermediate steps, a certain outcome follows from a set of initial conditions" (Mayntz 2004: 241, italics in the original). In other words, the term "mechanism" refers to "*causal generalizations about recurrent processes*" which connect specific initial conditions and outcomes, if the necessary conditions are given (Mayntz 2004: 241, italics in the original). Mechanisms thus allow for fine-grained and deep explanations (Hedström and Swedberg 1998: 8). However, mechanisms as such cannot be observed, they are analytical constructions (Bornmann 2010: 31). Their presence, mode of operation and *gestalt* can only be inferred based on the observation of empirical situations and "their description is bound to contain concepts that do not occur in empirical data" (Bunge 2004: 200).

The starting point for mechanism-based research is always empirical in nature, namely "an observed or suspected regularity; a correlation; or a puzzling event, structure or process" (Mayntz 2004: 253). Mechanisms are then formulated by means of a retrospective hypothetical reconstruction of causal processes which lead to a given outcome, including the identification of necessary initial conditions and inputs (Mayntz 2004: 244).

Frequently cited examples of social mechanisms are the self-fulfilling prophecy, by which an initially wrong definition of the situation (e.g., the bankruptcy of a business) makes it come true, or the diffusion of innovation through networks in which actors adopt novel practices due to the observation that others have done so before. Both rely on the observation of the behaviour of other actors which shapes individuals' propensity for similar action, which, in turn, signals appropriateness to further actors (Davis and Marquis 2005: 336). According to Weiss (2000), the identification and application of social mechanisms is an integral part of the analysis of policy interventions, too. She identified "three basic mechanisms . . . that are powerful over very broad ranges of social behavior and social circumstances: incentives, authority, and ideas" (Weiss 2000: 87–93). She goes on to define incentives "as the direct or indirect use of sanctions or inducements to alter the calculus of costs and benefits associated with given behavior for the target individuals" (Weiss 2000: 88). In what follows, I will argue that all cases under investigation create impact by means of an incentive-based mechanism. In particular, I will argue for the crucial role of *resources* in these processes.

11.2 The Role of (Additional) Resources

Resources are one of the central components in the model of problem solving introduced in Chapter 3. But while I have explored the role of the other elements, namely actors, problems, barriers and goal-states as well as interventions, the role of resources has remained underexposed. It is this question I will now turn to.

I have repeatedly argued that processes of social innovation do not rely on philanthropic money only, as they also require the availability of a wide range of other resources. I have further pointed at the need to enhance capacity as a major requirement of successful problem solving because, in the case of complex social problems, single actors usually lack the necessary resources to tackle them effectively. Hence, philanthropic actors need to mobilize a broad set of additional *external* resources provided by other organisations or individuals. For instance, the CFoI made use of the files of public bureaucracies, The Chance relies on the workforce of adult youths and vacant jobs in regional firms, the Nuffield Foundation mobilised the knowledge and competencies of experts in the Council and its working parties, and the approach of Foundation Interkultur/Foundation anstiftung rests on the combination of the commitment and knowledge of gardeners on the one hand, and pieces of land on the other. In all these cases, foundations made use of assets they did not and could not possibly have at their own command. Yet, these very resources proved to be key to the solution of the problem they tackled.

11.3 Problem Solving as Door Opening and the Role of Resource Mobilisation

The successful cases in my sample were all based on a common operating "principle" (Mayntz 1997: 149) which relies on supply-demand relations. All interventions created social dynamics by means of *opening access to external resources*. The social problem to be solved was caused by the lack of resources on the part of a target group that valued those resources highly. The solution consisted in the identification of a pool of external resources apt to satisfy the needs of the target group, and in opening up access. In consequence, the target group actively and autonomously made use of the new opportunity. Philanthropic actors thus satisfied social demands by making accessible a wide array of resources or goods needed by the target group— be it social or legal status, information, support, knowledge or, of course, money—by applying the door-opening principle. By these means, they also solved the dilemma of limited funds and thus considerably limited their own financial contribution.[2] Figure 11.1 illustrates the elements and processes which constitute the mechanism.

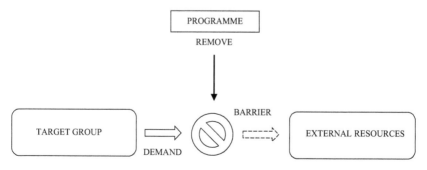

Figure 11.1 The Door-Opener Mechanism[3]

Put in somewhat metaphorical terms, the basic function of all four problem-solving interventions was to open up the doors for members of the target group who had a high self-interest in passing through the gate to get access to goods philanthropic actors do not and cannot provide themselves. If philanthropic organisations either establish or make use of such a situation, they set free or catalyse social dynamics in which new social configurations emerge that are driven by the interests of the actors involved; hence, they may become quite stable (Thümler and Bögelein 2010).

This circumstance has most clearly been perceived by The Chance which makes frequent references to this function. For instance, Foundation staff reported that they tell their trainees: "I am your door opener and I lay the red carpet to the firm for you". These findings confirm the results of implementation research which posit that programme success is more probable if an intervention aims at realising a state of affairs that the target group would aspire to achieve anyhow (Mayntz 1983: 22). Of course, this principle may also work the other way around and undermine programme success. For instance, philanthropic actors might mistakenly assume the existence of an urgent demand which is actually not there.

Importantly, there is not only one way to trigger the mechanism. In different problem situations, different barriers may inhibit access to resources. Depending on the kind of barrier, four different types of door-opener mechanisms could be identified. Sometimes, members of the target group cannot make use of existing resources because of a barrier that prohibits access. In these cases, philanthropic actors need to *open up access* to the resources. Sometimes, target groups lack the capabilities to make use of freely available resources. In this case, *capacity development* is the method of choice. Sometimes the necessary resources do not yet exist and need to be generated in the first place. Hence, philanthropic actors need to engage in *resource production*. Finally, actors may already have established access to available resources, but the process of resource mobilisation remains slow. Under these conditions, the process may need to be *catalysed* to enhance momentum.

11.3.1 Access Creation

Depending on the nature of the barrier, access can be facilitated by means of *brokering* activities. In case of resistance, however, it needs to be *enforced*. The ability of foundations to play a brokering role by virtue of being embedded in different social networks or fields has frequently been observed by scholars of philanthropy, and linked to the ability to generate innovations (Adloff 2010: 399). The role of brokers consists in the establishment of previously unconnected individuals, networks or organisations (Tilly 2001: 25–26; Adloff 2010: 398–399). The particular phenomenon of *resource brokerage* has mainly been discussed in studies of urban poverty. Brokers, be they organisations or individuals, bridge the gap between resource-rich actors such as businesses or public agencies and their target groups and thus enable the transfer of resources to the latter (Small 2006: 274, 277). My data show that the phenomenon of resource brokerage plays an important role for processes of philanthropic problem solving as well. In such cases, foundations open up access to resources that are—at least in principle— freely available by building a gateway between resources, or the keepers of the resources, and the target group. For instance, The Chance created a gateway for adolescents to access the labour market and thus enabled them to take vacant jobs. Staff described their contribution as follows:

> I do not realize my own ideas but take up those of the adolescents, their dreams, and derive concrete measures and give them hints as to where this could work, so that finally doors open up for them . . . they haven't seen before at all.

In other cases, however, the gatekeepers to resources resist the opening up of access. Under these conditions, mere brokerage does not work. Door opening requires the essentially political task of mobilising support and neutralising opponents to enforce access. This is what happened when Rowntree supported the CFoI's lobbying efforts for a Freedom of Information Act. Once the legislation was established, it opened up access to governmental files for journalists and citizens. These files pre-existed in their repositories, but only after a change of law could they be accessed and used.

The data further suggest that it makes a big difference if a programme has to overcome resistance, or not. In the case of the CFoI it did not suffice to realize access once and for all. Due to the contentious nature of the endeavor, it proved to be necessary to guard the Act permanently against attempts to constrict or abandon it altogether. The CFoI's role thus changed from a door opener to a door guardian. What is more, the activities required much more time to succeed (21 years) than any other programme. This is consistent with the insight of implementation research that programmes can be more easily implemented, the less resistance they provoke (Mayntz 1983: 22).

11.3.2 Capacity Development

Sometimes, members of the target group are unable to make use of existing resources, even though they can access them freely and without hindrance. Under these conditions, philanthropic actors need to build capacity in order to help them to access and use resources, which can happen in different ways. The importance of this principle is widely acknowledged both in the literature and in practice. It is defined as "the process through which individuals, organizations and societies obtain, strengthen and maintain the capabilities to set and achieve their own development objectives over time" (UNDP 2009: 4). Importantly, capacity development cannot be reduced to an instrumental function but also has an ethical dimension. For instance, in the case of Foundation Interkultur/Foundation anstiftung, gardeners stressed the need to change the situation of living through one's own efforts. One of them said:

> This is precisely . . . the empowerment-approach, that you don't feed the people and send them to the . . . food bank and say: Go and get your food. Then you will be doing fine. As recipients of alms. But they are rather supposed to look and ask: How can I change [the situation] myself?

In the case of The Chance, however, a different and particularly demanding variety of capacity development was employed which I will label "scaffolding". In principle, the necessary conditions for the door-opener mechanism to work were given as apprenticeship positions were available and most adolescents were able to apply and graduate successfully. However, Foundation staff reported that disadvantaged youths frequently suffered from a lack of personal discipline and perseverance in cases of problems which needed to be overcome for them to be able to make use of available positions. Hence, it is not enough to support them, for example by pointing out adequate vocations or by teaching them necessary skills. Rather, dysfunctional personal *routines* had to be addressed and changed. This was achieved by means of a complex regime of push and pull mechanisms which combine control and support elements. This aims at strengthening youths to cope with the difficulties of the process themselves, but also to set clear behavioural barriers and to enforce them. Senior staff illustrated this principle by means of the following example. Adolescents would sometimes contact the head of the Foundation at weekends, and also in the middle of the night:

> Then I say: "You are unemployed, well, all right, [call me] on Monday morning between 8 a.m. and 8.30 a.m. and not a minute later". . . . And it has never happened, nobody has ever been late. With one exception, and I gave him time for consideration as well and said: "Come back to me in one month".

11.3.3 Resource Generation

In the case of the CFoI and The Chance, resources are simply there and ready to be tapped. If, however, resources are unavailable, they must be organised, generated or produced in such a way as to complete the necessary elements for the door-opener mechanism to work. This is what the Nuffield Foundation did. It reacted to the call of practitioners who regarded a lack of independent and informed advice in the field of bioethics as a major problem for their work. The existence of an urgent need for this type of resource could thus be taken as given. The programme was further embedded in a professional environment which clearly disposed of the necessary capacities to make use of high-quality information and advice. As the Council joins experts in different collaborative formats, who have the expertise required to identify and discuss problematic issues and to prepare reports as well as to make recommendations, it taps and pools expert knowledge in such a way as to create the necessary resources which are then freely distributed to practitioners, researchers and the wider public. In a similar vein, the establishment of an intercultural garden by local activists can be regarded as the creation and provision of a very complex set of resources, including plots of land, which are then used by the gardeners in autonomous ways.

11.4 Catalysis, Overlap and Change

Sometimes, the process of access to resources has been started by the target group and the gateway has been set up independently of a foundation's intervention. In these cases, the process may be supported, intensified or enhanced. Foundation Interkultur did so by providing financial support, scientific expertise, public relations and networking opportunities to a self-organized type of gardening that had already developed on its own. It thus employed a catalysing role, combining the different tasks of capacity builder on the one hand, for example through networking and the generation and distribution of knowledge, and door opener, through modest financial support, on the other. It thus helped to create favourable conditions for the intercultural garden movement to emerge and for the number of gardens to increase.

A similar diagnosis applies to all those cases in which new problem-solving arrangements have been successfully established by philanthropic organisations. This demonstrates that the different roles may be combined, and they may also change over time. For instance, the CFoI focussed on building access to public files for 21 years. At the same time it aimed at creating a better, more adequate gateway by means of intense research processes. Beyond that, it worked towards raising the awareness and appetite of the media as one of its major target groups. Later in the process, and after the law had been implemented, its role changed. The organisation now focuses on preserving and catalysing the established process. While the CFoI keeps protecting the FOI law, it also increasingly engages in capacity building on behalf of requesters and civil servants to enhance the operation of the system and the quality of its work. In a similar vein, the Nuffield Council has started an education programme to enhance the understanding of and interest in bioethics among students in schools.

The case of the CFoI further demonstrates that the gateway can be shaped in different ways, and over time. As a result of its lobbying activities, the British government chose to implement a law that was at first perceived as rather restrictive. Yet, CFoI staff reported that it was interpreted in rather liberal ways and thus proved to be better than expected. Scotland, on the other hand, adopted a more encompassing FOI legislation with lower restrictions to access right from the beginning.

Importantly, the door-opener mechanism need not necessarily be conceived as a one-way street, as might be the case in emergency relief programmes. Members make best use of the newly available assets if they mobilize their own resources. By the combination of both, impact comes about. For instance, in the case of intercultural gardens, interviewees emphasised the importance of prior migrant knowledge:

> we must assume that a lot of knowledge is there and it can be made fruitful anew, if . . . you get public actors such as cities or the churches, to provide land . . . for this specific purpose which furthers the common purpose.

In the case of the Nuffield Foundation, the newly generated knowledge, ideas and recommendations are not valuable per se, either. They are only meaningful if they are integrated in the much more comprehensive professional practice of public policymakers or researchers. Similarly, in the case of the CFoI, access to governmental files is particularly influential if journalists make professional use of the information. Finally, in the case of The Chance, a clear win-win situation emerges as firms provide economic resources to their new staff, while trainees contribute their workforce. The door-opener mechanism thus helps to recognise that the members of the target group are not simply recipients of help. Instead, they contribute their own resources and thus become an active part of the solution, rather than

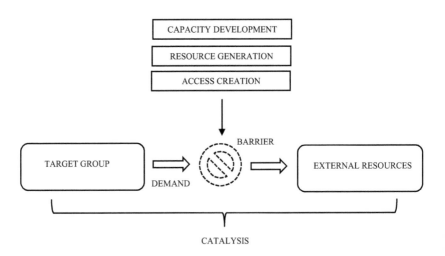

Figure 11.2 Triggers of the Door-Opener Mechanism

being conceived as part of the problem only. Figure 11.2 illustrates these multiple dimensions of the mechanism as well as the different ways to trigger it.

11.5 Impact as Access to Advantage

Based on these considerations, I conclude that social impact occurs if the activities of philanthropic actors open up, broaden or preserve access to resources to the members of a particular target group, given that such access is perceived as a desirable state of affairs by the target group and other relevant stakeholders in a particular field, whereas a lack of access is regarded as a social problem. This definition entails a number of important implications.

First, interventions do not aim at creating benefits directly, but at enhancing the capabilities of the members of the target group.[4] Under these conditions, a significant number of beneficiaries will make use of these newly won opportunities, but not necessarily all of them. Philanthropy as a largely non-coercive exercise that lacks democratic legitimacy profits from this emphasis on individual autonomy: if the creation of social impact is basically about the generation of opportunities with the intention to open up access to external resources, it is left to the members of the target group to decide if they make use of them or not. The approach thus works against tendencies to paternalism as one of the inherent weaknesses of philanthropy (Anheier 2005: 131).

Second, the chosen approach suggests a conception of social impact which may include long-term as well as short-term effects. In the literature there is an inclination to exclude the short-term outputs of non-profit action and rather conceive it in terms of "more fundamental, long-term effects" (Flynn and Hodgkinson 2001: 7). Against this, Roche defines impact as "significant or lasting changes in people's lives, brought about by a given action or series of actions" (Roche 1999: 21), arguing that in cases of emergency relief only these former effects are required. Assuming that this type of short-term support may often be a necessary condition for the solution of individual problems, for instance, in cases of emergency relief, short-term impact is certainly an important option for prosocial philanthropists.

Third, consistent with pragmatist theory, impact may occur in a variety of different forms. The resource-mobilisation model is thus compatible with different conceptions of impact which have been put forward in the literature. For instance, in the context of research on social movements, impact has been determined as collective benefits realised for a group of beneficiaries (Giugni 1999: xxii). Proponents of effective altruism, on the other hand, put particular emphasis on benefits at the individual level (Pogge 2011). The latter notion of social impact as an individual benefit has been put forward in a variety of different ways. Frequently, benefits are defined as the degree to which the well-being of clients or beneficiaries is enhanced or to which previously unmet human needs are satisfied (Provan and Milward 1995; Howaldt and Schwarz 2010; Caulier-Grice et al. 2012; Kroeger and Weber 2014). Others argue that the concept of social impact should be reserved for broader processes of social change, such as change at the community level (Turrini et al. 2010: 533–534), systemic or even nationwide change (Liket 2014: 49). The resource-based model of impact is compatible with all of these positions. For instance, in the case of The Chance, the intervention primarily aims at the generation of individual advantage. However, the organisation also emphasises the collective benefits which result out of its work. In the case of the CFoI, the focus is in the opposite direction: the approach primarily aims at the generation of a more transparent society. Yet, this is achieved by means of action motivated by the satisfaction of individual preferences. These considerations suggest that no sharp differentiation between impact at the individual and at the collective level needs to be drawn. Rather, benefits occur at both levels and, depending on emphasis, either the one or the other will be the focus of attention.

11.6 Conclusion

I have argued that social impact in a pragmatist sense can best be understood as a particular instance of successful social problem solving. In the cases under investigation, the generation of impact can be explained by means of the philanthropic door-opener mechanism. It is activated if philanthropic interventions render accessible valued resources to their target groups by different means. They thus create states of affairs which are regarded as advantageous from the point of view of the target group and the societal environments in which foundations operate. Seen that way, explications of why impact occurs, and of why it matters in normative terms, coincide. At the same time, the model explains why processes of growth, which are frequently regarded as a major managerial challenge, play such a moderate role in all the four cases.

However, an important task still remains open. The *structural* preconditions and consequences of the pragmatist model of action need to be explored in more depth. In what follows I will show that and how the concept of "niches" can be applied to the cases under investigation. Equipped with a more nuanced understanding of the strategies which play a role in processes of social innovation and of how interventions create value, based on the exploitation of external resources, I can now determine the nature and role of innovative niches in more depth.

Notes

1 Coupling may occur between a broad array of different kinds of elements, such as individuals, organisations, environments (Orton and Weick 1990: 208), means

and ends (Weick 1976: 4; Bromley and Powell 2012) as well as intentions and actions (Weick 1976: 4).

2 At the heart of the door-opener mechanism there lies the principle of rational choice. Put in the words of Coleman, the role of philanthropic organisations consists in the redistribution of the control over resources. They assist actors with a high interest in, yet no or low control over, particular resources to gain and keep exercising control. As the initial discrepancy is reduced, they further a social equilibrium in terms of a situation that enhances the satisfaction of all participants and thus create an overall "better-off" state of affairs (Coleman 1990: 28–40).

3 Adapted from Thümler and Bögelein (2010).

4 In these regards the model is highly consistent with the capability approach as developed by Amartya Sen (e.g., Sen 1980; 1985; 1993) and others. Sen claims that in assessing the well-being of persons, we should focus on the opportunities they actually have to lead the lives they value, and have reason to value (Robeyns 2006: 351). Hence, social impact in a meaningful sense occurs if the activities of philanthropic actors either enhance the overall capability sets of the members of its target group or the capabilities of society at large.

12 Towards a Model of Philanthropic Niches and Intelligent Niching

In Chapters 10 and 11, I have explored the strategies and mechanisms which are conducive to social problem solving. I have found that problems as non-routine situations require a departure from habitual types of action and the exploration of more effective novel practices, which are then stabilised and exploited. I further proposed that the preconditions for social impact are created in the course of this process as philanthropic organisations open up access to a pool of external resources to target groups whose members value these resources highly. In other words, a major avenue for foundations and their grantees to achieve desirable effects consists in the establishment of the door-opener mechanism by means of experimental action and its subsequent exploitation through continuous use.

In what follows I will substantiate my claim that niche structures render these functions possible in the first place. I will demonstrate how, through the lens of strategic niche management, the sample cases can be interpreted as instances of philanthropic niches and that the related activities of philanthropic organisation can meaningfully be described as niching behaviour. I will further demonstrate how philanthropic niches differ in kind and in purpose from the niches introduced in SNM and go on to develop a notion of philanthropic niches as an analytical category which is sui generis.

Finally, I will show how the organisations which were introduced in my sample cases can be differentiated along a typology of niche actors, depending on the niche level on which they operate and the contributions they provide.

12.1 Philanthropic Niches

In Chapter 5, I introduced transformation research and the approach of SNM as major instruments for the analysis and management of the structural aspects of radical socio-technological innovation. I proposed that, while SNM has not been created to cover bounded processes of social problem solving like those investigated in this study, it can be modified in such a way as to be applicable to my data.

When it comes to the explanation and design of processes of radical innovation, the literature on SNM assigns particular relevance to innovative niches in terms of protected, bounded and stable social spaces in which emerging innovations are shielded from unfavourable selection mechanisms for longer periods of time until they can compete and survive under mainstream conditions. They are created, maintained and modified for purposes of the experimental generation of novel knowledge, practices and artefacts.

As a first step I will investigate if and to what degree boundaries, protection and stability as major properties of niches apply to the cases under investigation. This conceptual transfer is not least suggested by the foundations' statements about their work. For instance, Foundation Interkultur made extensive use of spatial metaphors, referring to intercultural gardens as "oases" which open up a public realm for free autonomous engagement, (inter)action, participation and encounter with a diversity of people: "the precise opposite of a space oriented towards consumption". Senior staff of the Nuffield Foundation explicitly referred to the concept of niches to emphasise the relevance of claiming uncontested societal terrain to avoid resistance by the incumbents of power: "we see our niche as being one that isn't filled by other bodies, so I don't think we're in competition with them".

12.1.1 The Role of Boundaries

Boundaries play an essential role in the creation and maintenance of niches as they define those characteristics which both distinguish niches from and position them in their societal environments. Importantly, similar to ecological niches, innovative niches are not exhaustively described by locating interventions in time and space. In the cases under investigation, the demarcation of territory vis-à-vis organisational environments occurs along geographic, cognitive and social lines. Niche boundaries are a function of the locus of activities, be it on the local, regional or national level; the actors, including major target groups and stakeholders; and the issues, including problem definitions and goal situations.

The Chance is a rather straightforward case in point. The scale and scope of its operations is limited by geographic (six cantons in Eastern Switzerland) and thematic (youth unemployment) boundaries as well as by a clearly defined target group. Over time, these boundaries have been extended to a very limited degree only. While the organisation now accepts graduates of higher secondary schools, its target group is still defined as youth aged 15 to 22 with a "positive attitude" who leave school without a contract for an apprenticeship position or who are about to quit their trainee position (The Chance 2015a). The Nuffield Foundation and the Campaign for the Freedom of Information (CFoI) are both engaged at a national level and their target groups are rather broad, in the case of the Nuffield Council increasingly so. Yet, both organisations are committed to well-defined issues, as the Council chose bioethics as a limited domain in the highly diverse field of medical and technological ethics, whereas the CFoI not only specialised in the issue of freedom of information, but, more specifically, on the establishment, protection and enhancement of a particular piece of legislation.

In important respects, boundaries are neither a simple matter of definition, nor clear cut and stable. Rather, they are created, maintained and revised by means of active boundary work. Organisational narratives play an important role in these processes, which are sometimes highly political in nature, as they may conflict with the interests of external as well as internal stakeholders (Santos and Eisenhardt 2009; Smith and Raven 2012: 1032).

Take the case of Foundation Interkultur/Foundation anstiftung: boundaries were constituted by a definition of the issue, that is, support of the particular organisational template of intercultural gardens. However, as the Foundation chose a very wide approach to further its aims, which includes a broad variety of different activities, boundaries were all but self-evident. Under these conditions, the importance of a continual negotiation and determination of focus increases and boundary work was regarded as a key task of organisational leadership. Senior staff said:

> Clarity is very important. That is, to have a clear organisational direction, to keep defining it anew in daily practice . . . and thus also to distinguish between practice worthy of support and practice which may lead astray. Where you say: No, this does not belong to it. . . , I'd say that this is my main task, to sharpen the ability to distinguish . . . and to keep making clear decisions, in which direction we are going and in which direction we are not.

The relevance of boundaries is further signalled by the fact that niching organisations such as The Chance: Foundation for Vocational Practice in Eastern Switzerland, Nuffield Council on Bioethics, Foundation Interkultur and the Campaign for Freedom of Information all demarcate the terrain on which they operate in their *names*. They thus contrast with the Foundations anstiftung, Nuffield and Rowntree, which all pursue much more general purposes.

The cases further show that niche boundaries are neither contingent nor disadvantageous nor a result of organisational disability. On the contrary, they serve important functions. In particular, they limit problem complexity as they reduce uncertainty, contention and the need for material resources, and thus enhance control over the problem situation and the intervention.

The cognitive advantages of niching are illustrated by the difference between Rowntree's large and growing Democracy programme, and the much stronger focus of the CFoI which facilitates action and makes the chosen problem more tractable. This observation is consistent with Weick's emphasis on "the importance of *limits* for both the solution and the problem to distinguish the solution of small wins from the larger, more open-ended solutions that define problems more diffusely" (Weick 1984: 43, italics in the original).

Organizations such as The Chance profit from these limitations as they reduce the need to mobilise resources on an overly large scale. Nuffield senior staff also underlined this function, suggesting that instead of expanding its operations as suggested by the Council, it should best be "sticking to the actual substance of the things . . . because [otherwise] it could consume a lot of energy".

For the Nuffield Foundation, the drawing of thematic boundaries served an important political function, as well. Knowing that the new activities were potentially conceived with scepticism by established stakeholders in the field, "a lot of diplomacy and politics" was involved in the early stages of the process. In particular, clear boundaries needed to be drawn vis-à-vis the medical domain: "that was part of the early politics, because the . . . medical bodies would have been very unhappy . . . about some third party pronouncing on clinical ethics". Today, the Council has become an established actor in its field. At the same time, however, it is part of a densely populated environment of similar bodies. According to Foundation staff, this reaffirms the need to take care that boundaries, even as the Council expands in terms of target groups, are maintained in such a way as not to tread on other's actors terrain. The restriction to issues of bioethics thus had a dual function. It helped to demarcate "an important territory for us, a distinctive territory for us, but also thereby not threatening or cutting across the territory that belonged to others".

Importantly, boundaries are drawn on different levels, establishing different types of niches. In the case of local niching, foundations or their grantees determine the limits of particular interventions as they define the problem, the target groups and major stakeholders, and the field of operation. This happened when The Chance chose to limit its operations to unemployed adolescents in Eastern Switzerland. In the case of niching behaviour on a global level, boundaries demarcate the totality of different interventions which serve a similar purpose. The creation of the association Check Your Chance represents the attempt to create a field of similar non-profit organisations tackling youth unemployment across the whole of Switzerland, based on a different and much wider definition of problem, stakeholders and geography.

12.1.2 The Role of Protection

The notion of protection refers to all those activities which are supposed to help niches to become established, and to prevail. *Passive protection* is achieved by positioning interventions in favourable societal environments which are not crowded by other actors, in order to avoid competition or resistance.

For instance, The Chance purposefully chose an intermediate position between the systems of public education and of private business, which can be regarded as an important prerequisite for their freedom of manoeuvre. Intercultural gardens are not positioned on the most valuable building areas but on urban wasteland or property which is freely provided by public authorities or private supporters.

Niches further profit from a focus on uncontentious themes and the avoidance of controversy. Such passive protection may also be practised through the co-option of potential opponents. In the case of the Nuffield Foundation, senior staff reported that:

> one of the early decisions was to get the then president of the Royal College of Physicians onto the Council. . . . I suspect, for her, it was quite a big decision, to back this horse rather than to try and persuade her own college they should do it themselves.

These findings are consistent with prior research on the relevance of niches in processes of systemic innovation under conditions of both uncertainty and contention. For instance, Thümler (2015) found that actors who sought to develop a new model of regional educational governance in the German state of North Rhine-Westphalia pursued a "cheese dome-strategy". The project purposefully designed activities in such a way as to remain under the radar of potential opponents in order to facilitate learning processes and stabilise results. An informant described the approach as follows:

> We put a cheese dome on the region, . . . which is transparent. . . . Everybody can look inside if one wants to. You can also lift it. But I only lift it, if I am supposed to do so. And this protection from certain preventive influences which come too early has obviously facilitated developments, which could not be reversed.
>
> (Thümler 2015: 63)

Active protection refers to all activities intended to shield niches through the defence of external threats. In the cases of Nuffield and Interkultur, this included attempts at discouraging potential competitors as well as resistance to friendly take-overs. This is remarkable, because operating foundations often aim at the adoption of their innovations by other, preferably public, actors in order to set free resources for new processes of innovation. This was different in the sample cases. For instance, when the Nuffield Council was under threat of being replaced by a public body, Foundation staff tried to intervene early on to prevent this from happening. Senior staff reported that, when they "got wind" of plans to create a governmental council on issues of bioethics, they quickly sought a conversation with the official in charge of this project so as to highlight the unfavourable consequences this might have for government. In their view, this intervention was successful:

> You could see him thinking: actually, there are a lot of advantages to us in not having to do all that, and in having reports that we can, frankly,

take or leave. . . . [The official] was clearly thinking: this will be a bloody nuisance.

However, possible competition was also perceived from other angles. Senior Foundation staff said:

there're now big networks of clinical research ethics committees . . . sometimes they sort of drive towards that, and we kind of push them back again and say: actually, your terms of reference are about medical and scientific research and what comes out of it.

In a similar vein, Foundation Interkultur sought to protect its niche as they opposed attempts by other organisations to claim responsibility for it or intervene in this field. Senior staff said:

there were two foundations, they wanted to take over . . . what we set up. They said: Yes, a good idea, we'll do it. And then they began to act in this direction. . . . After consultation with us, they let it be. . . . Then there was an attempt by environmental organisations to rebrand all of that as intercultural-ecological gardens. . . . We had talks as well and that's over now, too. So, time and again there have been a number of small attempts at take-overs.

The Foundation also sought to provide support to more precarious gardens, for example in cases of conflict regarding their land, be it by means of direct support and advice or, indirectly, by mobilising the support of powerful stakeholders such as local politicians.

The cases further show that the integrity of boundaries may also be put under pressure from *internal* stakeholders who seek to expand their favourite aspects of the intervention, or the intervention as a whole. In the context of foundations, this involves protection from the founder himself, if still alive and active. In the case of grantees, it refers to freedom from interventions of the funding foundation. This is due to the fact that foundation management and founders are frequently laymen in the fields in which they operate. In the case of The Chance, for instance, the founder purposefully decided not to be directly involved in operations. Instead, he described his role as a mere facilitator: "I was delighted by the professional work of Foundation staff. I have catered for the necessary financial resources, so that work could go on" (The Chance 2014a: 6).

Compared with protection, philanthropic foundations are more obvious candidates for niche support through processes of *nurturing*. All the cases did this by mobilising a considerable and broad amount of material, social and cultural resources. Without this support, some would not have been created in the first place, and nor would they have prevailed. However, with the exception of Rowntree, they did much more than this. The activities of Interkultur/anstiftung are a prime example of this broad spectrum of contributions, accompanied with the aim of broadening and deepening niche growth. The organisation triggered, sustained and deepened the processes of learning in and across local gardens through the generation, consolidation and distribution of context-free knowledge. It facilitated interaction among local actors through the building and maintenance of networks. More than all the other actors it engaged in the articulation of expectations about the potential returns of intercultural gardening.[1]

Finally, philanthropic actors *empower* niches if they try to make the innovation "fit and conform" with incumbent regimes in order to pave the way for entry in a regime that remains more or less unaltered otherwise (Kemp et al. 1998; Smith and Raven 2012: 1030). For instance, the CFoI pursued a comprehensive research programme with the intention of developing a law that was tailor-made to the situation in the UK. Furthermore, superior knowledge generated by research and continuous activity in the field helped to recognise potential threats at an early stage and to develop tailor-made defence strategies.

It needs to be acknowledged that the single dimensions discussed above are sometimes hard to distinguish. Some organisational activities may serve multiple purposes, depending on the stage of the process of innovation. For instance, the mobilisation of context-free knowledge through the CFoI helped to empower its activities by means of creating tailor-made drafts of freedom of information legislation. After the enactment of the Freedom of Information Act, knowledge served both the purposes of nurturing (to enhance the effectiveness of the established FOI system) and protection (to detect possible avenues of criticism and develop and substantiate counter-arguments).

The above discussion results in three important findings. First, the relevance of protection contrasts with mainstream philanthropic research and practice. When it comes to the interaction between foundations and public bureaucracies, foundations and philanthropists are frequently portrayed as actors who stage attacks on inertia-ridden systems, and who prevail if they exhibit proactive "bold" leadership (Heifetz et al. 2004; Tayart de Borms 2003; Greene 2005; Hess 2005a; Clemens and Lee 2010; but see Ansell et al. 2009; Reckhow 2013). The analysis of my cases paints a different picture as it portrays innovations as inherently unstable and vulnerable endeavours, particularly at the early stages of development. It reaffirms the relevance of protection from environmental threats, such as opposition by competitors.

Second, the broad range of activities required to sustain and nurture niche activities points to the need for a more comprehensive and more targeted understanding of how foundations may contribute to the performance of grantees; obviously, this requires much more than simply writing cheques. Consistent with the findings on grassroots' niches discussed in Chapter 5, my data analysis also reaffirms the diagnosis that the use of different modes of protection and support depends on the properties of the problem situation, along with the values, interests and motivations of actors. If, in the case of Interkultur/anstiftung, niching is supposed to contribute to the emergence of an alternative to incumbent regimes, and if actors are outright opposed to the prevailing rules and norms, empowerment is clearly no reasonable option.

Third, protection and support do not necessarily come from outside the niche. Local niche actors actively seek to protect themselves, nurture learning processes and empower their niche, if necessary. They are supported by niche actors at the global level—sometimes in similar, sometimes in different, ways.

12.1.3 The Role of Stability and Growth

The literature on SNM emphasises the relevance of the stability of niches. It is argued that processes of evolutionary learning and the co-evolution of complex socio-technological arrangements require considerable time. Furthermore, niche actors who aim at regime change are dependent on favourable environmental developments in terms of regime crises which are beyond their control. Hence, under conditions of unfavourable selection mechanisms, innovative niches need to be stabilised over long periods of time.

Stability is characteristic of the cases under investigation as well. For instance, in the case of the Joseph Rowntree Charitable Trust (JRCT), interviewees emphasised the role of long-term funding for processes of advocacy and learning as this willingness "preserved the resource of knowledge over the years". What is more, boundaries remained quite stable over time in all the cases. This is regarded as an important precondition for experimental organisational learning processes, because the detection of causal relations between organisational action and its environmental effects is dependent on the stability of the problem situation (Van de Ven et al. 2008: 80).

However, the cases also suggest that stability matters for different reasons and in different respects. To begin with, all the foundations pursued an open-ended niching strategy, tackling the chosen problem long term. This is evident in the case of the JRCT, which provided 21 years of funding to the CFoI to achieve the enactment of an FOI law, and still sustains its support. The evaluation of its Power and Responsibility programme (the successor to the Democracy programme) concluded that the ability of funding long term instead of going for quick and cheap wins was an important reason for the Trust's social impact. In the case of the CFoI, the author further highlighted the importance of the fact that the Trust continued to provide support although, once the FOIA was enacted, the "mission accomplished" box could have been ticked and support withdrawn (Ellis 2012).

This stands in contrast to a widely shared, yet rather problematic, conviction that foundations should operate as innovators who serve as the developers of new solutions to public problems which are then adopted and rolled out by public authorities (e.g., Gerber 2006; Bacchetti and Ehrlich 2007; Person et al. 2009). This was not the case here. All foundations in my sample shared the conviction that public actors are not supposed to take over because philanthropic actors did what public actors "cannot, will not or should not do" (senior staff of Nuffield Foundation). For instance, The Chance was convinced that public bureaucracies cannot provide similar services as they lack the flexibility and commitment necessary for this kind of work. Nuffield and its partners argued that there was value in the autonomous organisation of the process of ethical inquiry, which should be shielded from both political and corporate interests. The CFoI clearly responded to the observation that government was not willing to introduce a comprehensive FOI legislation and reliably sustain it. For Interkultur/ anstiftung, all three "don'ts" may have played a role.

Stability also applies to the scale and scope of the niches. In all cases except for Interkultur/anstiftung, organisations exhibited limited to moderate levels of growth only, and they all kept operating in the thematic confines of the chosen niche, rather than diversifying their activities. This can be explained by a number of different reasons. First, except for urban gardening, actors were embedded in densely populated environments of similar public and (increasingly) private bodies which prohibits expansion. Second, growth is inhibited by a lack of resources. In economic theory, niches are regarded as places characterised by unserved needs or demands. The richer they are in resources, the more attractive it becomes for firms to serve them. The discussion of the door-opener mechanism demonstrated that philanthropic niches also involve target populations with a high, yet unsatisfied, need for different types of resources. Niches further contain resources of different kinds which are mobilised as a means to solve the problem under attack—be it governmental files, gardens, apprenticeships and jobs, or information and advice in the field of bioethics. Yet, while firms reap the resources available in the niches they serve themselves, non-profits don't, but their beneficiaries do. While the satisfaction of unserved needs by means of the provision of untapped external resources is a highly efficient technique, it is still dependent on a steady provision of material resources. The CFoI and The Chance have their own, if moderate, sources of income through fees for services, but they do not cover full costs in either case. Opposed to business firms, philanthropic niches do not promise a sufficient return on investment, which is why they are served by non-profit organisations in the first place. At the same time, this is why their growth implies an increase in costs, which sets limits to the degree of potential expansion.

The Chance provides a further reason for the virtue of stability in terms of size. Its expansion to two additional cantons was made possible by substantial additional funding. At the same time, the organisation refused to cover the whole of Switzerland, arguing that this would overwhelm organisational capacities and undermine the very capabilities which were regarded as a prerequisite for effectiveness, namely a highly flexible organisation capable of maintaining a very close relationship with adolescents and firms and the availability of large informal networks. The following events showed that the Foundation's judgement was right as even the moderate dimension of growth posed subsequent problems in terms of sustainability, once the additional funding ended.

Finally, further growth may simply not be desirable. In the case of the CFoI, it saw no need to expand its activities because new actors emerged in the field who provided additional services on their own. The CFoI further claims that an increase in the numbers of requests would be detrimental to its cause, for this might result in higher overall costs of the FOI system. Moreover, it could result in more "frivolous" (i.e., meaningless or overly huge) requests, all of which would make the system of FOI vulnerable to criticism. According to Campaign staff, it would be better if figures remained stable and if the quality of requests rather than the quantity of use increased.

12.2 Niche Actors and Types of Niching

SNM further posits that there are two types of niche levels: local and global. They correspond with two different types of niche actors. These distinctions do not refer to geography, Rather, they designate essentially different types of roles and contributions. "Local" niche actors are the *developers* of innovation and the *producers* of value, whereas global actors play a more indirect, intermediary role. They seek to create or support populations of local actors by means of the generation of favourable ecosystems which provide a broad spectrum of supportive external conditions. Recall the model of problems and problem solving in Chapter 3. In case of success, local actors organise and sustain the transfer of a particular problem situation into the goal state. This process is dependent on contextual conditions in important regards, because environments contain institutions, interests, resources and opportunity structures which may support or undermine problem solving. While local niche actors may actively try to cope with, influence or change their environments, these are often beyond their reach. Global niche actors such as intermediary organisations may be better positioned to do so, and to do it in different ways. The case studies show that there is another, different type of actor which does not fit in either category. Organisations of this type are active across many niches, specializing in none. Hence, they operate on supra niche level and provide distinct services to actors on local and intermediary levels. Let me discuss this distinction in more detail.

12.2.1 Local Actors as Producers of Value

Local actors are the "carriers" of innovation and the producers of value. They create innovative arrangements which generate the desired outcomes. For these purposes they develop novel knowledge, practices and artefacts in processes of experimentation and bricolage and sustain them over time. However, their activities are limited to tackling chunks of much broader problems. Also, their contributions may remain idiosyncratic to the specific local situation and they frequently remain small in size as they lack access to sufficient resources and support by incumbents of regime positions.

The Chance is a straightforward instance of such a local niche actor. It engages in a process of continuous production of value through the provision of long-term support to its trainees. For these purposes, it developed new practices and capacities which are composed in such a way as to expose their trainees to a complex regime of support and control mechanisms for a considerable period of time. All these activities are highly dependent on and adapted to its regional situation.

For most of its existence, though, The Chance remained an organisational loner. The recent creation of the intermediary association Check Your Chance demonstrates vividly how outside actors may help transcend the limitations of local or regional actors through the promotion of a new understanding of hitherto separate organisations as members of a common endeavour. Today, The Chance regards itself as part of the global niche of non-profit organisations active in the field of transition from school to labour. The connection with other local actors in a global network further strengthened the organisation through the possibility of exchanging information and seeking advice. Finally, it profited from the creation of a common representative body which helps to gain access to resourceful regime actors on a national level.

Similar to The Chance, the Nuffield Council engages in production activities as it organises and facilitates the process of the generation and distribution of knowledge. It does so by creating an environment which is tailor-made for the production of these particular outcomes. Senior staff said that "the creative thing is to develop environments in which these connections can emerge and then to find the description and the structure or the framework in which they can continue, then, to function together".

In doing so, it is part of the much larger field of organisations which address ethical problems in the sciences and, particularly, medicine. However, while the field is populated by regime actors only, the Council has carved out its own, private niche of which it is the only inhabitant, as it were.

12.2.2 Intermediary Actors as Shapers of Favourable Ecosystems

Global niche actors seek to build favourable environments with the purpose of facilitating the work of local niche actors. They do so by providing *global niche support* through the creation of networks among single actors on the one hand and regime actors on the other. They further build supportive infrastructure as they engage in the generation of context-free knowledge, its storage and distribution; advocate by means of expectation management;

and enhance local managerial or organisational capacity. At the same time, they are detached from concrete local niche activities and lack the means to directly influence them, hence their contributions may go astray or spin in the void. Global niche actors thus seek to enhance the ecosystem surrounding single interventions in order to support the effectiveness, sustainability and, potentially, the growth of the niche population.

Foundation Interkultur pursued such an approach as it did not run projects on its own but chose to support the activities of local activists who create and maintain intercultural gardens as the locus of value creation. As opposed to Rowntree, however, the Foundation did not restrict its contribution to the financial support of a multitude of actors and causes. Rather, it mobilised the entire toolkit of intermediary organisations as described in the SNM literature. This way, it provided a broad array of support to an increasing number of local niche actors, from financial funding to the provision of knowledge and advice. In particular, however, it strengthened the *global* niche level by means such as networking, aggregation and distribution of knowledge and advocacy—not least through the development of the successful generic label of "intercultural" gardens.

Similar to Foundation Interkultur, the CFoI does not engage in production activities itself, and never has. As a result of a long process of advocacy, it contributed to the emergence of the newly established FOI system in the UK. Like Interkultur, the CFoI employs the wide range of SNM instruments such as networking, advocacy, knowledge distribution and advice to support the activities of a variety of different actors who now populate the niche. The case of the CFoI is special in that the FOI system has become an established part of the legal and administrative system in the UK. Following the logic of SNM, this might lead to the opening up of the niche and the withdrawal of protection, which is precisely what Rowntree, as the major funder, had planned. However, regardless of its institutionalisation, the FOI system is still the object of attempts to constrain its scope and to limit rights of those making requests of it. Although the innovation may have become an integral part of the dominant regime, it may still require continuous protection and support.

12.2.3 Actors on Supra Niche Level

Organisations such as Foundation anstiftung, the Joseph Rowntree Charitable Trust and Nuffield Foundation cannot properly be qualified as local niche actors because none of them engages in the direct production of value on a local level. They are not proper intermediaries, either. Organisations such as Rowntree do not exhaust the full potential of intermediary options for action. If they do, as with the Foundation anstiftung, they support a rather broad range of activities instead of a particular type such as intercultural gardens. Most importantly, they are not specialised in the support of

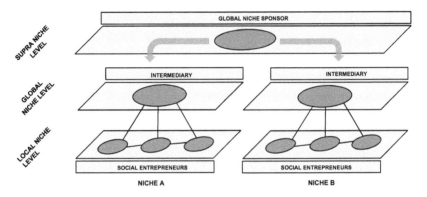

Figure 12.1   Niche Structure

a particular niche. Rather, they all operate on a higher level of abstraction, spanning different niches. While they may entertain direct contact with both intermediary and local actors, they themselves operate from a somewhat detached position. However, as generalists rather than specialists, they may profit from a broader thematic horizon which covers developments in different fields of society. Compared with activists such as the CFoI or local gardeners, they are in a better position to access societal elites in order to mobilise resources. The cases of Interkultur, The Chance and the Nuffield Council demonstrate that they may also be well positioned to create new intermediary organisations. Figure 12.1 illustrates the interplay between organisations on the three different niche levels.

12.3 Niche Management and Control

I have argued that local, global and supra niche actors pursue different targets and fulfil different functions. There is yet another important dimension which distinguishes the three: they operate under different conditions in terms of managerial control—an issue that has been identified as a research gap in the literature on complex social problem solving in Chapter 3. This pertains both to the production of value as well as to organisational governance structures.

For instance, both the CFoI and the Nuffield Council exert a substantial degree of control over the process of value production, although they rely on the collaboration with autonomous actors such as trainees and contributors to working parties. In the case of The Chance, this is due to the fact that trainees are disciplined by means of the technique of scaffolding which was introduced earlier as a particular type of capacity development.

The Nuffield Council, on the other hand, has no authority over its contributors whatsoever. Furthermore, it keeps addressing new topics in each report. Hence, the precise outcomes of this work can never be specified in advance. Yet, processes and outputs are highly standardised in formal regards, which serves as an established coupling mechanism and results in enhanced conformity of behaviour of their contributors (Firestone 1984: 10–11). Nuffield Council staff described their function as the provision of a structured space which renders possible creative, yet targeted and productive, interaction. They talked of a "box in which people then know their position and their relation to each other, when they do have to work in a common environment".

The situation is fundamentally different for Foundation Interkultur and the CFoI. They both rely on the contributions of entirely autonomous actors as well, but neither organisation can make use of direct coupling mechanisms. Hence, both are confronted with manifest control problems. Based on my data, it is impossible to attribute causally the adoption and the recurrent system of FOI legislation in the UK to the activities of the CFoI alone. Neither would it be possible to explain the growth of the intercultural garden movement exclusively by recourse to the activities of Foundation Interkultur. In both cases, similar events might have occurred anyway. At the same time, however, the data also suggest that the two intermediary activities may have accelerated and enhanced these processes, resulting in more comprehensive, more effective and more sustainable local niche activities.

On a supra niche level, organisations exert the lowest degree of control over the production of value. They provide important resources to local or intermediary actors in order to help them survive and thrive or even engage in the establishment of new organisations, again, both on a local or intermediary level. However, they are too far removed from the locus of value production to be able to influence it in direct ways.

With regard to control in terms of governance structures, it was remarkable that the establishment of new solutions and the creation of value was not realised by established foundations as supra niche organisations. In all the cases, this was the task of independent or semi-independent bodies, endowed with considerable degrees of autonomy and independence from the funding organisation(s). These "niche organisations" were staffed by experts and led by highly competent and committed managers, particularly in the early stages of their lives. This type of governance arrangement shifts the locus of power and control and confirms the image of guerrilla warfare in terms of small and rather independent operating units which are directed by field commanders rather than central headquarters. These entities are well acquainted with the terrain in which they operate; they can best judge the local situation and may move swiftly to evade attacks as well as to perceive and exploit opportunities.

The relevance of this enhanced room for manoeuvre was noticed by many of the interviewees. Recall, for instance, the metaphor of Foundation Inter- kultur as a temporarily independent "submarine". Senior staff of the Nuff- ield Council said: "I've worked in government departments . . . and what I've seen is people who work within fairly tight parameters". Opposed to that, in the Council:

> there is probably more room for creative approaches and for a kind of wider and richer engagement with things than sometimes the civil ser- vice displays. . . . This environment that I'm in now, the boundaries are much wider and the freedoms are much greater.

This reduction of control goes along with a heightened relevance of trust on the side of Foundation management, which was frequently mentioned as a key characteristic of the Foundation's operating policy. For instance, senior staff of the Nuffield Council reaffirmed that collaboration was guided by:

> a notion of trust that the trustees place in us as individuals or as a part of the organisation, a good measure of trust that we will do things that are designed to achieve the broad aims that the foundation is there for.

On the other hand, the data suggest that niche organisations may be more tightly coupled within, exerting a higher degree of control over internal pro- cesses, structures and resources. Particularly if compared with large foun- dations with their broad and diverse programme portfolios, organisations such as Interkultur or the CFoI were characterised by a better understanding of problems and a clearer definition of ends. Control is further enhanced by the fact that the leaders of niche organisations were often characterised as being particularly strong. Foundation Interkultur was even described as being more hierarchical than the parental Foundation anstiftung. This may point to a need to combine a high degree of flexibility with a high degree of unity, which is also reflected in the limited size of these units. With a perma- nent staff of 11, the Nuffield Council was the largest of my sample organ- isations. The CFoI employed two staff members only while Interkultur and The Chance both had eight. Niche organisations thus seem to replace the control of processes and outcomes with control of purpose and boundaries and thus serve as adequate vehicles to steer through rugged, unknown and volatile problem landscapes in experimental yet persistent ways.

Yet, the data analysis also showed that governance structures may change during the process of innovation. In the beginning, niches required most freedom for manoeuvre, combined with a high degree of slack resources. As the uncertainty regarding the organisational "business model" gave way to more stable routines, the coupling between foundations and their off- spring increased. This is obvious in the case of Interkultur which was inte- grated in the larger parental organisation after some years of operation. The development of the Nuffield Council shows that the expectations of funders with regard to accountability and evidence for performance may increase over time. While the Foundation used to claim that its funding was based on a logic of trust rather than control, this language has recently shifted. While the Foundation retains the length of the funding cycles, it now describes its own work as "strategic", which implies an emphasis on outcomes and impact, including the Council's duty to prove that they produce value for money. The Foundation further puts increasing emphasis on its ability to set the terms of reference within which the Council has to operate and under-lines that it does not have a completely free rein. This might be regarded as the inevitable price for substantial long-term funding, but it may also be an expression of the rationalisation of charity by which trust and autonomy are reduced in favour of the need to demonstrate social impact—including problematic cases such as this, in which the organisation cannot control the ultimate impact of its work.

12.4 Conclusion

My data confirm the proposition that the cases under investigation can be regarded as instances of philanthropic niches as they share important simi-larities with the niche concept developed by research on socio-technological transitions. The case analysis demonstrates the relevance of boundaries vis-à-vis societal environments as well as the importance of protection and support and the necessity to sustain niches over time. Niches, thus conceived, serve as the locus of variation as they provide leeway for experimental attempts to develop novel arrangements. Due to their stability they also change the con-ditions of selection and retention of novel solutions to social problems. Three different niche levels were identified. On local level, experiments are con-ducted and value is produced in case of success. Actors open up the doors to resources for their target groups, be it by means of brokering or by enforcing access, developing capacity or producing assets. On an intermediary level, specialised actors seek to build favourable ecosystems in order to trigger or support the work of local niche actors. Organisations on supra niche level support existing organisations in different fields, or help to create new ones.

At the same time, there are also important distinctions. The cases under investigation are not radical but reformist in character as they tackle prob-lems of middle range and seek to generate small wins rather than disrup-tive change. These philanthropic niches do not serve as incubators for the experimental development of alternatives to prevailing systems and they do not aim at the widespread change of large systems. Rather, they function as "simple niches" (Seyfang and Smith 2007: 593) which are assigned an intrinsic value and function as permanent instruments for the production of value in their own right. They are constructed and supported to satisfy the unserved needs of their target populations by means of the mobilisation of untapped resources of different kinds in which these niches are rich.

Hence, the process towards impact is largely consensual, rational and collaborative. The scale and scope of the resulting change is moderate and its pace is incremental. The niches are thus situated at the middle of the innovative spectrum: they lack the potential to "save the world" or to generate disruptive practices, but they are also limited in terms of uncertainty, contention and risk and the degree of required resources.

My considerations further show how philanthropic niches combine the virtues and characteristics of socio-technological and commercial niches. Similar to technological niches, they are conceived as protected environments which provide necessary conditions for the experimental development of novelty. Similar to business niches, they are created and sustained with the ultimate purpose of satisfying unmet individual needs through the exploitation of external resources.

Commercial actors cannot serve those niches because they are either too poor in economically relevant resources, or because these resources cannot be exploited. Public authorities do not provide such services, either, because philanthropic niche actors focus on issues they "cannot, will not or should not" address. I conclude that philanthropic niches can serve as a distinct model for the analysis of processes of social impact and innovation driven by civil society actors.

Note

1 This may be due to the fact that the outcomes and benefits of urban gardens are less straightforward and more diverse than those of the other organisations. Hence, there might be a higher need to point out these benefits to external audiences. At the same time, this variety may make it easier to connect to different discourses such as those on the integration of migrants or the development of alternatives to capitalist economies. However, the Foundation may also have recognised more clearly the need for the formulation and communication of expectations for purposes of niche support.

13 Conclusion and Outlook

In this study I have investigated the questions of how and why philanthropic organisations succeed in solving complex social problems in novel ways. I asked for the kinds of outcomes that satisfy both prosocial organisational intentions and corresponding societal expectations, and I have presented successful examples of innovative philanthropic action and sought to explain them. In particular, I have reconstructed the characteristic interrelations between problem situations, strategies and structures that render this particular kind of organisational action comprehensible, possible and, sometimes, result in social impact.

13.1 Pragmatic Philanthropy as Problem-Solving Action

I have maintained that my cases can be characterised as instances of intelligent social action in the pragmatist understanding of the term. This type of action is problem-driven, that is, motivated by the immediate perception of social problems which elude standardised responses and thus interrupt habitual organisational behaviour. These problems were not identified by means of systematic processes of search nor defined by strategy departments. Neither were foundations the first actors to recognise them. Rather, problems arose, and were tackled, in social fields in which philanthropic organisations were embedded, or in communities to which foundations entertained a close and permanent contact. In the cases under investigation, philanthropic action was further characterised by the attempt to address a particular class of problems, namely problems of "middle range" which exhibited medium degrees of complexity and societal relevance. Accordingly, the barriers actors were confronted with were high but not unsurmountable. Furthermore, the social impact of philanthropic action depended on the development and sustenance of effective new solutions. These solutions could not be characterised as large-scale, disruptive or systemic changes, but rather as bounded but quite concrete "small wins" (Weick 1984)—a phenomenon that deserves attention and study in its own right.

There is not the *one* effective strategy to effectively tackle these types of problems and they are not enacted by one actor only. Instead, diverse actors chose different procedures, the adequacy of which was contingent on the problem situation. If these situations were completely unclear and opaque, explorative strategies were used. Exploration contributes to a deeper understanding of the problem and helps to discover possible options for action. Drawing on Van de Ven et al.'s (2008) metaphor of "innovation journeys", they can be equated with expeditions through unknown terrain. They are not employed to reach a given objective, but rather to get acquainted with the landscape and to identify a reasonable goal in the first place. Once that had been achieved, problem solvers chose experimental methods to probe more or less well-known paths towards sufficiently clear goals based on processes of trial and error. In other words, experimental behaviour was required to develop bespoke remedial practices which both adapted to the particular problem situation and transformed it as they effectively reduced the different types of barriers between problem state and goal state.

In all my cases, value was created long term as philanthropic actors sustained these arrangements to exploit the newly established organisational capabilities. In this phase of "habitualization" (Tolbert and Zucker 1996), the journey increasingly became routinised and stable and organizational action was oriented towards the bureaucratic model. This observation highlights the fact that the pragmatic theory of action does not privilege one particular strategy of action over the other. Rather, it favours the use and concatenation of different strategies, dependent on the problem situation at hand.

Just like pragmatist theory predicts, both the definition of problems and their solution by means of different types of remedial action is a collective and distributed endeavour, based on the co-construction of new practices and the co-production of solutions, and change is largely consensual and collaborative in nature. This presupposes the existence of interactive and interdependent, committed and competent communities of inquiry as problem-solving agents.

In the sample cases, foundations were embedded in networks of different types which served as important sources of information on current and future developments in the field. At the same time, they mobilised a broad variety of resources which were beyond the reach of any single organisation. Hence, networks were created and maintained as major tools for all phases of the process of social innovation.

Yet, the mere circumstance *that* and *how* new instruments for the solution of problems were developed does not sufficiently explain *why* social impact occurs and *why and for whom* these effects can be regarded as beneficial.

The analysis showed that the occurrence of social impact relied on the activation of the door-opener mechanism by which members of a target group gain access to resources they value highly. In principle it is based on a simple model of rational choice. Following Coleman, the observed impact can be explained as the distribution of control over particular resources to actors who value these resources highly. In my cases, these included urban gardens (anstiftung and Interkultur), apprenticeship positions and regular jobs (The Chance), high-quality advice on problems of bioethics (Nuffield) as well as governmental files (Rowntree and CFoI). The generation of social impact further relied on the assumption that such access is perceived as desirable by relevant societal audiences, whereas a lack of access is regarded as a social problem. The mechanism can be triggered in three different ways. First, if the intervention opens up access to resources which used to be off limits, as in the case of the Campaign for Freedom of Information. Second, if philanthropic actors engage in the production of the valued resources, as the Nuffield Council does. Third, if the capacity of members of the target group to make use of available resources is enhanced, which is the approach chosen by The Chance.

The mechanism illustrates the nature of the value that is created, it explains why effects come about in the first place and why they can be sustained. Moreover, it suggests a plausible new understanding of the concept of "leverage" which might underpin the notion of "high" social impact. Although the assets which are invested by foundations and the external resources which are mobilised are of a different nature and thus incommensurable, the examples illustrate that a comparatively small intervention may open up access to a very large pool of external resources.

In this study, I have further portrayed philanthropic organisations as niche strategists and I have demonstrated how the niche concept can be made fruitful for the understanding of those structures, which render possible the experimental development and continuous production of solutions in the first place. Similar to the niches in research on technology transitions, they are defined in terms of bounded, protected and stable spaces which provide leeway for long-term processes of social innovation. They are also akin to economic niches as they are rich in untapped resources. However, the philanthropic niches of my sample can be distinguished from both. They are niches sui generis because they neither aim at the change of systems nor seek to mobilise resources for themselves but for their target groups.

Niches play such an important role in problem-solving processes because they render experimental strategies possible in the first place and thus help to establish "fit" between intervention and the problem situation. As niches are essentially bounded entities, they help satisfy the problem-solving principle of complexity reduction and make it easier to sustain and exploit novel arrangements over long periods of time. Niches further rely on networks and thus enhance the capacity of problem solvers.

A closer analysis of the internal structure of niches revealed that philanthropic organisations played different roles and provided different contributions, depending on the niche level on which they were active. On a local level, they organised the routinised production of goods or services. The Chance and the Nuffield Council as operating single-purpose organisations engaged in this type of action. Grant-making foundations such as the Joseph Rowntree Charitable Trust operated on a supra niche level.

As "global sponsors", their activities spanned different societal domains, addressing a multiplicity of issues and themes. At the same time, and as a result of this position, the organisations were rather far removed from the realm of practice.

Organisations on an intermediary level such as the Foundation Interkultur or the CFoI did not produce goods and services on their own but they were not detached from their target groups, either. They sought to create favourable ecosystems intending to facilitate, encourage and support the desired behaviour of local actors in a variety of different ways and with the intention of thus altering the field of force in which the members of their target group operated. This role was labelled "advocacy". My analysis suggests that this may be a particularly promising option for philanthropic foundations. Intermediaries combine operating and grant-making behaviour and retain a close contact to practice. Thus, they avoid the overly detached role of mere grant-making, yet leave the concrete work on a local level to practitioners who may be much better acquainted with the circumstances of the problem. At the same time, key strengths of philanthropy such as the ability to act as an honest broker, convene disconnected actors and establish bridges between different societal fields are exploited.

The discussion further showed that philanthropic niches are versatile instruments. They need to be designed in such a way as to meet the variable and changing requirements of problem situations in order to generate the desired results. Intelligent niche management thus becomes a major task for philanthropic actors and a necessary condition for the enactment of a pragmatic approach to philanthropy.

13.2 Pragmatic Philanthropy in Evolutionary Perspective

Following the summary of those elements of the pragmatic model which reside on the micro-level (the door-opener mechanism) and meso-level (organisational strategies and structures), I would like to take up the question of how the work of philanthropic organisations might be adequately framed in a more macro-perspective.

As opposed to portraits of philanthropy as a major force for systemic and disruptive processes of change on a large scale, I found that the organisations under investigation could be characterised as niche actors which addressed problems of moderate scale and scope. My findings further discouraged voluntary conceptions of philanthropic action which conceive of society as a kind of playground for unconstrained social entrepreneurs who refashion their environments at will, imposing ready-made solutions on society. Neither are philanthropists wanderers through a landscape full of gaps and voids which need to be filled by means of strategic action like an unfinished giant "jigsaw puzzle" (Sarasvathy et al. 2008: 332), always assuming that public actors will step in when it comes to sustaining their solutions.

Instead, the discussion underlines the heuristic value of a quasi-evolutionary framework of philanthropic action. In modern societies, philanthropic organisations operate in rather crowded yet increasingly dynamic societal fields, the evolution of which results in new or increased social problems. Some of these are fundamental and systemic in nature, while others are of a more moderate scale. Pragmatism recommends that both be seen as windows of opportunity for meaningful action, but it is only the latter that are suitable candidates for the pragmatic approach to problem solving which was developed in this book.

Intelligent philanthropic actors thus respond to and harness societal developments which occur independently of their work, making use of dynamics which constitute a fundamental datum for pragmatist thought. Dewey (LW 14: 113) wrote: "change is going to occur anyway, and the problem is the control of change in a given direction".

In the evolutionary perspective, philanthropic organisations need to connect to their environments in such a way as to be able to recognise relevant developments. They are further assigned the role to create variation in terms of the experimental development of diverse new solutions. They best enact this role if they operate as specialised repair units which may fill some of the emerging or widening gaps quicker, more effectively and even more legitimately than other actors—particularly in the case of those problems which, for good reasons, reside beyond the reach of both public actors and the markets. This diagnosis echoes and confirms the position of the Nuffield Foundation which described its societal role in terms of a niche actor, endowed with the particular advantage of the independence "to contribute to areas which are difficult or impossible or indeed wrong for governments and others to take the lead on".

However, the focus on novelty and innovation alone is obviously insufficient. The evolutionary perspective puts equal emphasis on the relevance of selection and retention of innovative arrangements. The cases suggest that this may be achieved in two different ways. Endowed foundations are in the privileged situation of being able to "pick winners" out of the diverse population of innovative projects and support or run them long term or even open ended. In many cases, however, these two mechanisms can only be enacted by wholly independent external actors. This is where the advocacy function of philanthropy comes into play. Organisations such as the Campaign for the Freedom of Information and Foundation Interkultur succeeded in convincing policymakers and urban gardeners to select the model solutions they favoured. Either way, though, foundations needed to engage in a very long-term perspective. For the adoption of novel arrangements by external actors alone did not guarantee sustainability, let alone prosperity and growth of innovations. Even the most successful innovative niche arrangements did not reach complete stability and there remained the constant need to nurture and protect them to preserve the tools by means of which individual and societal value was created.

This diagnosis does not exclude the possibility of meaningful alternative options for philanthropic action. For instance, instead of engaging in processes of innovation, foundations may very well generate social impact by supporting well-established and effective non-profit organisations. At the other end of the spectrum, research on educational philanthropy in the United States suggests that coalitions of foundations may also make a systemic impact. However, the feasibility of the former approach is limited if there are too few effective solutions, as in the case of school improvement. In the latter case, societal changes are often judged very controversially by external stakeholders and observers. Hence, the question arises of whether these broad innovations can be regarded as being beneficial in individual and societal regards at all.

I maintain that the pragmatic model of philanthropic action is superior to its rivals in these respects because it explains how solutions to social problems emerge in situations where there were none before, and why these innovations can be regarded as positive. However, this does not come without consequences for the concept of social impact. In the proposed framework, it loses the central position it is assigned in conventional discussions on rational philanthropic action. Instead, impact now is regarded as the potential result of a particular and rather limited segment of philanthropy. Hence, it can no longer serve as a key concept and a measure for rational philanthropic action per se.

13.3 Open Questions

I began this study with the diagnosis of the philanthropic predicament and set out to suggest a viable alternative. However, I did not aspire to replace the misleading recipes of strategic philanthropy with a new panacea. I acknowledge that the pragmatic model of intelligent niching is restrained to the creation of more and better islands of success and that this is not all that can be said about the societal role of philanthropy.

Given these limitations, I would like to suggest a number of avenues for further research. I put particular emphasis on the question of how those broader and complex problems can be addressed, which require systemic change on a large scale. From the discussion on socio-technological transformations it should have become obvious that philanthropic action directed at tackling the wicked and even "super-wicked" problems (Levin et al. 2012) of the contemporary world should be informed by the approach of SNM, as sketched in Chapter 5. However, this has yet to be made fit to deal with problems which reside: (a) outside of socio-technological domains, such as education; (b) across systems, such as migration and integration and (c) on an international scale, such as global finance. Yet, while this study bracketed the question of what it means for philanthropic organisations to act in such a broad transformative perspective, I hope to have put forward a number of helpful suggestions of how parts of this approach might be applied by future problem solvers.

Second, while the door-opener mechanism implies a number of important advantages for philanthropic actors, and while it can be found in a wide range of very different fields, it is no panacea for philanthropic action, either. In particular, it relies on the availability of resource-rich niches which may not always be given, particularly in developing countries. Furthermore, it obviously requires a high demand on behalf of the target group and fails if this is not the case. The example of The Chance shows that members of the target group must be willing and able to become active in the first place. If they completely lack motivation, mental or physical stability, this simple mechanism will not work and other methods will have to be applied. Furthermore, this observation points at the fact that the door-opener mechanism is certainly not the only relevant tool available to philanthropic actors. More advanced and complete knowledge on other such mechanisms is urgently needed. For instance, the "Strategies for Impact in Philanthropy" sample also included campaigning and framing activities, that is, attempts to change public attitudes and/or the course of public discourse. In these cases, the essential prerequisites of the resource-mobilisation model are not given since the initial problem situation is not characterised by demand on behalf of the target group (activities seem more to be driven by considerations of supply). In these cases, the decisive question is: what leads people to change their beliefs and attitudes and how can this process be influenced in targeted ways (provided that it can—or should—be influenced by philanthropic actors at all)? Since no cases of demonstrably successful philanthropic agenda setting could be found, the question must remain open.

I have also pointed at a number of implications in terms of organisational structure and culture, including questions of competencies, motivations and attitudes of senior staff. These consequences would be quite far-reaching for philanthropic foundations, in particular, suggesting that they would have to restrain their autonomy and independence in favour of the discipline required for social problem solving (Ansell 2011: 75). However, I have touched on these issues only cursorily. Hence, the questions of how philanthropic niche organisations must be organised and staffed, and which organisational mindset and capabilities would be needed to underpin strategies and structures, to detect problems of the middle range and to cope with them effectively, have remained open and could not be discussed in more depth. At the same time, an investigation into the organisational preconditions of innovative action would have to deal with the fact that adequate problem-solving behaviour was very much the exception rather than the rule in the very many cases of philanthropic action that were explored in the context of SIP. Hence, it would also be highly worthwhile to explore organisational pathologies[1] in terms of those ideological, managerial or psychological factors which systematically inhibit more responsive, responsible and effective social action.

The discussion also pointed to the need to explore normative questions more systematically. I concede that the pragmatist perspective is only one possible way to make sense of the beneficial nature of philanthropic effects, while other normative theories, such as the capability approach or Rawlsian conceptions of justice as fairness, would arrive at different propositions of what makes philanthropic action worthwhile.

In terms of method, it would be desirable to investigate all these new fields of inquiry in a much longer time horizon which should reach far beyond the multi-year duration of projects. Important innovative developments take decades to unfold. Hence, longitudinal studies similar to Van de Ven et al. (2008) would be desirable to trace developments in a long-term perspective. They should be complemented with historical case studies to trace the fate of social innovation over even longer periods of time.

All these possible future avenues have one thing in common, though: their pursuit would require a much tighter integration of the study of philanthropy with other strands of social science. This would strengthen the connections between these different worlds, help philanthropy studies come up to the standards of established empirical and theoretical research, and thus contribute to a richer and more coherent, if possibly more realistic and sober, portrait of the consequences and contributions of philanthropic action.

Note

1 I owe this point to Wolfgang Seibel and Christian Seelos.

Appendix A
List of Cases

No.	Foundation	Country	Programme/Project
1.	Aga Khan Foundation	Portugal	K'Cidade
2.	Atlantic Philanthropies	UK/Ireland	Disadvantaged Children and Youth Programme/Preparing for Life Programme
3.	Bank of Sweden Tercentenary Foundation	Sweden	PhD Schools
4.	Barrow Cadbury Trust	UK	Migrants Rights Network
5.	Bernard van Leer Foundation	Netherlands	Social Inclusion and Respect for Diversity Programme
6.	Cariplo Foundation	Italy	Community Foundations
7.	City Bridge Trust	UK	First Night in Custody
8.	Compagnia di San Paolo	Italy	Social Microcredit
9.	Dag Hammarskjöld Foundation	Sweden	*Unit of analysis was no single programme but the foundation*
10.	Deutsche Bank Stiftung/ Deutsche Kinder- und Jugendstiftung	Germany	Youth Banks
11.	Foundation Interkultur	Germany	Intercultural Gardens
12.	Fryshuset Foundation	Sweden	Easy Street
13.	Gulbenkian Foundation	Portugal	Recognition of the Qualification of Immigrant Doctors
14.	Joseph Rowntree Charitable Trust	UK	Campaign for Freedom of Information
15.	King Baudouin Foundation	Belgium	General Report on Insecurity
16.	Mercator Foundation	Germany	Developmental instruction
17.	Nuffield Foundation	UK	Nuffield Council on Bioethics
18.	Start Foundation	Netherlands	Labour Market Integration

(Continued)

Appendix A (Continued)

No.	Foundation	Country	Programme/Project
19.	The Chance Foundation[1]	Switzerland	*Unit of analysis was no single programme but the foundation*
20.	Young Foundation	UK	Transforming Neighbourhoods

Note
1 The case of The Chance was prepared in the context of the project "Strategies for Impact in Education". It was the immediate follow-up to SIP and conducted with similar intentions and with an almost identical methodology.

Appendix B
Interview Schedule

The interview covers eight major topics:

1 Opening: Background of those involved in the activity
  Ask respondent about his/her function in the foundation, relevant training and background and how he/she fits into the foundation's idea of good staff members.

2 Status quo and development
  Ask respondent to describe the current state of unit of analysis, how the activity came about, how it developed over time and how it fits into the foundation's other activities.

3 Social impact
  Ask respondent about the impact that was achieved: what kind or scope of impact was envisioned, what impact did come about and why does it last?

4 Strategies & process leading to high impact
  Ask respondent about the design of the process leading to impact. What resources were needed and how did they contribute to success? Was there a clear understanding of those mechanisms leading to success?

5 Critical success factors
  Ask respondent for the reasons that made the unit of analyses so successful, about the role of internal structures, the role of the media and if there were risks and failures on the way.

6 Environment
  Ask respondent whether the social environment was favourable or unfavourable, if their intervention was seen as legitimate, what role public attention and media would play and about their relations and their comparative advantages in regard to the other stakeholders.

7 Partners
  Ask respondent about the role and importance of other stakeholders and partners in achieving the goals, which frictions occurred and what made the collaborations productive and successful in the end.

8   Closing

Ask respondent if there is anything to add and whether you can follow up with them in the future.

I   Opening: Professional background

1   What is your current function in the foundation?
2   For how long have you been working in this foundation?
3   What is your relevant academic and personal background?
4   What is the model for a good staff member in the foundation and how do you fit in this scheme?

II   Status quo and development

5   Describe what has been done to date.
6   Why did the foundation take up the issue?
7   What was the point of departure for the programme/project and how did the idea of the chosen approach emerge?
8   Were alternatives to the chosen approach being discussed and why were they discarded?
9   Is the activity part of a greater internal goal system?

III   Social impact

10   If your activity had been entirely successful—how would the desired social state of affairs look like? Please describe as detailed as possible.
11   Was it explicitly named before the programme started and did you think about growth or ways to enhance impact in the beginning?
12   How is the situation now? Which specific social impact did the activity have so far?

• Qualitative and quantitative description of the social impact
• What evidence for impact is there (reports of evaluation, annual reports, press releases, etc.)?

13   Did the foundation guarantee sustainability? If so, how?

IV   Process leading to high impact

14   What has been the financial input so far? How high is it today?
15   What other resources were needed to achieve your goals?

• foundation's reputation
• social networks of the foundation
• human resources strategy
• special training for those involved
• other

16 How would you describe the way from input to results?

- Did the project follow a certain idea of how to bring about change or could you tell a story that explains what steps needed to be taken in order to achieve your aims?

V Critical success factors

17 What are the crucial factors that made the activity successful?
18 How important were organisational structure, culture and management styles of the foundation?

- Was there any kind of systematic strategic controlling along the way?

19 What did the organisational structure within the programme look like and how important was it for overall success?
20 Was there systematic marketing or public relations work?

- If so: how important was it?
- If not: why not?

21 Did you take risks as a foundation in taking up this issue or in pursuing your goals?
22 Are there any systematic or acute weaknesses or failures connected to the activity that you would like to mention?
23 What were the lessons learned from those failures?

VI Environment

24 How would you describe the social and institutional environment of the activity and was it favourable or unfavourable?
25 What kind of barriers were there and which obstacles did you have to overcome?
26 Has there been public criticism of any kind?
27 Has your activity been seen as legitimate?
28 What was the role of the media?

- Did you have to create attention or was there attention towards the issue before the intervention of the foundation?

29 Are there key initiatives undertaken by other players?
30 Is there a division of labour and what does it look like?
31 Was there something the foundation did that no other player could have done?

VII Partners

32 Who are your main partners in the unit of activity?
33 What is their essential contribution to success?
34 Were there frictions during cooperation and if so, why?

35 What factors are important for successful cooperation with partners?

36 What is their overall rating of the activity and what do *they* see as crucial for success or failure of the activity?

VIII Closing

37 We are coming to the end of our interview; is there anything you would like to add?

- Check notes for things left out

38 May I follow up with you in the future?

- Next steps

References

Adam, Silke; Kriesi, Hanspeter (2007): The Network Approach. In: Paul A. Sabatier (ed.): *Theories of the Policy Process*, 2nd ed., Boulder, CO: Westview Press, pp. 129–154.

Adloff, Frank (2004): Wozu sind Stiftungen gut? Zur gesellschaftlichen Einbettung des Deutschen Stiftungswesens. In: *Leviathan* (2), pp. 269–285.

Adloff, Frank (2005): *Zivilgesellschaft: Theorie und politische Praxis.* Frankfurt am Main, New York: Campus.

Adloff, Frank (2010): *Philanthropisches Handeln: Eine historische Soziologie des Stiftens in Deutschland und den USA.* Frankfurt am Main: Campus.

Adloff, Frank; Sigmund, Steffen (2005): Die gift economy moderner Gesellschaften. Zur Soziologie der Philanthropie. In: Frank Adloff and Steffen Mau (eds.): *Vom Geben und Nehmen: Zur Soziologie der Reziprozität.* Frankfurt/Main, New York: Campus, pp. 211–235.

Alberg-Seberich, Michael; Meibom, Aletta von (2009): Chocolate Eggs for Swiss Nuns? In: *Alliance Magazine* 14 (1), pp. 41–42.

Allen, Craig R.; Gunderson, Lance H. (2011): Pathology and Failure in the Design and Implementation of Adaptive Management. In: *Journal of Environmental Management* 92 (5), pp. 1379–1384.

Almog-Bar, Michal; Schmid, Hillel (2014): Advocacy Activities of Nonprofit Human Service Organizations: A Critical Review. In: *Nonprofit and Voluntary Sector Quarterly* 43 (1), pp. 11–35.

Alvord, Sarah H.; Brown, L. David; Letts, Christine W. (2004): Social Entrepreneurship and Societal Transformation: An Exploratory Study. In: *Journal of Applied Behavioral Science* 40 (3), pp. 260–282.

Amburgey, Terry L.; Dacin, Tina (1994): As the left foot follows the right? The dynamics of strategic and structural change. In: *Academy of Management Journal*, 37(6), pp. 1427–1452.

Andersen, Ole Johann (2008): A Bottom-Up Perspective on Innovations: Mobilizing Knowledge and Social Capital Through Innovative Processes of Bricolage. In: *Administration & Society* 40 (1), pp. 54–78.

Anderson, Elizabeth (2014): Dewey's Moral Philosophy. In: Edward N. Zalta (ed.): *The Stanford Encyclopedia of Philosophy.* Retrieved from http://plato.stanford.edu/archives/spr2014/entries/dewey-moral/.

Andreoni, James (1990): Impure Altruism and Donations to Public Goods: A Theory of Warm-Glow Giving. In: *The Economic Journal* 100 (401), pp. 464–477.

Anheier, Helmut K. (2005): *Nonprofit Organizations: Theory, Management, Policy.* London, New York: Routledge.

Anheier, Helmut K. (2012): Zivilgesellschaft und Krisen: Dahrendorf'sche Reflektionen. In: *Leviathan,* pp. 421–440.

Anheier, Helmut K.; Daly, Siobhan (2007a): Comparing Foundation Roles. In: Helmut K. Anheier and Siobhan Daly (eds.): *The Politics of Foundations: A Comparative Analysis.* London, New York: Routledge, pp. 27–44.

Anheier, Helmut K.; Daly, Siobhan (2007b): Philanthropic Foundations in Modern Society. In: Helmut K. Anheier and Siobhan Daly (eds.): *The Politics of Foundations. A Comparative Analysis.* London, New York: Routledge, pp. 3–26.

Anheier, Helmut K.; Freise, Matthias (2004): Der Dritte Sektor im Diskurs des Dritten Weges. In: Jens Beckert, Julia Eckert, Martin Kohli and Wolfgang Streeck (eds.): *Transnationale Solidarität: Chancen und Grenzen.* Frankfurt/Main, New York: Campus Verlag, pp. 109–125.

Anheier, Helmut K.; Leat, Diana (2006): *Creative Philanthropy: Towards a New Philanthropy for the Twenty-First Century.* London: Routledge.

Anheier, Helmut K.; Toepler, Stefan (1999): Why Study Foundations? In: Helmut K. Anheier and Stefan Toepler (eds.): *Private Funds, Public Purpose: Philanthropic Foundations in International Perspective.* New York: Plenum Press, pp. 255–259.

Ansell, Christopher K. (2011): *Organizing Pragmatist Democracy: Evolutionary Learning as Public Philosophy.* Oxford: Oxford University Press.

Ansell, Christopher K.; Bartenberger, Martin (2015): *Expanding the Toolkit of Experimentation.* Retrieved from http://ssrn.com/abstract=2475844 or http://dx.doi.org/10.2139/ssrn.2475844.

Ansell, Christopher K.; Reckhow, Sarah; Kelly, Andrew (2009): How to Reform a Reform Coalition: Outreach, Agenda Expansion, and Brokerage in Urban School Reform. In: *The Policy Studies Journal* 37 (4), pp. 717–743.

anstiftung (2015a): http://anstiftung.de/.

anstiftung (2015b): *Strategiepapier 2015.* Unpublished internal document of anstiftung foundation.

Anthony, Robert N.; Herzlinger, Regina E. (1975): *Management Control in Nonprofit Organizations.* Homewood, IL: R. D. Irwin.

Bacchetti, Ray; Ehrlich, Thomas (2007): Foundations and Education: Introduction. In: Ray Bacchetti and Thomas Ehrlich (eds.): *Reconnecting Education & Foundations: Turning Good Intentions Into Educational Capital.* San Francisco: Wiley, pp. 3–20.

Baier, Andrea; Müller, Christa (n.d.): *Vom Haus der Eigenarbeit zur Stadt der Commonisten.* Zum Forschungsverständnis der anstiftung.

Banerjee, Abhijit V.; Duflo, Esther (2011): *Poor Economics. A Radical Rethinking of the Way to Fight Global Poverty.* New York: Public Affairs.

Banisar, David (2006): *Freedom of Information Around the World 2006: A Global Survey of Access to Government Information Laws.* Edited by Privacy International. London. Retrieved from www.humanrightsinitiative.org/programs/ai/rti/international/laws_papers/intl/global_foi_survey_2006.pdf.

Bartelborth, Thomas (1996): *Begründungsstrategien: Ein Weg durch die analytische Erkenntnistheorie.* Berlin: Akademie Verlag.

Beckert, Jens (2009): *Pragmatismus und wirtschaftliches Handeln.* Working Paper 09/4. Köln: Max-Planck-Institut für Gesellschaftsforschung.

Bekkers, René; Wiepking, Pamala (2011): A Literature Review of Empirical Studies of Philanthropy: Eight Mechanisms That Drive Charitable Giving. *Nonprofit and Voluntary Sector Quarterly* 40 (5), pp. 924–973.

Beller, Annelie (2014): *Jacobs Summer Camp* and *DeutschSommer*: Making a Difference with Summer Camp Programmes. In: Ekkehard Thümler, Nicole Bögelein, Annelie Beller, Helmut K. Anheier (eds.): *Philanthropy and Education: Strategies for Impact*. Basingstoke: Palgrave Macmillan, pp. 47–64.

Bethmann, Stefan, 2014. The Chance: A Systemic Approach to Integrate Adolescents Into the Job Market. In: Ekkehard Thuemler, Nicole Boegelein, Annelie Beller, Helmut K. Anheier (eds.): *Philanthropy and Education. Strategies for Impact*. Basingstoke: Palgrave Macmillan, pp. 65–83.

Bierhoff, Hans-Werner (2002): *Prosocial Behaviour*. New York: Psychology Press.

Bierhoff, Hans-Werner (2010): *Psychologie prosozialen Verhaltens. Warum wir anderen helfen*. 2nd ed. Stuttgart: Kohlhammer (Kohlhammer-Urban-Taschenbücher, 418).

Bishop, Matthew; Green, Michael (2008): *Philanthrocapitalism: How the Rich Can Save the World*. New York: Bloomsbury Press.

Blanco, Hilda (1994): *How to Think About Social Problems: American Pragmatism and the Idea of Planning*. Westport, CT: Greenwood Press.

Blumer, Herbert (1971): Social Problems as Collective Behavior. In: *Social Problems* 18 (3), pp. 298–306.

Boli, John (2005): Contemporary Developments in World Culture. In: *International Journal of Comparative Sociology* 46 (5–6), pp. 383–404.

Borman, Geoffrey D. (2002): Experiments for Educational Evaluation and Improvement. In: *Peabody Journal of Education* 77 (4), pp. 7–27.

Bornmann, Lutz (2010): Die analytische Soziologie: Soziale Mechanismen, DBO-Theorie und Agentenbasierte Modelle. In: *Österreichische Zeitschrift für Soziologie* 35 (4), pp. 25–44.

Bourdieu, Pierre (1982): *Die feinen Unterschiede: Kritik der gesellschaftlichen Urteilskraft*. Frankfurt/Main: Suhrkamp.

Bower, Joseph L. (1986): *Managing the Resource Allocation Process: A Study of Corporate Planning and Investment*. Boston, MA: Harvard Business School Press.

Braun-Thürmann, Holger (2005): *Innovation*. Bielefeld: Transcript Verlag.

Brest, Paul; Harvey, Hal (2008): *Money Well Spent: A Strategic Plan for Smart Philanthropy*. New York: Bloomberg Press.

Brest, Paul; Roumani, Nadia; Bade, Jason (2015): *Problem Solving, Human-Centered Design, and Strategic Processes*. Conference Paper. Retrieved from http://pacscenter.stanford.edu/sites/all/files/Brest%20Roumani%20Bade%20Solving%20and%20Strategic%20Processes%20v%2015a.docx%205.17.15.pdf.

Bromley, Patricia; Powell, Walter W. (2012): From Smoke and Mirrors to Walking the Talk: Decoupling in the Contemporary World. *The Academy of Management Annals* 6 (1), pp. 483–530.

Brunsson, Nils (2006): *The Organization of Hypocrisy: Talk, Decisions and Actions in Organizations*. 2nd ed. Malmö: Copenhagen Business School Press.

Bruun, Henrik; Sierla, Seppo (2008): Distributed Problem Solving in Software Development: The Case of an Automation Project. In: *Social Studies of Science* 38 (1), pp. 133–158.

Bunge, Mario (2004): How Does It Work? The Search for Explanatory Mechanisms. *Philosophy of the Social Sciences* 34 (2), pp. 182–210.

Burke, F. Thomas; Hester, D. Micah; Talisse, Robert B. (2002): Editor's Introduction. In: F. Thomas Burke, D. Micah Hester and Robert B. Talisse (eds.): *Dewey's Logical Theory: New Studies and Interpretations*. Nashville: Vanderbilt University Press, pp. xi–xxiv.

Burns, Tom; Stalker, George M. (1961): *The Management of Innovation*. London: Tavistock.

Camic, Charles (1986): The Matter of Habit. In: *American Journal of Sociology* 91(5), pp. 1039–1087.

Campaign for Freedom of Information (CFoI) (2007): Application to the Joseph Rowntree Charitable Trust, April 2007.

Campaign for Freedom of Information (CFoI) (2015): www.cfoi.org.uk/.

Campbell, Donald T. (1969): Reforms as experiments. In: *American Psychologist* 24 (4), pp. 409–429.

Campbell, Donald T. (1991): Methods for the Experimenting Society. In: *American Journal of Evaluation* 12, pp. 223–260.

Campbell, James (1992): *The Community Reconstructs: The Meaning of Pragmatic Social Thought*. Urbana: University of Illinois Press.

Caniëls, Marjolein C.J.; Romijn, Henny A. (2008): Actor Networks in Strategic Niche Management: Insights from Social Network Theory. In: *Futures* 40 (7), pp. 613–629.

Cartwright, Timothy J. (1973): Problems, Solutions and Strategies: A Contribution to the Theory and Practice of Planning. In: *Journal of the American Institute of Planners* 39 (3), pp. 179–187.

Caulier-Grice, Julie; Davies, Anna; Patrick, Robert; Norman, Will (2012): *Defining Social Innovation*. London: The Young Foundation.

Caves, Richard E.; Porter, Michael E. (1977): From Entry Barriers to Mobility Barriers: Conjectural Decisions and Contrived Deterrence to New Competition. In: *The Quarterly Journal of Economics* 91 (2), pp. 241–261.

Chandler, Alfred D. (1962): *Strategy and Structure: Chapters in the History of the American Industrial Enterprise*. Cambridge, MA: MIT Press.

Chisholm, Donald (1992): *Coordination Without Hierarchy: Informal Structures in Multiorganizational Systems*. Berkeley, CA: University of California Press.

Chisholm, Donald (1995): Problem Solving and Institutional Design. In: *Journal of Public Administration Research and Theory* 5 (4), pp. 451–491.

Cho, Albert Hyunbae (2006): Politics, Values and Social Entrepreneurship: A Critical Appraisal. In: Johanna Mair, Jeffrey A. Robinson and Kai Hockerts (eds.): *Social Entrepreneurship*. Basingstoke: Palgrave Macmillan, pp. 34–56.

Christensen, Karen S. (1985): Coping with Uncertainty in Planning. In: *Journal of the American Planning Association* 51 (1), pp. 63–73.

Clemens, Elisabeth; Lee, Linda C. (2010): Catalysts for Change? Foundations and School Reform, 1950–2005. In: Helmut K. Anheier, David C. Hammack (eds.): *American Foundations. Roles and Contributions*. Washington, DC: Brookings Institution, pp. 51–72.

Cockrall-King, Jennifer, 2012. *Food and the City: Urban Agriculture and the New Food Revolution*. New York: Prometheus Books.

Cohen, David K.; Peurach, Donald J.; Glazer, Joshua L.; Gates, Karen E.; Goldin, Simona (2014): *Improvement by Design: The Promise of Better Schools*. Chicago, London: University of Chicago Press.

Cohen, Michael D. (2007): Reading Dewey: Reflections on the Study of Routine. In: *Organization Studies* 28 (5), pp. 773–786.

Cohen, Michael D.; March James G.; Olsen Johann Peder (1972): A Garbage Can Model of Organizational Choice. In: *Administrative Science Quarterly* 17 (1), pp. 1–25.

Coleman, James S. (1990): *Foundations of Social Theory*. Cambridge, MA and London: The Belknap Press of Harvard University Press.

Corrigan, Oonagh P. (2005): Pharmacogenetics, Ethical Issues: Review of the Nuffield Council on Bioethics Report. In: *Journal of Medical Ethics* 31 (3), pp. 144–148.

Courtney, Hugh; Kirkland, Jane; Viguerie, Patrick (1997): Strategy Under Uncertainty. In: *Harvard Business Review* 75 (6), pp. 67–79.

Creswell, John W. (2007): *Qualitative Inquiry & Research Design: Choosing Among Five Approaches*. 2nd ed. Thousand Oaks, CA: Sage Publications.

Crozier, Michel (1982): *Strategies for Change: The Future of French Society*. Cambridge, MA: MIT Press.

Cutler, David (2009): *The Effective Foundation—A Literature Review*. London: The Baring Foundation.

Damon, William (2006): Introduction: Taking Philanthropy Seriously. In: William Damon and Susan Verducci (eds.): *Taking Philanthropy Seriously: Beyond Noble Intentions to Responsible Giving*. Bloomington and Indianapolis: Indiana University Press, pp. 1–11.

Davies, Jonathan S. (2004): The Foundation as a Political Actor: The Case of the Joseph Rowntree Charitable Trust. In: *The Political Quarterly* 75 (3), pp. 275–284.

Davis, Gerald F.; Marquis, Christopher (2005): Prospects for Organization Theory in the Early Twenty-First Century: Institutional Fields and Mechanisms. In: *Organization Science* 16 (4), pp. 332–343.

Dees, Gregory; Anderson, Beth Battle; Weiskillern, Jane (2004): Scaling Social Impact: Strategies for Spreading Social Innovations. In: *Stanford Social Innovation Review*, pp. 24–32.

Deuten, J. Jasper (2003): *Cosmopolitanizing Technology: Studies of Four Emerging Technological Regimes*. PhD thesis, University of Twente.

Dewey, John (1969–1991): *The Collected Works of John Dewey: The Early Works, The Middle Works (MW), The Late Works (LW)* (37 vols.). Jo Ann Boydston (Ed.), Carbondale: Southern Illinois University Press.

Dewey, John (2011 [1910]): The Influence of Darwinism on Philosophy. In: Robert B. Talisse and Scott F. Aikin (eds.): *The Pragmatism Reader: From Peirce Through the Present*. Princeton and Oxford: Princeton University Press, pp. 141–149.

Dewey, John (2011 [1917]): The Need for a Recovery of Philosophy. In: Robert B. Talisse and Scott F. Aikin (eds.): *The Pragmatism Reader: From Peirce Through the Present*. Princeton and Oxford: Princeton University Press, pp. 109–140.

Dewey, John (2011 [1939]): Creative Democracy – The Task Before Us. In: Robert B. Talisse and Scott F. Aikin (eds.): *The Pragmatism Reader: From Peirce Through the Present*. Princeton and Oxford: Princeton University Press, pp. 150–154.

DiMaggio, Paul J. (2001): Measuring the Impact of the Nonprofit Sector on Society Is Probably Impossible but Possibly Useful: A Sociological Perspective. In: Patrice Flynn and Virginia A. Hodgkinson (eds.): *Measuring the Impact of the Nonprofit Sector*. New York: Kluwer Academic/Plenum Publishers, pp. 249–272.

DiMaggio, Paul J.; Powell, Walter W. (1991): The Iron Cage Revisited: Institutional Isomorphism and Collective Rationality in Organizational Fields. In: Walter W. Powell and Paul J. DiMaggio (eds.): *The New Institutionalism in Organizational Analysis*. Chicago, London: The University of Chicago Press, pp. 63–82.

Dorado, Silvia; Ventresca, Marc J. (2012): Crescive Entrepreneurship in Complex Social Problems: Institutional Conditions for Entrepreneurial Engagement. In: *Journal of Business Venturing* 28 (1), pp. 69–82.

Dörner, Dietrich (2007): *Die Logik des Misslingens: Strategisches Denken in komplexen Situationen.* 6th ed. Reinbek: Rowohlt.

Dosi, Giovanni (1982): Technological Paradigms and Technological Trajectories. In: *Research Policy* 11 (3), pp. 147–162.

Ebrahim, Alnoor; Rangan, V. Kasturi (2010): *The Limits of Nonprofit Impact: A Contingency Framework for Measuring Social Performance.* Cambridge, MA: Harvard Business School General Management Unit Working Paper, 10–99.

Ebrahim, Alnoor; Rangan, V. Kasturi (2014): What Impact? In: *California Management Review* 56 (3), pp. 118–141.

Edwards, Michael (2010): *Small Change: Why Business Won't Save the World.* San Francisco: Berrett-Koehler.

Ellis, Fiona (2012): *Impact Study of the Joseph Rowntree Charitable Trust's Power and Responsibility Programme.* Unpublished report.

Elster, Jon (1989): *Nuts and Bolts for the Social Sciences.* Cambridge: Cambridge University Press.

Emerson, Jed; Wachowicz, Jay; Chun, Suzi (1999): Social Return on Investment: Exploring Aspect of Value Creation in the Nonprofit Sector. In: Roberts Enterprise Development Fund (ed.): *Social Purpose Enterprises and Venture Philanthropy in the New Millennium, Vol. 2.* San Francisco: REDF, pp. 131–173.

Engelen, Ewald; Ertürk, Ismail; Froud, Julie; Johal, Sukhdev; Leaver, Adam; Moran, Michael (Eds.) (2011): *After the Great Complacence. Financial Crisis and the Politics of Reform.* Oxford: Oxford University Press.

Esser, Hartmut (1996): Die Definition der Situation. In: *Kölner Zeitschrift für Soziologie und Sozialpsychologie* 48 (1), pp. 1–34.

European Foundation Centre (2008): *Foundations in the European Union: Facts and Figures.* Report on work by EFC Research Task Force. Brussels.

European Union (2003): *Directive 2003/98/EC of the European Parliament and of the Council of 17 November 2003 on the Re-use of Public Sector Information.*

Farla, Jacco; Markard, Jochen; Raven, Rob; Coenen, Lars (2012): Sustainability Transitions in the Making: A Closer Look at Actors, Strategies and Resources. In: *Technological Forecasting and Social Change* 79 (6), pp. 991–998.

Feffer, Andrew (1993): *The Chicago Pragmatists and American Progressivism.* Ithaca: Cornell University Press.

Feldman, Martha S.; Pentland, Brian T. (2003): Reconceptualizing Organizational Routines as a Source of Flexibility and Change. In: *Administrative Science Quarterly* 48 (1), p. 94.

Fine, Gary Alan (2006): The Chaining of Social Problems: Solutions and Unintended Consequences in the Age of Betrayal. In: *Social Problems* 53 (1), pp. 3–17.

Fioramonti, Lorenzo; Thümler, Ekkehard (2011): The Financial Crisis and the Nonprofit Sector: Can Philanthropic Foundations Support the Creation of a Civic Watchdog of International Finance? In: *The International Journal of Not-For-Profit Law* 13 (3), pp. 33–42.

Fioramonti, Lorenzo; Thümler, Ekkehard (2013): Accountability, Democracy, and Post-growth: Civil Society Rethinking Political Economy and Finance. In: *Journal of Civil Society* 9 (2), pp. 117–128.

Firestone, William A. (1984): *The Study of Loose Coupling: Problems, Progress, and Prospects.* Paper presented at the Annual Meeting of the American Educational Research Association. Philadelphia: Research for Better Schools, Inc.

Fleishman, Joel L. (2007): *The Foundation: A Great American Secret*. New York: PublicAffairs.

Flynn, Patrice; Hodgkinson, Virginia A. (2001): Measuring the Contributions of the Nonprofit Sector. In: Patrice Flynn and Virginia A. Hodgkinson (eds.): *Measuring the Impact of the Nonprofit Sector*. New York: Kluwer Academic/Plenum Publishers, pp. 3–16.

Foundation Center (2012): *Aggregate Fiscal Data of Grants from FC 1000 Foundations, 2012*. Retrieved from http://data.foundationcenter.org/#/fc1000/subject:all/all/total/trends:amount/2012.

Freedom of Information Unit (1998): *Your Right to Know: Freedom of Information*. White Paper. London: Freedom of Information Unit at the Cabinet Office.

Frensch, Peter A.; Funke, J. (1995): Definitions, Traditions, and a General Framework for Understanding Complex Problem Solving. In: Peter A. Frensch and J. Funke (eds.): *Complex Problem Solving—The European Perspective*. Hillsdale, NJ: Lawrence Erlbaum, pp. S. 3–26.

Friedeburg, Ludwig von (1992): *Bildungsreform in Deutschland: Geschichte und gesellschaftlicher Widerspruch*. Frankfurt am Main: Suhrkamp.

Friedland, Roger; Alford, Robert R. (1991): Bringing Society Back In: Symbols, Practices, and Institutional Contradictions. In: Walter W. Powell, Paul J. DiMaggio (eds.): *The New Institutionalism in Organizational Analysis*. Chicago, London: The University of Chicago Press, pp. 232–263.

Friedrichs, Jürgen (1983): *Methoden empirischer Sozialforschung*. 11th ed. Opladen: Westdeutscher Verlag.

Fritschi, Tobias; Oesch, Thomas and Jann, Ben (2009): *Gesellschaftliche Kosten der Ausbildungslosigkeit in der Schweiz*. Bern: BASS.

Frumkin, Peter (2000): Philanthropic Leverage. In: *Society* 37 (6), pp. 40–46.

Frumkin, Peter (2003): Inside Venture Philanthropy. Symposium: The Third Sector in Transition. In: *Society* 40 (4), pp. 7–15.

Frumkin, Peter (2006): *Strategic Giving: The Art and Science of Philanthropy*. Chicago, London: The University of Chicago Press.

Funke, Joachim (2003): *Problemlösendes Denken*. Stuttgart: Kohlhammer.

Funke, Joachim (2006): Lösen komplexer Probleme. In: Joachim Funke, Peter A. Frensch (eds.): *Handbuch der Allgemeinen Psychologie—Kognition*. Göttingen: Hogrefe, pp. 439–445.

Funke, Joachim; Frensch Peter A. (2007): Complex Problem Solving: The European Perspective—10 Years After. In: David H. Jonassen (eds.): *Learning to Solve Complex Scientific Problems*. New York and London: Lawrence Erlbaum, pp. 25–47.

Garud, Raghu; Van de Ven, Andrew H. (1992): An Empirical Evaluation of the Internal Corporate Venturing Process. In: *Strategic Management Journal* 13 (S1), pp. 93–109.

Geels, Frank W. (2002): Technological Transitions as Evolutionary Reconfiguration Processes: A Multi-Level Perspective and a Case Study. In: *Research Policy* 31 (8–9), pp. 1257–1274.

Geels, Frank W.; Deuten, J. Jasper (2006): Local and Global Dynamics in Technological Development: A Socio-Cognitive Perspective on Knowledge Flows and Lessons from Reinforced Concrete. In: *Science and Public Policy* 33 (4), pp. 265–275.

Geels, Frank W.; Hekkert, Marko P.; Jacobsson, Staffan (2008): The Dynamics of Sustainable Innovation Journeys.In: *Technology Analysis & Strategic Management*, 20(5), pp. 521–536.

Geels, Frank W.; Raven, Rob (2006): Non-Linearity and Expectations in Niche-Development Trajectories: Ups and Downs in Dutch Biogas Development (1973–2003). In: *Technology Analysis & Strategic Management* 18 (3–4), pp. 375–392.

Gerber, Pia (2006): Der lange Weg der sozialen Innovation—Stiftungen und sozialer Wandel: Unternehmensnahe Stiftungen in der Bundesrepublik als Innovationsagenturen im Feld der Bildungs- und Sozialpolitik am Beispiel der Freudenberg Stiftung. Frankfurt/Main: Peter Lang.

Giugni, Marco (1999): How Social Movements Matter: Past Research, Present Problems, Future Developments. In: Marco Giugni, Doug McAdam and Charles Tilly (eds.): *How Social Movements Matter*. Minneapolis and London: University of Minnesota Press, pp. xiii–xxxiii.

Glouberman, Sholom; Zimmerman, Brenda (2002): Complicated and Complex Systems: What Would Successful Reform of Medicare Look Like? *Romanow Papers*, 2, pp. 21–53.

Gordon, Teresa P.; Knock, Cathryn L.; Neely, Daniel G. (2009): The Role of Rating Agencies in the Market for Charitable Contributions: An Empirical Test. In: *Journal of Accounting and Public Policy* 28 (6), pp. 469–484.

Grant, Robert M. (2003): Strategic Planning in a Turbulent Environment: Evidence From the Oil Majors. In: *Strategic Management Journal* (24), pp. 491–517.

Greene, Jay P. (2005): Buckets Into the Sea: Why Philanthropy Isn't Changing Schools, and How It Could. In: Frederick M. Hess (ed.): *With the Best of Intentions: How Philanthropy Is Reshaping K-12 Education*. Cambridge, MA: Harvard Education Press, pp. 49–76.

Gupta, Anil K.; Smith, Ken G.; Shalley, Christina E. (2006): The Interplay Between Exploration and Exploitation. In: *Academy of Management Journal* 49 (4), pp. 693–706.

Hall, Peter D. (1992): Paper Ephemera: Managers, Policymakers, Scholars, and the Future of American Philanthropy. In: Peter Dobkin Hall (ed.): *Inventing the Nonprofit Sector and Other Essays on Philanthropy, Voluntarism and Nonprofit Organizations*. Baltimore, London: Johns Hopkins University Press, pp. 221–231.

Hammack, David C.; Anheier, Helmut K. (2010): American Foundations: Their Roles and Contributions to Society. In: Helmut K. Anheier and David C. Hammack (eds.): *American Foundations: Roles and Contributions*. Washington, DC: Brookings Institution, pp. 3–27.

Hanleybrown, Fay; Kania, John; Kramer, Mark R. (2012): Channeling Change: Making Collective Impact Work. In: *Stanford Social Innovation Review*, pp. 1–8.

Hargreaves, Tom; Hielscher, Sabine; Seyfang, Gill; Smith, Adrian (2013): Grassroots Innovations in Community Energy: The Role of Intermediaries in Niche Development. In: *Global Environmental Change* 23 (5), pp. 868–880.

Harrow, Jenny (2010): Philanthropy. In: Rupert Taylor (ed.): *Third Sector Research*. New York etc.: Springer, pp. 120–138.

Harrow, Jenny; Jung, Tobias (2015): Debate: Thou Shalt Have Impact, Total Impact—Government Involvement in Philanthropic Foundations' Decision-Making. In: *Public Money & Management* 35 (3), pp. 176–178.

Hattie, John A.C.; Anderman, Eric M. (Eds.) (2013): *International Guide to Student Achievement*. New York: Routledge.

Hayes, Robert H. (1985): Strategic Planning-Forward in Reverse. In: *Harvard Business Review* 63 (6).

Hedström, Peter; Swedberg, Richard (1998): Social Mechanisms: An Introductory Essay. In: Peter Hedström and Richard Swedberg (eds.): *Social Mechanisms*. Cambridge: Cambridge University Press pp. 1–31.

Heifetz, Ronald A.; Kania, John V.; Kramer, Mark R. (2004): Leading Boldly: Foundations Can Move Past Traditional Approaches to Create Social Change Through Imaginative—and Even Controversial—Leadership. In: *Stanford Social Innovation Review*, pp. 21–31.

Hernes, Gudmund (1998): Real Virtuality. In: Peter Hedström and Richard Swedberg (eds.): *Social Mechanisms* Cambridge: Cambridge University Press, pp. 74–101.

Hess, Frederick M. (2005a): Introduction. In: Frederick M. Hess (ed.): *With the Best of Intentions: How Philanthropy Is Reshaping K-12 Education*. Cambridge, MA: Harvard Education Press, pp. 1–17.

Hess, Frederick M. (2005b): Conclusion. In: Frederick M. Hess (ed.): *With the Best of Intentions. How Philanthropy Is Reshaping K-12 Education*. Cambridge, MA: Harvard Education Press, pp. 295–312.

Hippel, Eric von (1994): "Sticky Information" and the Locus of Problem Solving: Implications for Innovation. In: *Management Science* 40 (4), pp. 429–439.

Hofstede, Geert (1981): Management Control of Public and Not-for-Profit Activities. In: *Accounting, Organizations and Society* 6 (3), pp. 193–211.

Howaldt, Jürgen; Schwarz, Michael (2010): *"Soziale Innovation" im Fokus. Skizze eines gesellschaftstheoretisch inspirierten Forschungskonzepts.* Bielefeld: transcript.

Human, Sherrie E.; Provan, Keith G. (2000): Legitimacy Building in the Evolution of Small-Firm Multilateral Networks: A Comparative Study of Success and Demise. In: *Administrative Science Quarterly* 45 (2), pp. 327–365.

Hutchinson, G. Evelyn (1957): Concluding Remarks. In: *Cold Spring Harbor Symposium on Quantitative Biology* 22, pp. 415–427.

Hwang, Hokyu; Powell, Walter W. (2009): The Rationalization of Charity: The Influences of Professionalism in the Nonprofit Sector. In: *Administrative Science Quarterly* 54 (2), pp. 268–298.

Ilten, Carla (2009): *Strategisches und soziales Nischenmanagement: Zur Analyse gesellschaftspolitisch motivierter Innovation.* Wiesbaden: VS Verlag für Sozialwissenschaften.

Institute for Philanthropy (2009): *Supportive to the Core: Why Unrestricted Funding Matters.* Retrieved from www.tpw.org/images/files/supportive_to_the_core.pdf.

Internationale Gärten (2015): www.internationale-gaerten.de/.

Jamrozik, Adam; Nocella, Luisa (1998): *The Sociology of Social Problems. Theoretical Perspectives and Methods of Intervention.* Cambridge: Cambridge University Press.

Jennings, Edward T.; Ewalt, Jo Ann G. (1998): Interorganizational Coordination, Administrative Consolidation, and Policy Performance. In: *Public Administration Review* 58 (5), p. 417.

Joas, Hans (1992): *Die Kreativität des Handelns.* Frankfurt am Main: Suhrkamp.

Jonassen, David H. (2000): Toward a Design Theory of Problem Solving. In: *Educational Technology Research and Development* 48 (4), pp. 63–85.

JRCT (2015): www.jrct.org.uk/about us.

Kail, Angela; Lumley, Tris (2012): *Theory of Change: The Beginning of Making a Difference.* London: Edited by New Philanthropy Capital.

Kania, John; Kramer, Mark R. (2011): Collective Impact. In: *Stanford Social Innovation Review* 9 (1), pp. 36–41.

Kania, John; Kramer, Mark R. (2013): Embracing Emergence: How Collective Impact Addresses Complexity. In: *Stanford Social Innovation Review,* pp. 1–7.

Kania, John; Kramer, Mark R.; Russell, Patty (2014): Strategic Philanthropy for a Complex World. *Stanford Social Innovation Review,* pp. 26–33.

Katz, Stanley N. (2005): What Does It Mean to Say That Philanthropy Is 'Effective'? The Philanthropists' New Clothes. In: *Proceedings of the American Philosophical Society* 149 (2), pp. 123–131.

Kaufmann, Franz-Xaver (1999): Konzept und Formen sozialer Intervention. In: Günter Albrecht, Axel Groenemeyer and Friedrich W. Stallberg (eds.): *Handbuch soziale Probleme.* Opladen, Wiesbaden: Westdeutscher Verlag, pp. 921–940.

Kemp, René; Rip, Arie; Schot, Johan W. (2001): Constructing transition paths through the management of niches. In Raghu Garud and Peter Karnoe (eds.): *Path Dependence and Creation.* Mahwah (N.J.) and London: Lawrence Erlbaum, pp. 269–299

Kemp, René; Schot, Johan; Hoogma, Remco (1998): Regime Shifts to Sustainability Through Processes of Niche Formation: The Approach of Strategic Niche Management. In: *Technology Analysis & Strategic Management* 10 (2), pp. 175–195.

Kern, Thomas (2008): *Soziale Bewegungen: Ursachen, Wirkungen, Mechanismen.* Wiesbaden: VS Verlag für Sozialwissenschaften.

Kettl, Donald F. (2009): *The Next Government of the United States: Why Our Institutions Fail Us and How to Fix Them.* 1st ed. New York: W. W. Norton & Co.

Kitcher, Philip (2005): The Hall of Mirrors. In: *Proceedings of the American Philosophical Society* 79 (2), pp. 67–84.

Kitcher, Phillip (2009): Education, Democracy, and Capitalism. In: *The Oxford Handbook of Philosophy of Education,* pp. 300–318.

Kitsuse, John I.; Spector, Malcom (1973): Toward a Sociology of Social Problems: Social Conditions, Value-Judgments, and Social Problems. In: *Social Problems* 20 (4), pp. 407–419.

Knott, Jack H.; McCarthy, Diane (2007): Policy Venture Capital: Foundations, Government Partnerships and Child Care Programs. In: *Administration & Society* 39 (3), pp. 319–353.

Kohn, Melvin L. (1976): Looking Back—A 25-Year Review and Appraisal of Social Problems Research. In: *Social Problems* 24 (1), pp. 94–112.

Kroeger, Arne; Weber, Christiane (2014): Developing a Conceptual Framework for Comparing Social Value Creation. In: *Academy of Management Review* 39 (4), pp. 513–540.

Krüger, Susanna (2010): *The "Intercultural Gardens" of the Foundation "Interkultur",* Germany. Unpublished case report.

Kurz, Bettina; Kubek, Doreen (2013): *Kursbuch Wirkung: Das Praxishandbuch für Alle, die Gutes noch besser tun wollen.* Berlin: Phineo.

Landau, Martin; Stout, Russel, J.R. (1979): To Manage Is Not to Control: Or the Folly of Type II Errors. In: *Public Administration Review* 39 (2), pp. 148–156.

Lawrence, Paul R.; Lorsch, Jay William (1986): *Organization and Environment: Managing Differentiation and Integration.* Boston: Harvard Business School Press.

Leat, Diana (2005): *Foundations and Policy Involvement: Creating Options.* York: Joseph Rowntree Charitable Trust.

Leat, Diana (2008): *The Nuffield Foundation and the Nuffield Council on Bio-Ethics*. Unpublished Casereport.

Levin, Kelly; Cashore, Benjamin; Bernstein, Steven; Auld, Graeme (2012): Overcoming the Tragedy of Super Wicked Problems: Constraining Our Future Selves to Ameliorate Global Climate Change. In: *Policy Sciences* 45 (2), pp. 123–152.

Levine, Donald N. (1995): *Visions of the Sociological Tradition*. Chicago, London: University of Chicago Press.

Levinthal, Daniel A. (1997): Adaptation on Rugged Landscapes. In: *Management Science* 43 (7), pp. 934–950.

Levinthal, Daniel A. (1998): The Slow Pace of Rapid Technological Change: Gradualism and Punctuation in Technological Change. In: *Industrial and Corporate Change* 7 (2), pp. 217–247.

Levinthal, Daniel A.; Warglien, Massimo (1999): Landscape Design: Designing for Local Action in Complex Worlds. In: *Organization Science* 10 (3), pp. 342–357.

Light, Paul C. (2006): Reshaping Social Entrepreneurship. In: *Stanford Social Innovation Review* 4 (3), pp. 47–51.

Liket, Kellie (2014): *Why Doing Good Is Not Good Enough: Essays on Social Impact Measurement*. Doctoral Dissertation, Rotterdam, PhD Series in Research in Management 307.

Lindblom, Charles E. (1959): The Science of "Muddling Through". In: *Public Administration Review* 19 (2), pp. 79–88.

Lindblom, Charles E. (1979): Still Muddling, Not Yet Through. In: *Public Administration Review* 39 (6), pp. 517–526.

List, Regina (2009): *The Joseph Rowntree Charitable Trust and the Campaign for Freedom of Information*. Unpublished case report.

Lock, Stephen (1990): Towards a National Bioethics Committee. In: *British Medical Journal* 300 (6733), pp. 1149–1150.

McCaskey, Michael B. (1974): A Contingency Approach to Planning: Planning With Goals and Planning Without Goals. In: *Academy of Management Journal* 17 (2), pp. 281–291.

March, James G. (1978): Bounded Rationality, Ambiguity, and the Engineering of Choice. In: *The Bell Journal of Economics* 9 (2), pp. 587–608.

March, James G. (1991): Exploration and Exploitation in Organizational Learning. Special Issue: Organizational Learning: Papers in Honor of (and by) James G. March. In: *Organization Science* 2 (1), pp. 71–87.

Martin, Andy; Tweed, Helen; Hughes, Ruthann and van der Hoeven, Ilse (2015): *Nuffield Council on Bioethics Evaluation*. London: Firetail Ltd. Unpublished report.

Martin, Roger L.; Osberg, Sally (2007): Social Entrepreneurship: The Case for Definition. In: *Stanford Social Innovation Review* 5 (2), pp. 27–39.

Mayntz, Renate (1983): Zur Einleitung: Probleme der Theoriebildung in der Implementationsforschung. In: Renate Mayntz (ed.): *Implementation politischer Programme II: Ansätze zur Theoriebildung*. Opladen: Westdeutscher Verlag, pp. 7–24.

Mayntz, Renate (1997): The Conditions of Effective Public Policy. In: Renate Mayntz (ed.): *Soziale Dynamik und politische Steuerung: theoretische und methodologische Überlegungen*. Frankfurt am Main, New York: Campus, pp. 143–167.

Mayntz, Renate (2004): Mechanisms in the Analysis of Social Macro-Phenomena. In: *Philosophy of the Social Sciences* 34 (2), pp. 237–259.

Mead, George H. (1929): National-Mindedness and International-Mindedness. In: *International Journal of Ethics* 39 (4), pp. 385–407.

Meier, Kenneth J.; O'Toole, Laurence J. (2003): Public Management and Educational Performance: The Impact of Managerial Networking. In: *Public Administration Review* 63 (6), pp. 689–699.

Merton, Robert K. (1936): The Unanticipated Consequences of Purposive Social Action. In: *American Sociological Review* 1 (6), pp. 894–904.

Merton, Robert K. (1968): On Sociological Theories of the Middle Range. In: Robert K. Merton (ed.): *Social Theory and Social Structure*. New York: Free Press, pp. 29–72.

Merton, Robert K. (1976): Introduction: The Sociology of Social Problems. In: Robert K. Merton, Robert Nisbet (eds.): *Contemporary Social Problems*. 4th ed. New York: Harcourt Brace Jovanovich, pp. 3–43.

Miller, Danny (1988): Relating Porter's Business Strategies to Environment and Structure: Analysis and Performance Implications. In: *Academy of Management Journal* 31 (2), pp. 280–308.

Mills, C. Wright (1966): *Sociology and Pragmatism: The Higher Learning in America*. New York: Oxford University Press.

Ministry of Justice (2014): *Freedom of Information Statistics: Implementation in Central Government*. Retrieved from www.gov.uk/government/uploads/system/uploads/attachment_data/file/423487/foi-statistics-oct-dec-2014-annual.pdf.

Mintzberg, Henry (1979a): Patterns in Strategy Formation. In: *International Studies of Management & Organization* 9 (3), pp. 67–86.

Mintzberg, Henry (1979b): *The Structuring of Organizations: A Synthesis of the Research*. Englewood Cliffs, NJ: Prentice-Hall.

Mintzberg, Henry (1990): The Design School: Reconsidering the Basic Premises of Strategic Management. In: *Strategic Management Journal* 11 (3), pp. 171–195.

Mintzberg, Henry; Quinn, J.; Ghoshal, Sumantra (1998): *The Strategy Process*. Revised European Edition. Hertfordshire: Prentice Hall.

Mitroff, Ian I.; Emshoff, James R.; Kilmann, Ralph H. (1979): Assumptional Analysis: A Methodology for Strategic Problem Solving. In: *Management Science* 25 (6), pp. 583–593.

Monroe, Kristen Renwick (1994): A Fat Lady in a Corset: Altruism and Social Theory. In: *American Journal of Political Science* 38 (4), pp. 861–893.

Moore, Mark H. (2000): Managing for Value: Organizational Strategy in for-Profit, Nonprofit, and Governmental Organizations. In: *Nonprofit and Voluntary Sector Quarterly* 29 (1), pp. 183–204.

Moore, Michele-Lee; Westley, Frances (2011): Surmountable Chasms: Networks and Social Innovation for Resilient Systems. In: *Ecology and Society* 16 (1), p. 5.

Moulaert, Frank; Martinelli, Flavia; Swyngedouw, Erik; González, Sara (2005): Towards Alternative Model(s) of Local Innovation. In: *Urban Studies* 42 (11), pp. 1969–1990.

Müller, Christa (2002): *Wurzeln schlagen in der Fremde—Die internationalen Gärten und ihre Bedeutung für Integrationsprozesse*. München: oekom.

Müller, Christa (2012): Interkulturelle Gärten als innovative Antwort auf soziale Entwurzelung. In: G. Beck and C. Kropp (eds.): *Gesellschaft innovativ. Wer sind die Akteure?* VS Verlag für Sozialwissenschaften, pp. 103–117.

Murphey, Murray G. (1983): Introduction. In: *The Collected Works of John Dewey, Vol. 14: 1922. Human Nature and Conduct.* Carbondale: Southern Illinois University Press, pp. 4–11.

Nagl, Ludwig (1998): *Pragmatismus.* Frankfurt am Main: Campus.

Nelson, Richard R.; Winter, Sidney G. (1977): In: Search of Useful Theory of Innovation. In: *Research Policy* 6 (1), pp. 36–76.

Neuenschwander, Markus P. (2014): Coaching und Schulung sind wirksam. In: *Panorama* 2/2014, pp. 30–31.

Nickel, Patricia Mooney; Eikenberry, Angela M. (2009): A Critique of the Discourse of Marketized Philanthropy. In: *American Behavioral Scientist* 52 (7), pp. 974–989.

Nielsen, Waldemar N. (1972): *The Big Foundations.* New York and London: Columbia University Press.

Nill, Jan; Kemp, René (2009): Evolutionary Approaches for Sustainable Innovation Policies: From Niche to Paradigm? In: *Research Policy* 38 (4), pp. 668–680.

Nuffield Council (2000): *Nuffield Council on Bioethics 1992–99.* Retrieved from http://nuffieldbioethics.org/wp-content/uploads/REVIEW.pdf.

Nuffield Council (2012): *Strategic Plan 2012–2016: Exploring Ethical Issues in Biology and Medicine.* Retrieved from http://nuffieldbioethics.org/wp-content/uploads/2014/06/Strategic_Plan_2012-2016.pdf.

Nuffield Council (2013): *Annual Report.* Retrieved from: http://nuffieldbioethics.org/annualreport2013/index.php.

Nuffield Foundation (2011): *Nuffield Council on Bioethics 1991–2011: 20 Years of Investigating and Illuminating Ethical Issues in Biology and Medicine.* London: Nuffield Foundation.

Nuffield Foundation (2015): www.nuffieldfoundation.org/.

Oelkers, Jürgen (2008): Eine pragmatische Sicht auf Schulentwicklung. In: *Journal für Schulentwicklung* 12 (2), pp. 7–13.

Offe, Claus (2002): Wessen Wohl ist das Gemeinwohl? In: Herfried Münkler and Karsten Fischer (eds.): *Gemeinwohl und Gemeinsinn: Rhetoriken und Perspektiven sozial-moralischer Orientierung.* Berlin: Akademie Verlag, pp. 55–76.

Ogliastri, Enrique; Jäger, Urs P.; M. Prado, Andrea (2015): Strategy and Structure in High-Performing Nonprofits: Insights from Iberoamerican Cases. In: *Voluntas* 27 (1), pp. 1–27.

Orton, J. Douglas; Weick, Karl E. (1990): Loosely Coupled Systems: A Reconceptualization. In: *Academy of Management Review* 15 (2), pp. 203–223.

O'Toole, Laurence J. (1997): Treating Networks Seriously: Practical and Research-Based Agendas in Public Administration. In: *Public Administration Review* 57 (1), pp. 45–52.

Pape, Helmut (2000): The Unity of Classical Pragmatism: Its Scope and Its Limits. In: *The Proceedings of the Twentieth World Congress of Philosophy* 8, pp. 233–244.

Parsons, Talcott (1968): *The Structure of Social Action: A Study in Social Theory with Special Reference to a Group of Recent European Writers.* Vol. I. New York: Free Press.

Peirce, Charles S. (2011 [1877]): The Fixation of Belief. In: Robert B. Talisse and Scott F. Aikin (eds.): *The Pragmatism Reader: From Peirce Through the Present.* Princeton and Oxford: Princeton University Press, pp. 37–49.

Pepall, Lynne (1992): Strategic Product Choice and Niche Markets. In: *Journal of Economics & Management Strategy* 1 (2), pp. 397–417.

Peters, Helge (2002): *Soziale Probleme und soziale Kontrolle.* Wiesbaden: Westdeutscher Verlag.

Phineo (Ed.) (2012): *Engagement mit Wirkung.* Berlin. Retrieved from www.phineo. org/downloads/PHINEO_Engagement_mit_Wirkung.pdf.

Piliavin, Jane Allyn; Charng, Hong-Wen (1990): Altruism: A Review of Recent Theory and Research. In: *Annual Review of Sociology* 16 (1), pp. 27–65.

Pogge, Thomas (2011): How International Nongovernmental Organizations Should Act. In: Patricia Illingworth, Thomas Pogge and Leif Wenar (eds.): *Giving Well.* New York and Oxford: Oxford University Press, pp. 46–66.

Porter, Michael E. (1980): *Competitive Strategy: Techniques for Analyzing Industries and Competitors.* New York: Free Press.

Porter, Michael E. (1996): What Is Strategy? In: *Harvard Business Review,* pp. 61–78.

Porter, Michael E.; Kramer, Mark R. (1999): Philanthropy's New Agenda: Creating Value. In: *Harvard Business Review* 77 (6), pp. 121–130.

Portes, Pedro R. (2005): *Dismantling Educational Inequality: A Cultural-Historical Approach to Closing the Achievement Gap.* New York: P. Lang.

Powell, Walter W.; Koput, Kenneth W.; Smith-Doerr, Laurel (1996): Interorganizational Collaboration and the Locus of Innovation: Networks of Learning in Biotechnology. In: *Administrative Science Quarterly* 41 (1), pp. 116–145.

Power, Michael (1999): *The Audit Society: Rituals of Verification.* Oxford: Oxford University Press.

Prewitt, Kenneth (2006): Foundations. In: Walter W. Powell and Richard Steinberg (eds.): *The Nonprofit Sector. A Research Handbook.* 2nd ed. New Haven, London: Yale University Press, pp. 355–377.

Provan, Keith G.; Kenis, Patrick (2008): Modes of Network Governance: Structure, Management, and Effectiveness. In: *Journal of Public Administration Research and Theory* 18 (2), pp. 229–252.

Provan, Keith G.; Lemaire, Robin H. (2012): Core Concepts and Key Ideas for Understanding Public Sector Organizational Networks: Using Research to Inform Scholarship and Practice. In: *Public Administration Review* 72 (5), pp. 638–648.

Provan, Keith G.; Milward, Brinton H. (1995): A Preliminary Theory of Interorganizational Network Effectiveness: A Comparative Study of Four Community Mental Health Systems. In: *Administrative Science Quarterly* 40 (1), pp. 1–33.

Provan, Keith G.; Sebastian, Juliann G. (1998): Networks Within Networks: Service Link Overlap, Organizational Cliques, and Network Effectiveness. In: *Academy of Management Journal* 41 (4), pp. 453–463.

Rauscher, Olivia; Schober, Christian; Millner, Reinhard (2012): *Social Impact Measurement und Social Return on Investment (SROI)-Analyse. Wirkungsmessung neu?* Working Paper. NPO-Kompetenzzentrum WU Wien. Wien.

Raven, Rob; Geels, Frank W. (2010): Socio-Cognitive Evolution in Niche Development: Comparative Analysis of Biogas Development in Denmark and the Netherlands (1973–2004). In: *Technovation* 30, pp. 87–99.

Reckhow, Sarah (2013): *Follow the Money: How Foundation Dollars Change Public School Politics.* New York, Oxford: Oxford University Press.

Rittel, Horst W.J.; Webber, Melvin M. (1973): Dilemmas in a General Theory of Planning. In: *Policy Sciences* 4 (2), pp. 155–169.

Robeyns, Ingrid (2006): The Capability Approach in Practice. In: *The Journal of Political Philosophy* 14 (3), pp. 351–376.

Roche, Chris (1999): *Impact Assessment for Development Agencies: Learning to Value Change*. Oxford: Oxfam.

Roelofs, Joan (2003): *Foundations and Public Policy: The Mask of Pluralism*. Albany, NY: State University of New York Press.

Rowan, Brian (2002): Rationality and Reality in Organizational Management: Using the Coupling Metaphor to Understand Educational (and Other) Organizations— a Concluding Comment. In: *Journal of Educational Administration* 40 (6), pp. 604–611.

Rowan, Brian; Miller, Robert J. (2007): Organizational Strategies for Promoting Instructional Change: Implementation Dynamics in Schools Working With Comprehensive School Reform Providers. In: *American Educational Research Journal* 44 (2), pp. 252–297.

Salamon, Lester M. (2014): *Leverage for Good: An Introduction to the New Frontiers of Philanthropy and Social Investment*. Oxford, New York: Oxford University Press.

Santos, Filipe M.; Eisenhardt, Kathleen M. (2009): Constructing Markets and Shaping Boundaries: Entrepreneurial Power in Nascent Fields. In: *Academy of Management Journal* 52 (4), pp. 643–671.

Sarasvathy, Saras D. (2001): Causation and Effectuation: Toward a Theoretical Shift from Economic Inevitability to Entrepreneurial Contingency. In: *Academy of Management Review* 26 (2), pp. 243–263.

Sarasvathy, Saras D.; Dew, Nicholas; Read, Stuart; Wiltbank, Robert (2008): Designing Organizations That Design Environments: Lessons from Entrepreneurial Expertise. In: *Organization Studies* 29 (3), pp. 331–350.

Schambra, William (2014): The Coming Showdown Between Philanthrolocalism and Effective Altruism. *Philanthropy Daily*. Retrieved from www.philanthropy daily.com/the-coming-showdown-between-philanthrolocalism-and-effective-altruism/.

Scheffler, Israel (1974): Four Pragmatists: A Critical Introduction to Peirce, James, Mead, and Dewey. London, New York: Routledge and Kegan Paul.

Schetsche, Michael (2008): *Empirische Analyse sozialer Probleme: Das wissenssoziologische Programm*. Wiesbaden: VS Verlag für Sozialwissenschaften.

Schimank, Uwe (2002): Handeln und Strukturen: Einführung in die akteurthoretische Soziologie. Weinheim und München: Juventa.

Schöller, Oliver (2006): Bildung geht stiften. Zur Rolle von Think Tanks in der Wissensgesellschaft. In: Uwe H. Bittlingmayer and Ullrich Bauer (eds.): *Die "Wissensgesellschaft". Mythos, Ideologie oder Realität?* Wiesbaden: VS Verlag für Sozialwissenschaften, pp. 285–320.

Schön, Donald A. (1971): *Beyond the Stable State*. New York: Norton.

Schön, Donald A. (1987): *Educating the Reflective Practitioner*. San Francisco: Jossey-Bass.

Scholte, Jan A. (2013): Civil Society and Financial Markets: What is Not Happening and Why. *Journal of Civil Society*, 9 (2), pp. 129–147.

Schot, Johan (1998): The usefulness of evolutionary models for explaining innovation. The case of the Netherlands in the nineteenth century. In: *History and Technology* 14(3), pp. 173–200.

Schot, Johan; Geels, Frank W. (2007): Niches in Evolutionary Theories of Technical Change. In: *Journal of Evolutionary Economics* 17 (5), pp. 605–622.

Schot, Johan; Geels, Frank W. (2008): Strategic Niche Management and Sustainable Innovation Journeys: Theory, Findings, Research Agenda, and Policy. In: *Technology Analysis & Strategic Management* 20 (5), pp. 537–554.

Schumpeter, Joseph A. (2012): *The Theory of Economic Development: An Inquiry Into Profits, Capital, Credit, Interest, and the Business Cycle.* New Brunswick, NJ: Transaction Publishers.

Sebeok, Thomas A.; Umiker-Sebeok, Jean (1979): "You Know my Method": A Juxtaposition of Charles S. Peirce and Sherlock Holmes. In: *Semiotica* 26 (3–4), pp. 203–250.

Seelos, Christian; Mair, Johanna (2014): Organizational Closure Competencies and Scaling: A Realist Approach to Theorizing Social Enterprise. In: *Research Methodology in Strategy and Management* 9, pp. 147–187.

Seibel, Wolfgang (1994): *Funktionaler Dilettantismus.* Baden-Baden: Nomos.

Seibel, Wolfgang (1996): Successful Failure: An Alternative View on Organizational Coping. In: *American Behavioral Scientist* 39 (8), pp. 1011–1024.

Sen, Amartya (1980): Equality of What? In: Sterling M. McMurrin (ed.): *The Tanner Lectures on Human Values.* Salt Lake City: University of Utah Press, pp. 197–220.

Sen, Amartya (1985): Well-Being, Agency and Freedom: The Dewey Lectures 1984. In: *The Journal of Philosophy* 82 (4), pp. 169–221.

Sen, Amartya (1993): Capability and Well-Being. In: Martha C. Nussbaum and Amartya Sen (eds.): *The Quality of Life.* Oxford: Clarendon, pp. 30–53.

Seyfang, Gill; Haxeltine, Alex (2012): Growing Grassroots Innovations: Exploring the Role of Community-Based Initiatives in Governing Sustainable Energy Transitions. In: *Environment and Planning C: Government and Policy* 30 (3), p. 381.

Seyfang, Gill; Longhurst, Noel (2013): Desperately Seeking Niches: Grassroots Innovations and Niche Development in the Community Currency Field. In: *Global Environmental Change* 23 (5), pp. 881–891.

Seyfang, Gill; Smith, Adrian (2007): Grassroots Innovations for Sustainable Development: Towards a New Research and Policy Agenda. In: *Environmental Politics* 16 (4), pp. 584–603.

Shear, Linda; Means, Barbara; Mitchell, Karen; House, Anne; Gorges, Torie; Joshi, Aasha; Smerdon, Becky; Shkolnik, Jamie (2008): Contrasting Paths to Small-School Reform: Results of a 5-Year Evaluation of the Bill & Melinda Gates Foundation's National High Schools Initiative. In: *Teachers College Record* 110 (9), pp. 1986–2039.

Sigmund, Steffen (2000): Grenzgänge: Stiften zwischen zivilgesellschaftlichem Engagement und symbolischer Anerkennung. In: *Berliner Journal für Soziologie* 10 (3), pp. 333–348.

Sigmund, Steffen (2004): Solidarität durch intermediäre Institutionen: Stiftungen. In: Jens Beckert, Julia Eckert, Martin Kohli and Wolfgang Streeck (eds.): *Transnationale Solidarität: Chancen und Grenzen.* Frankfurt am Main, New York: Campus Verlag, pp. 95–108.

Simon, Herbert A. (1962): The Architecture of Complexity. In: *Proceedings of the American Philosophical Society* 106 (6), pp. 467–482.

Simon, Herbert A. (1973): The Structure of Ill Structured Problems. In: *Artificial Intelligence 4*, pp. 81–201.

Singer, Peter (1972): Famine, Affluence, and Morality. In: *Philosophy & Public Affairs* 1 (3), pp. 229–243.

Small, Mario Luis (2006): Neighborhood Institutions as Resource Brokers: Childcare Centers, Interorganizational Ties, and Resource Access Among the Poor. In: *Social Problems* 53 (2), pp. 274–292.

Smith, Adrian; Raven, Rob (2012): What Is Protective Space? Reconsidering Niches in Transitions to Sustainability. In: *Research Policy* 41 (6), pp. 1025–1036.

Snowden, David J.; Boone, Mary E. (2007): A Leader's Framework for Decision Making. In: *Harvard Business Review*, pp. 1–9.

Stanat, Petra; Becker, Michael; Baumert, Jürgen; Lüdtke, Oliver; Eckhardt, Andrea G. (2012): Improving Second Language Skills of Immigrant Students: A Field Trial Study Evaluating the Effects of a Summer Learning Program. In: *Learning and Instruction* 22 (3), pp. 159–170.

Stinchcombe, Arthur L. (1991): The Conditions of Fruitfulness of Theorizing About Mechanisms in Social Science. In: *Philosophy of the Social Sciences* 21 (3), pp. 367–388.

Streeck, Wolfgang (2011): The Crises of Democratic Capitalism. In: *New Left Review* (71), pp. 5–29.

Sulek, Marty (2010): On the Modern Meaning of Philanthropy. In: *Nonprofit and Voluntary Sector Quarterly* 39 (2), pp. 193–212.

Swailes, Heather (1988): *Democracy, Power and Justice in the UK*. Report to the Trustees of the Joseph Rowntree Charitable Trust. Unpublished Paper.

Sydow, Momme von (2013): Metaphysics, Darwinian. In: *Encyclopedia of Sciences and Religions*. New York: Springer, pp. 1306–1314.

Talisse, Robert B.; Aikin, Scott F. (2008): *Pragmatism: A Guide for the Perplexed*. London, New York: Continuum.

Talisse, Robert B.; Aikin, Scott F. (Eds.) (2011): *The Pragmatism Reader: From Peirce Through the Present*. Princeton and Oxford: Princeton University Press.

Tayart de Borms, Luc (2003): *Foundations: Creating Impact in a Globalised World*. Chichester: John Wiley.

Thaler, Richard H.; Sunstein, Cass R. (2008): *Nudge: Improving Decisions About Health, Wealth, and Happiness*. New Haven, CT: Yale University Press.

Thayer, Horace S. (1981): *Meaning and Action. A Critical History of Pragmatism*. Indianapolis: Hackett.

The Chance (2010): *Jahresbericht 2010*. Retrieved from www.die-chance.ch/down load/pictures/60/s197owqlk19wq4u064strgxmuw0xwg/jahresbericht2010.pdf.

The Chance (2012): *Jahresbericht 2012*. Retrieved from www.die-chance.ch/down load/pictures/f9/2ctv5a8hbfcj4osiqgm9uotdpl9fy9/jahresbericht2012.pdf.

The Chance (2013): *Jahresbericht 2013*. Retrieved from www.die-chance.ch/down load/pictures/8b/pl2gjl4t5b7m73fgysvn4m4emwb28t/l_geschaftsbericht_dc-2013.pdf.

The Chance (2014a): *Jahresbericht 2014*. Retrieved from www.die-chance.ch/ download/pictures/a6/6d016rwt72n4r4c3nkc6gf8r2cqr7g/l_geschaeftsbericht_dc_2014.pdf.

The Chance (2014b) *Strategischer Rahmen 2014–2016*. Unpublished document.

The Chance (2015a): www.die-chance.ch/.

The Chance (2015b): Reporting 2014/15. Gründung des Dachvereins "Check Your Chance".

Thornton, Patricia H.; Ocasio, William (2008): Institutional Logics. In: Royston Greenwood, Christine Oliver, Roy Suddaby and Kerstin Sahlin-Andersson (eds.): *The Sage Handbook of Organizational Institutionalism*. London: Sage, pp. 99–129.

Thümler, Ekkehard (2010): Nuffield Foundation. In: Helmut K. Anheier and Stefan Toepler (eds.): *International Encyclopedia of Civil Society*. New York: Springer, pp. 1103–1104.

Thümler, Ekkehard (2011): Foundations, Schools and the State: School Improvement Partnerships in Germany and the United States as Legitimacy-Generating Arrangements. In: *Public Management Review* 13 (8), pp. 1095–1116.

Thümler, Ekkehard (2015): *Erfolgsbedingungen Staatlich-Philanthropischer Bildungspartnerschaften*. Project report. Heidelberg: Centre for Social Investment.

Thümler, Ekkehard (2016): Financialization of Philanthropy: The Case of Social Investment. In: Jenny Harrow, Tobias Jung and Susan Phillips (eds.): *The Routledge Companion to Philanthropy*. London: Routledge, pp. 362–374.

Thümler, Ekkehard; Bögelein, Nicole (2010): Strategies for Impact in Philanthropy Teil 2: Ein pragmatisches Modell der Problemlösung durch Stiftungen. In: *Stiftung & Sponsoring* 6, pp. 38–41.

Thümler, Ekkehard; Bögelein, Nicole (2012): Sind Stiftungen Soziale Investoren? Zur Anwendbarkeit eines ökonomischen Begriffs auf die Tätigkeit gemeinnütziger europäischer Stiftungen. In: Helmut K. Anheier, Andreas Schröer and Volker Then (eds.): *Soziale Investitionen. Interdisziplinäre Perspektiven*. Wiesbaden: VS Verlag für Sozialwissenschaften, pp. 257–275.

Thümler, Ekkehard; Bögelein, Nicole; Beller, Annelie (2014a): Education Philanthropy in Germany and the United States. In: Ekkehard Thümler, Nicole Bögelein, Annelie Beller and Helmut K. Anheier (eds.), *Philanthropy and Education. Strategies for Impact*. Basingstoke: Palgrave Macmillan, pp. 3–28.

Thümler, Ekkehard; Bögelein, Nicole; Beller, Annelie (2014b): Philanthropic Impact and Effectiveness in Education. In Ekkehard Thümler, Nicole Bögelein, Annelie Beller and Helmut K. Anheier (eds.), *Philanthropy and Education. Strategies for Impact*. Basingstoke: Palgrave Macmillan, pp. 207–235.

Thümler, Ekkehard; Nelles, Mattia (2015): Die Chance: Stiftung für Berufspraxis in der Ostschweiz. In: Ekkehard Thümler: *Erfolgsbedingungen Staatlich-Philanthropischer Bildungspartnerschaften*. CSI Project Report, Heidelberg, pp. 25–27.

Tilly, Charles (2001): Mechanisms in Political Processes. In: *Annual Review of Political Science* 4 (1), pp. 21–41.

Timmer, Karsten (2005): *Stiften in Deutschland: die Ergebnisse der StifterStudie*. Gütersloh: Bertelsmann Stiftung.

Tisdell, Clem; Seidl, Irmi (2004): Niches and Economic Competition: Implications for Economic Efficiency, Growth and Diversity. In: *Structural Change and Economic Dynamics* 15 (2), pp. 119–135.

Tolbert, Pamela S.; Zucker, Lynne G. (1983): Institutional Sources of Change in the Formal Structure of Organizations: The Diffusion of Civil Service Reform, 1880–1935. In: *Administrative Science Quarterly* 28 (1), pp. 22–39.

Tolbert, Pamela S.; Zucker, Lynne G. (1996): The Institutionalization of Institutional Theory. In: Stewart R. Clegg, Cynthia Hardy, Walter R. Nord (eds.): *Handbook of Organization Studies*. London: Sage, pp. 175–190.

Tomasello, Michael (2009): *Why We Cooperate*. Cambridge, MA: MIT Press.

Tsoukas, Haridimos (1989): The Validity of Idiographic Research Explanations. In: *Academy of Management Review* 14 (4), pp. 551–561.

Tsoukas, Haridimos (1994): What Is Management? An Outline of a Metatheory. In: *British Journal of Management* 5 (4), pp. 289–301.

Turrini, Alex; Cristofoli, Daniela; Frosini, Francesca; Nasi, Greta (2010): Networking Literature About Determinants of Network Effectiveness. In: *Public Administration* 88 (2), pp. 528–550.

Tyack, David; Cuban, Larry (1995): *Tinkering Toward Utopia: A Century of Public School Reform*. Cambridge, MA: Harvard University Press.

Tyre, Marcie J.; Hippel, Eric von (1997): The Situated Nature of Adaptive Learning in Organizations. In: *Organization Science* 8 (1), pp. 71–83.

United Nations Development Programme (Ed.) (2009): *Supporting Capacity Development: The UNDP Approach*. Retrieved from www.undp.org/content/dam/aplaws/publication/en/publications/capacity-development/support-capacity-develop ment-the-undp-approach/CDG_Brochure_2009.pdf, checked on 3/09/2015.

Van de Ven, Andrew H.; Polley, Douglas E.; Garud, Raghu; Venkataraman, Sankaran (2008): *The Innovation Journey*. Oxford, New York: Oxford University Press.

Van de Ven, Andrew H.; Poole, Marshall Scott (1995): Explaining Development and Change in Organizations. In: *The Academy of Management Review* 20 (3), pp. 510–540.

Verheul, Hugo; Vergragt, Philip J. (1995): Social Experiments in the Development of Environmental Technology: A Bottom-Up Perspective. In: *Technology Analysis & Strategic Management* 7 (3), pp. 315–326.

Wagner, Richard K. (1991): Managerial Problem Solving. In: Robert J. Sternberg and Peter Frensch (eds.): *Complex Problem Solving. Principles and Mechanisms*. Hillsdale, NJ: Lawrence Erlbaum, pp. 159–222.

Weaver, R. Kent (2014): Compliance Regimes and Barriers to Behavioral Change. In: *Governance* 27 (2), pp. 243–265.

Weber, Christina; Kröger, Arne; Kunz, Linda; Lambrich, Kathrin; Peters, Maria; Labitzke, Gerald (2013): *Skalierung sozialer Wirkung: Handbuch zu Strategien und Erfolgsfaktoren von Sozialunternehmern*. Gütersloh: Bertelsmann Stiftung.

Weber, Eric Thomas (2011): What Experimentalism Means in Ethics. In: *The Journal of Speculative Philosophy* 25 (1), pp. 98–115.

Weber, Klaus (2006): From Nuts and Bolts to Toolkits: Theorizing With Mechanisms. In: *Journal of Management Inquiry* 15 (2), pp. 119–123.

Weick, Karl E. (1976): Educational Organizations as Loosely Coupled Systems. In: *Administrative Science Quarterly* 21, pp. 1–19.

Weick, Karl E. (1984): Small Wins: Redefining the Scale of Social Problems. In: *American Psychologist* 39 (1), pp. 40–49.

Weisbrod, Burton A. (1998): The Nonprofit Mission and Its Financing: Growing Links Between Nonprofits and the Rest of the Economy. In: Burton A. Weisbrod (ed.): *To Profit or Not to Profit: The Commercial Transformation of the Nonprofit Sector*. Cambridge: Cambridge University Press, pp. 1–22.

Weiss, Janet A. (2000): From Research to Social Improvement: Understanding Theories of Intervention. In: *Nonprofit and Voluntary Sector Quarterly* 29 (1), pp. 81–110.

Wernicke, Jens; Bultmann, Torsten (eds.) (2007): *Netzwerk der Macht—Bertelsmann. Der medial-politische Komplex aus Gütersloh*. 2nd ed. Marburg: BdWi-Verlag.

West, Cornel (1989): *The American Evasion of Philosophy: A Genealogy of Pragmatism*. Madison, WI: The University of Wisconsin Press.

Whitford, Josh (2002): Pragmatism and the Untenable Dualism of Means and Ends: Why Rational Choice Theory Does Not Deserve Paradigmatic Privilege. In: *Theory and Society* 31 (3), pp. 325–363.

Wikipedia (2015): *Nuffield Council on Bioethics*. Retrieved from https: en.wikipedia.org/wiki/Nuffield_Council_on_Bioethics.

Wiltbank, Robert; Dew, Nicholas; Read, Stuart; Sarasvathy, Saras D. (2006): Wha to Do Next? The Case for Non-Predictive Strategy. In: *Strategic Managemer Journal* 27 (10), pp. 981–998.

Yin, Robert K. (2003): *Case Study Research: Design and Methods*. 3rd ed. Thousan Oaks: Sage.

Zapf, Wolfgang (1989): Über soziale Innovationen. In: *Soziale Welt* 40 (1/2), pp. 170–18:

Zunz, Olivier (2012): *Philanthropy in America: A History*. Princeton, Oxforc Princeton University Press.

Index